The Social Development

of English Quakerism

1655–1755

The frontispiece of *War with Ye Devill* (1676) by Benjamin Kiffin

The Social Development
of English Quakerism
1655-1755

by Richard T. Vann

Harvard University Press

Cambridge, Massachusetts, 1969

Library of Congress Catalog Card Number 79-78524

SBN 674-81290-5

Printed in the United States of America

To my Mother and my Father

Preface

For those who wish to understand religious behavior histori-
cally there can be few questions more interesting than what
happens to religious urgency when it is stretched out over
time. The differences between the apostolic church and the
church under Constantine, or between the friends of St.
Francis of Assisi and the later Franciscan order, afford a
constant subject for ironical or melancholy contemplation.
I have chosen a comparable example, the Society of Friends
in eighteenth-century England, and have tried to find out
how, in less than a century, a group of vagrant and sometimes
naked preachers and their ecclesiastically subversive followers had reached a state of remarkably sober and decorous
piety.

There has been no lack of satirists and moralists to ridicule
or lament the passing away of primitive religious enthusiasm.
Without altogether abandoning the resources of indignation,
I have tried to be guided by the motto of Spinoza: "not to
ridicule or bewail, neither to despise, but to understand." To
understand eighteenth-century Quakerism, I have analyzed
in the first four chapters various aspects of the development
from its seventeenth-century origins. The first chapter deals
with the mode of becoming a Quaker, as narrated in the
spiritual histories of those who did so. The second chapter

examines the changing place of Quakerism within the social order. The dynamics of Quaker organization, particularly as a response to persecution, are discussed in the third chapter, and the fourth treats the history of the concept of membership, which sharpened the distinction between Quakers and the "world" which surrounded them. These four analytical chapters are a preface to the synoptic view of eighteenth-century Quakerism in the fifth chapter, and to the concluding discussion of what this part of the history of Quakerism may tell us about sectarian development in general.

I have chosen to write about the Quakers because of all the sects that have arisen within Christianity (with the possible exception of some contemporary ones) the Society of Friends has left us the most gratifying amount of evidence about its development. Puritanism in all its manifestations fostered a kind of moral accountancy, but nowhere else was it so thoroughly done. The number of spiritual autobiographies written by Quakers, for example, is probably greater than those by all other kinds of English Dissenters put together. "Church books," or formal records of church business, were kept by Independent and Baptist meetings in the Restoration period; [1] but these church books were mere isolated survivals compared with the unparalleled series of minute books kept by the Quaker meetings for business. Continuous records dating from the first "settling" of such meetings in 1667 are available from all parts of England. Again, Congregational, Baptist, and Presbyterian meetings also kept registers of baptisms, marriages, and burials, but few of them date before 1700 and they were not kept so methodically as those of the Quakers. Many Quaker registers give the place of residence, family relationships, and occupations of those entered — and the registers run back in almost perfect continuity to the

---

1. Such books from the Broadmead and Fenstanton Baptist churches provided Max Weber with a good deal of the not very extensive evidence from which he wrote *The Protestant Ethic and the Spirit of Capitalism.*

beginnings of Quakerism in the 1650's. There is in addition a source of evidence almost unique to Friends — the voluminous records of their sufferings under persecution. Often they were the earliest records of all, and since Friends so often suffered in their property, the inventory of goods carried away by a rapacious informer often provides invaluable information about the occupations and estates of the early Quakers.

This great mass of evidence allows, and indeed dictates, that it be attacked by considering samples of various kinds. I have done this first through local history: a good part of the book is based on a biographical analysis of all the Quakers in the counties of Buckinghamshire and Norfolk and the city of Norwich (areas chosen largely for the accessibility of their records, since I cannot argue that they or any other areas were "typical"). This analysis was made by filling out separate punch-cards (more than six thousand in all) for all Quakers mentioned in the registers of births, marriages, and burials or in the minute books and records of sufferings. Information from Quaker archives was then substantially supplemented from other sources, notably wills and letters of administration, ecclesiastical records, and the presentments of quarter sessions. To get the feeling of the spiritual struggles which preceded acceptance of the Quaker message and way of life, I read all the journals and spiritual autobiographies which Friends wrote during the first century of Quakerism. Finally, I tried to avoid the limitations of a purely biographical approach (whether individual or multiple) by studying the logic of Quaker institutions through a selection of minutes from the meetings which undertook the responsibility for the pastoral care of members and the exercise of discipline.

Many of the questions which this book raises were posed a half-century ago by the great historian, William Charles Braithwaite: "How long will the vital forces of genuine first-hand experience, and of fellowship and personal leadership remain supreme; how soon will they become subordinated to tradition and organization and authority? At what point will the preservation of a sect claim more attention than the propagation of a new way of life? How soon will the vision of a new heaven and a new earth fade into the light of common day?" [2] If I have made any advances towards answering them, it has been by going beyond the narrative mode and national scope appropriate for the general histories of Braithwaite and Rufus Jones to sample the riches of local evidence hardly touched even by the industrious historiography of the Society of Friends. It goes without saying that much more could doubtless be learned from a systematic exploitation of the local Quaker archives and a collation of evidence from Quaker sources with that available from ecclesiastical and judicial records. I hope that whatever merits or faults this book has, it will stimulate further work on these important and neglected documents, which, in my opinion, can tell us most of the inner life of this religious movement.

Without the unfailing help of the librarians of the Society of Friends' library at Friends' House, London — first John Nickalls and Muriel Hicks, and then Edward Milligan — I should probably have shared the fate of the first foreigner who tried to write a history of English Quakerism, the Dutch William Sewel, who "doubting of Some Things, and finding others defective" had to write to England for better information; "which having gotten at length after much Pains and long Waiting, I was Several Times obliged to lay aside Part of my former Description, and make a new one." [3] Since much of my work has been done with manuscripts, many of them in the care of local meetings or vicars, I had to make frequent demands on the time of others, which were always

2. William Charles Braithwaite, *The Beginnings of Quakerism*, 2nd ed., revised by Henry J. Cadbury (Cambridge, Eng.: Cambridge University Press, 1956), pp. 308–309.
3. William Sewel, *The History of the Rise, Increase, and Progress of the Christian People Called Quakers* (1722), Preface.

treated with more than routine courtesy; I shall particularly mention the help given me by Doris Eddington and D. E. H. James of Norwich, and George W. Edwards of Hayes, Kent. Susan Moger did a great deal of helpful work as a research assistant, both in England and in America. I should like to acknowledge the courtesy of Cambridge University Press for allowing me to use extracts from W. C. Braithwaite, *The Beginnings of Quakerism*, and Norman Penney, ed., *The Journal of George Fox*. I have benefited — perhaps not so much as I should have — from the comments of Hugh Barbour, W. K. Jordan, Edward Milligan, the late David Owen, David Swift, and Frederick Tolles, who have read my manuscript at various stages of its development, and above all, I am grateful for the continuous encouragement and criticism of my wife, to whom the book could have been dedicated were it not already so much her own.

Richard T. Vann

Middletown, Connecticut
November 1968

A Note on Style

The spelling and dating of seventeenth- and eighteenth-century documents presents some difficulties for the modern reader, but I have decided that it is worth seeing exactly what the writers said, even if it is sometimes incoherent or poorly spelled. Thus in all direct quotations from primary sources I have retained the original spelling and capitalization, and almost always the original punctuation as well. The obvious abbreviations in manuscripts ("ye" and "yt", for example), have been spelled out. Except in direct quotations, place names and surnames are given in the most common modern spelling; names of well-known Friends are spelled as in the catalog of the Friends' House Library. Seventeenth-century writers were lavish with italics, often using them where we would enclose the italicized words in quotation marks. I have generally retained these italics and have added none of my own.

Quakers, as is well known, rejected the Latin names of the months from January through August and the names of all the days of the week. In order to establish a standard chronological scheme, I have translated all dates from their Quaker form into the heathenish calendar that other Englishmen would have used and put all dates into New Style. In making citations, I have generally cited manuscripts by the date of the entry, rather than by any page number, since very few were paginated consistently or consecutively, whereas most were kept in chronological order. Wherever possible I have tried to make these citations in the text rather than in a footnote. Except for books published in the twentieth century, for which I have given complete citations, the place of publication, unless otherwise noted, is London, and I have provided only the date. I have had to curtail the gross prolixity of seventeenth-century titles, especially in the footnotes; a relatively full form of all titles will be found in the bibliography. One abbreviation is consistently used: *J.F.H.S.* for the *Journal of the Friends' Historical Society.*

Contents

Tables

The Social Development
of English Quakerism

I   The Theory and Practice of Conversion

An historical study of Quakerism begins with a paradox. The beliefs of the Quakers are almost uniquely hostile to history, yet they have written more of it than any other sect. "Historical" in early Quaker language almost always had a pejorative connotation, being implicitly contrasted to "living" or "vital." Faith, for Friends, was not "once delivered to the Saints"; it was and must be the response of the soul to the immediate inward presence of God. Tradition in the church was thus useless at best, since there was nothing God had said once that he would not say again, and there was no action that should not be authenticated by this living word. In fact, ecclesiastical tradition was a pernicious accretion of superstitions, serving to withdraw the soul from God, not fix it in the faith. By the same reasoning, the Bible itself was not essential to the Christian life; no amount of learning in the biblical languages, no mastery of the letter of scripture could avail if the inward voice of God were not heeded; and if it were, it would declare the same truth that it had imparted to the writers of the Bible.

Paradoxically, this emphasis on immediate personal spiritual experience eventually contributed to the mass of Quaker historiography. Quaker meetings for worship were silent except for spontaneous speaking, arising, as Friends believed, only from the direct promptings of God. Since there were no paid clergymen and no prepared sermons, Quaker devotional writing did not take the homiletical turn common to that of other Christians. Theology, in the conventional sense, was also less cultivated by Friends. Consequently, when they put pen to paper in the effort to reach the witness of God within other men, they shunned the artifices of rhetoric or syllogism. Instead, they related the story of their own experiences, and thus laid down the deposits of memory from which more general histories could be constructed.[1]

This meant that the origins of Quakerism were remembered in a special way. Mere idle reminiscence, informed by no moral purpose, would have struck Friends as profitless self-pleasing. But put to the service of evangelism, memory would be sanctified; and as memory was evoked for the edification of others, the experiences through which the first believers found their faith took on a certain normative coloration. These pious narrations lent themselves to at least half-consciously formulated generalizations about the ways that grace was likely to be received and perceived; for what the first Friends remembered, they expected others in some measure to relive. Therefore, as we make a brief sketch of early Quaker history and then study in more detail the circumstances in which the earliest Friends came to know the shining of the inward light, we are at the same time beginning to understand the Quaker mode and theory of conversion.

The First Preaching of Quakerism

To an eighteenth-century rationalist who proposed the founding of a new religion, Voltaire returned the useful but in-

---

1. Although there are sermons by the early Quakers in print (presumably taken down in shorthand) these were not authorized or regularly published by Friends. Formal theology among the early Friends was most cultivated by two Scots, Robert Barclay and George Keith. Scotland was notoriously inhospitable to Quakerism, and it is interesting that the English Quakers had to resort to Scotland for theological expertise.

complete advice to be crucified forthwith. The ability to conceive theological or metaphysical notions, handy as it is in the rational defense of a faith already received, has seldom fostered the discovery of new ways of religious life. Most of the men who have found these have done so only through stretching to its limits the religion in which they had been brought up. Only after exhausting the resources of the old religion — one thinks of St. Paul's zeal as a Pharisee and Luther's as a monk — were they led into fresh paths; and then, almost inevitably, they were persecuted by those who still held the old ways to be entirely adequate.

Such, at least, is the history of the origins of Quakerism. The matrix within which it was formed is that complex of beliefs and practices which we call Puritanism; the moment at which it emerged was that of the seeming triumph of the saints in the Protectorate of Oliver Cromwell. "Puritanism" was a word much used — and misused — in the seventeenth century, and it is hardly less misused in our time. Archbishop Whitgift, Sir Walter Raleigh, King James I, his son Charles I, the architect Inigo Jones, and even the minister of Charles I, the Earl of Strafford, were all called Puritans by some of their contemporaries.[2] Despite this bewildering variety of examples, it is possible to identify certain attitudes — moral, religious, and political — as Puritan. At the broadest definition, Puritans were those who felt that the English Reformation which took untidy shape during the reign of Elizabeth I had been incomplete. It was not so much its doctrines as contained in the Thirty-Nine Articles which they found unsatisfactory; indeed, the Puritans made great claim to be the upholders of the ancient doctrine of the English church against the "innovations" associated with that more relaxed version of Calvinism known as Arminianism. Their objection was rather

2. Christopher Hill, *Society and Puritanism in Pre-Revolutionary England* (London: Secker and Warburg, 1964), p. 16. The first chapter of this book is an excellent essay on the meanings of Puritanism.

that the Anglican settlement seemed to entrust the preaching of sound biblical doctrine to a clergy too sluggish, ignorant, and venial to proclaim the word, while the bishops appeared increasingly more concerned to smite the zealous preacher instead of the devil. Writing in 1637, Milton gave the most eloquent expression to this Puritan despair about the malignancy of some and the negligence of most clergy and bishops:

> How well could I have spar'd for thee, young swain,
> Anow of such as for their bellies sake,
> Creep and intrude, and climb into the fold?
> Of other care they little reck'ning make,
> Then how to scramble at the shearers feast,
> And shove away the worthy bidden guest;
> Blind mouthes! that scarce themselves know how to hold
> A Sheep-hook, or have learn'd ought els the least
> That to the faithfull Herdmans art belongs!
> What recks it them? What need they? They are sped;
> And when they list, their lean and flashy songs
> Grate on their scrannel Pipes of wretched straw,
> The hungry Sheep look up, and are not fed,
> But swoln with wind, and the rank mist they draw,
> Rot inwardly, and foul contagion spread:
> Besides what the grim Woolf with privy paw
> Daily devours apace, and nothing sed.[3]

Such feelings about the necessity for further reformation in the church inevitably required that the Puritans should have a distinctive political program, too; for in a national church in which an educated laity held serious religious convictions, political and religious questions were bound to be inextricably intertwined. Elizabeth I had tried to keep her actions as supreme governor of the church entirely free of parliamentary discussion, much less control. At the same time

3. John Milton, *Lycidas*, lines 113–129.

she took somewhat belated steps to counter the influence of Puritans in the church. Her successors, especially Charles I, completed the exclusion of Puritans from the centers of ecclesiastical power, but they were quite unable to stifle parliamentary discussion of their ecclesiastical policies. They might be excluded from the bench of bishops, but Puritans had by no means been harried out of the land, and their preaching had deeply influenced many lawyers (the Inns of Court had Puritan chaplains) and country gentlemen.[4] These men were the stuff of which the House of Commons was made, and during the eleven years from 1629 to 1640 when no parliaments were called, they beheld with increasing indignation the successes of Archbishop Laud's Anglo-Catholic policy in England and the supine failure of Charles I to go to the rescue of the hard-pressed Protestants of Germany. If the precarious finances of Charles I should compel him to call another parliament, they would be certain to call to account the authors of such anti-Christian policies. It was a reckoning which was to lead Strafford, then Laud, and finally Charles himself to the scaffold.

These political and ecclesiastical ambitions of the Puritans were the servants to a deeper desire to live in the fullest possible obedience to the will of God — an obedience constantly frustrated in an England where Laud and Strafford held sway. This life of obedience is the core of Puritanism — an ethic with powerful theological reinforcement. Plays such as *Twelfth Night* and *Bartholomew Fair* represent Puritan austerities as frequently ridiculous and their pieties as tinged with hypocrisy. We may be inclined to take these as contemporary evidence that Macaulay was right when he observed that the Puritans were opposed to bear-baiting on grounds of the pleasure that it gave to the spectators. It would, however,

---

4. The influence of Puritanism on the gentry is brilliantly discussed by Michael Walzer in *The Revolution of the Saints* (Cambridge, Mass.: Harvard University Press, 1965), pp. 232–267.

be a mistake to let our understanding of Puritans be colored by the stereotype of the hypocritical killjoy which, if it has any validity at all, is more nearly applicable to the nineteenth-century Nonconformist than to his Puritan predecessor. (The later Nonconformist differed from the Puritan, as Christopher Hill has remarked, rather in the way that vinegar differs from wine.) The Puritans who fought in the English Civil War had no objection to operas or masques, in themselves, or even to that "good creature," alcohol. They valued self-discipline, but not necessarily inhibition; they were serious but by no means always somber.

Religious beliefs which, like Puritanism, not only imposed a life of austere self-control but also left the believer baffled by the inscrutable will of God do not immediately commend themselves to modern taste. But, alien as they now may seem, we may suppose that Puritan ideas and morals allowed the Puritan to make superior sense of his life. To some extent, as Michael Walzer has suggested, Puritanism was one functional response to the kind of dislocation of society that we have learned to call "modernization." [5] Confronted by the bands of vagabonds and idle people thrown up by unequal industrial development and challenged by the threats to morality posed by both poverty and prosperity, the Puritan felt that the imposition of discipline and the abasement of pride was as essential to the right ordering of the commonwealth as to that of his own soul.

For whatever reasons, Puritanism for three generations was a viable and widespread style of life; and then, just at the time when the popish bishops had been scattered and the king's ungodly counsellors sent to exile or the block, just when it seemed that the Puritans could proceed to the creation of their Zion, their unity and cohesiveness disappeared. In part

5. See his article, "Puritanism as a Revolutionary Ideology," *History and Theory* 3 (1963), 59–90, and the review of *The Revolution of the Saints*, in *ibid.*, 7 (1968), 102–114.

this was the usual fate of a revolutionary opposition party come to power. In resistance to the bishops, the Puritans had been able to make common cause with those who were merely anticlerical, while enjoying the luxury of deferring the divisive question of what sort of rule in church and state should succeed that of Laud and Strafford. But this political weakness was reinforced, and ultimately made incurable, by a widespread personal defection. Men simply found that Puritanism could no longer organize life satisfactorily.

There can be no better example of this than the growth of sects. As early as 1641 there was published *A Discovery of 29 Sects here in London all of which except the First are divelish and damnable*. Among the diabolical twenty-eight were Saturnians, Bacchanalians, and Adamites. Ephraim Pagitt, a Puritan clergyman, unmasked, among others, the Pueris Similes, Deo-Relicti, Scattered Flock, and Familists, who came in both mountain and valley subdivisions. By 1646, when the Presbyterian minister Thomas Edwards turned the force of his encyclopedic loathing upon them, no less than 199 different sects were reckoned to be in England.

The time was fit for the efflorescence of these sects. Englishmen had lived through a decade of war and rumor of war in the course of the most profound civil disturbance in their turbulent history. Armies larger than had ever been seen in England had trampled the countryside, their plundering and disruption of markets adding to the miseries of an economic depression.[6] The man of blood, Charles Stuart, had been put to death — a great symbolic parricide producing the usual heady mixture of liberation and guilt. The English Revolution, perhaps spared its Reign of Terror, was embarked

6. Between 1640 and 1650 "the country was to experience a period of economic dislocation which was, for modern England, unique in kind." So writes Margaret James in *Social Problems and Policy during the Puritan Revolution* (London: G. Routledge and Sons, 1930), p. 35. The second chapter of the book is a full account of economic conditions between 1640 and 1660, though it relies almost entirely upon literary rather than statistical evidence.

on a Reign of Virtue which was scarcely less bracing. The handwriting of God seemed unusually plain in recent history; to the Roundhead the life and to the Royalist the death of Charles I was a punishment of the people for their sins.

Furthermore, the instruments of repression of unorthodox religious opinions, which had been used all too often against the Puritans, were dismantled by the Long Parliament. The favorite courts of royal action, High Commission and the Star Chamber, ceased to sit; censorship of the press utterly failed to cope with the flood of pamphlets and newspapers; and many preachers whose chief credentials were that they had been silenced by the bishops were now free to proclaim messages scarcely more welcome to new presbyter than to old priest. Yet it proved impossible to repair the repressive machinery of the state, and the Presbyterian system of church government was effective only in London and Lancashire. The orthodox ministers might fulminate and the House of Commons might savagely punish the occasional "heretic" who fell into their hands, but power lay with Oliver Cromwell, and the army would not allow the sects to be stamped out.

Thus it was within a society intensely preoccupied with religion, but deeply divided as to what external forms it should take, and scandalized (but also fascinated) by a babel of strange sectarian visions, that the first messengers appeared talking of what they simply called "Truth."

To contemporaries it appeared that most of these men were a peculiar kind of Baptist; Pagitt's *Heresiography* first saluted Quakers as "an upstart branch of the Anabaptists." Some of their more distinctive doctrines and customs, such as calling the months and days of the week by numbers and declining to take oaths, had indeed been anticipated by the Baptists. It was obvious from their accents that most of them were from the north of England. They lost no opportunity to proclaim that Christ himself, speaking directly to them, was their immediate leader; insofar as they had a system of organization, it appeared to rest on a few men who had more or less independently arrived at a new knowledge of God: William Dewsbury, Richard Farnworth, George Fox, and James Nayler.

We will not understand what these early Quaker preachers, the ones who came to be called "First Publishers of Truth," were up to if we let our attention focus entirely on Fox, the so-called founder of Quakerism. Fox can truly be said to have been the founder of Quakerism if "Quakerism" is regarded as the complex of institutions and traditions which grew up in the last third of the seventeenth century. In 1655, when the first Quaker preachers began to work in southern and eastern England, no one could know that Fox would live while Edward Burrough, Farnworth, Richard Hubberthorne, and Nayler — any of whom might have held an eminence comparable to that of Fox — would die before the end of 1662. To be sure, Swarthmoor Hall in Lancashire was the center of the evangelistic effort, and it had been Fox who converted Margaret Fell, the mistress of that house, to Quakerism. It was also Fox who alone was granted the length of days and the literary genius to write in his *Journal* the classic account of how a son of "righteous Christer," a Leicestershire weaver, wandered from town to town and from priest to "professor" until he heard that "there is one who can speak to thy condition, even Jesus Christ." But we should not think of Quaker evangelism primarily in terms of Fox's winning others to his distinctive beliefs. One consistent note in the accounts that the early Friends themselves gave of their conversions is that no man had made them a Quaker. In the words of William Sewel: "There were also some others who, by the like immediate way, as George Fox himself, were convinced in their minds . . . These unexpectedly and unawares came to meet with fellow-believers, which they were not acquainted with before." In one sense, there was no real effort at evangelism:

as Emilia Fogelklou rightly comments, "The first publishers of truth did not go out to make adherents. They went out 'to discover in all lands those who were true fellow-members with them.' " [7]

We may see this process in more detail if we study the way in which Quakerism came to the two areas I have selected for special attention, Norfolk and Buckinghamshire. The first sign that new winds of doctrine were about to be unloosed in Norfolk came from the arrival in the western part of the county of a woman called Anne Blaykling. In June 1655 she was arrested, as we learn from the papers of the Norfolk Quarter Sessions, "with a great concourse of people about her in the highway to the disturbance of the publique peace." Upon search the justices found on her person "divers papers . . . conteyning directions for travails into severall counties and places in this commonwealth." Treating this as a dangerous case of the detestable offense of vagabondage, made yet more disgusting by the sex of the prisoner, the justices committed her to the house of correction in Swaffham.[8]

Friends' records state that Anne Blaykling had come with Christopher Atkinson, James Lancaster, and George Whitehead — all from Westmorland — to preach in Norfolk and Norwich. Mary Fisher, John Whitehead, Dorothy Waugh, and William Dewsbury were the first to undertake the same mission in Buckinghamshire.[9] All of them undoubtedly

7. William Sewel, *History of the Christian People Called Quakers* (1722), p. 28, and William C. Braithwaite, *The Second Period of Quakerism* (London: Macmillan, 1919), xvii, both quoted in Emilia Fogelklou, "Quakerism and Democracy," *Journal of the Friends' Historical Society*, 42 (1950), 18.

8. Norfolk Quarter Sessions Indictments, 12 June 1655. In the indictment the name is given as "Blayning." This particular incident is probably the one referred to in a letter from Friends in Ely, Cambridgeshire, in August 1659. See *Extracts from State Papers Relating to Friends, 1654 to 1672*, ed. Norman Penney (London: Headley Brothers, 1913), pp. 108–109.

9. For most counties the establishment of Quakerism can be studied in a return which every quarterly meeting of Friends was asked to make in 1678, giving details of the "first publishers of Truth" in their area and

traveled with papers like those found on Anne Blaykling, containing not only a schedule of places to be visited and information about the roads, but also the names of those who might be especially inclined to listen to their message. We know that George Fox used to inquire in each town about those who were "disposed towards God"; he complains in Cornwall that his work there was hindered by the "Badness of the inn-keepers" in not performing this service, the publicans in that county evidently being more acquainted with the sinners.[10] Sometimes alterations and enhancement of the itinerary resulted from suggestions made by the newly converted. When John Stubbs and William Caton were leaving Luke Howard, who had just embraced Truth, he gave them the names of some towns and men along the sea coast, and when they subsequently visited these men, all of them received them.[11]

This speaks eloquently of the degree to which men in every part of England, disaffected from the ministrations of the orthodox churches and loosely in touch with one another, awaited some further light. To know the names on those lists, and why they were put there, would tell us a great deal about the spread of Quakerism. To what extent would the names

of those who were the first to receive them. These were published in *"The First Publishers of Truth" Being Early Records (Now First Printed) of the Introduction of Quakerism into the Counties of England and Wales*, ed. Norman Penney (London: Headley Brothers, 1907). Unfortunately the return for Buckinghamshire is not extant; the one for Norwich, written into the front of "A Booke of ye Sufferings of the People of God cald Quakers in the Citty of Norwich," was not discovered in time to appear in Penney's compilation. It was printed in the *J.F.H.S.*, 18 (1921), pp. 22–25. Besides the rich but thoroughly gleaned Swarthmore Manuscripts, the best source for the Quaker evangelization of Buckinghamshire is *Letters to William Dewsbury and Others*, ed. Henry J. Cadbury (London: Bannisdale Press, 1948). For Norwich the best manuscript source is the records of the Norwich Quarter Sessions, especially the Minute Book, vol. X, and the Indictments, vol. LXIII, for 1655.

10. L. V. Hodgkin, *A Quaker Saint of Cornwall: Loveday Hambly and her Guests* (London: Longmans, Green, 1927), p. 8.

11. Quoted in L. V. Hodgkin, *The Shoemaker of Dover* (London: Friends' Book Centre, 1943), p. 24.

be the same as those of the first converts? We can only speculate, since none of the lists have survived; like many priceless historical documents, they were probably considered too trivial to be worth keeping. But our speculations can to a degree be substantiated by reference to surviving correspondence which passed among the traveling ministers.

It seems likely that many of the networks of acquaintance exploited by the "first publishers of Truth" had arisen from previous association within the "gathered churches" (Congregationalists and Baptists). Often the visiting Friend was invited to speak to a Baptist or Congregational meeting; Stubbs and Caton, while they were in Kent, preached to such at Canterbury and Maidstone, with some effect.[12] John Whitehead, preaching in Buckinghamshire in January and February, 1656, had several meetings with the Baptists, who were especially numerous in the county.[13] Near Winslow he spoke to twelve Baptists assembled in the house owned by one of them; "Some of them was tender, but the greater part gaine said the truth," he wrote to William Dewsbury. Often public interest in the new doctrine and the combativeness of its opponents led to public disputations. After a general meeting at Wingrave, the Baptists issued a challenge to dispute the differences between them and Friends — a debate which was carried on, as Whitehead reports, "with moderation, and the deepest subtiltie that ever ever I mett with on their part, yett out of their snares in the power of truth I was preserved over them and it cleared it selfe to the single eye." Several days later he once again attended a Baptist meeting, disputing

12. *A Journal of the Life of William Caton* (1689), pp. 16, 20.

13. G. Lyon Turner states that in 1669 there were more Baptists in this county than in any other. He reaches this conclusion — a surprising one in view of the relatively small population of Buckinghamshire — from an analysis of the returns of the census of Dissenters ordered in 1669 by Archbishop Sheldon; see *Original Records of Early Nonconformity under Persecution and Indulgence* (London: T. F. Unwin, 1911), III, 136. By assigning 50 or 90 adults wherever a conventicle of unknown size was reported, Turner often overestimated the Nonconformist population.

with one William Hartley, an apothecary and lay preacher. In fact, Whitehead seems to have spoken almost as often among the Baptists as in specifically Quaker meetings.[14]

Commercial ties, especially in the cloth trade, were often converted into channels of evangelism. One of the reasons for the predominance of wholesale traders among early Friends (discussed in the next chapter) is that such men, as they made the trips required by their business, were exposed to new ideas; thus while traveling to Stourbridge Fair, Thomas Symonds of Norwich, a master worsted weaver, heard of Anne Blaykling, who was still in prison. By the time he had returned from his trip, during which he visited her, he had become a Friend, the first important adherent in Norwich.[15] Such things happened sufficiently often to cause the movement of clothiers to be identified with traffic in illicit ideas; during George Fox's imprisonment at Launceton in Cornwall, many clothiers entering the county were arrested as "sus-picious persons."[16]

Besides wholesale traders, another group particularly disposed to receive Friends was composed of former officers in the parliamentary armies. Captain Matthew Draper of Buckingham, though he soon moved to London, provided a meeting place for the Quakers in the northern parts of Buckinghamshire, an area where Quakerism flourished exceedingly, in part because the road from Swarthmoor Hall to

14. *Letters to Dewsbury*, pp. 43–45.
15. Symonds provides the only autobiographical account of the establishment of Quakerism in Norwich: *The Voyce of the Just Uttered: His Passing out of Aegypt through the Red Sea, Through the Wildernesse to the Promised Land, where rest and peace is Enjoyed* (1656).
16. George Fox, *The Journal of George Fox*, ed. Norman Penney (Cambridge, Eng.: Cambridge University Press, 1911), I, 231. Clothiers were the entrepreneurs in the textile trade; they "put out" wool for spinning and later for weaving, collecting the finished cloth from a wide area. These clothiers should not be confused with the men who did the actual weaving on their hand-operated looms, usually located in their houses. There was a long tradition of Lollardy and Separatism among weavers of this sort, but I do not regard this as especially pertinent in this context.

London carried visiting Friends through that part of the county. Many meetings in 1655 and 1656 were held in the house of Captain John Lawrence of Wramplingham in Norfolk, whereas one of the first to receive Friends in Norwich was Colonel Thomas Deney.[17] We know of one hundred Friends who had served in the armies (all but five in the parliamentary one) including six colonels, two majors, twenty-five captains, and nine other officers. Like the wholesale traders, they had broken out of a merely local mold and were the more susceptible to novel ideas brought by the strangers from other parts of England.

The adherence of one or two men of wealth and influence gave Friends some base of operations in the county and some protection against persecution by the justices. John Lawrence was clearly a man of considerable local influence which, after he left the Norwich Old Meeting (Independent) to join Friends, was used to support Quaker evangelism. Visiting ministers entered the county in considerable numbers after his conversion, usually staying with him and his brother Joseph Lawrence.[18] Something of the same service to Quakerism in Buckinghamshire was performed by John Raunce of High Wycombe and his wife Frances. Raunce was a physician and member of the common council of the borough of High Wycombe; his wife Frances became one of the "first publishers of Truth," traveling with Jane Waugh and preaching

17. Margaret E. Hirst, *The Quakers in Peace and War* (London: Swarthmore Press, 1923), Appendix A, pp. 527–529, gives a list of early Friends who had served in the army and navy. Other officers omitted there are mentioned in C. H. Firth and Godfrey Davies, *The Regimental History of Cromwell's Army* (Oxford: Clarendon Press, 1940), I, 272 and II, 440–441 and 659. I have added to the ninety-four names mentioned in these sources six more which were omitted there.

18. In 1669 we find John Lawrence joining in a petition to the Privy Council that a limit of time be set on "lotteries, puppet plays and shows . . . by the frequent resort to which of the meaner sort of people, we have been much damnified in our manufactures." (*Calendar of State Papers, Domestic 1668–1669*, p. 627.) See also *The Christian Progress of George Whitehead* (1725), pp. 53, 245–246, and *Calendar of State Papers, Domestic 1663–1664*, p. 650.

to the newly formed Quaker meeting at Turville Heath in Oxfordshire.[19] Probably the greatest single impetus to the growth of Quakerism in Buckinghamshire was the conversion of Isaac Penington the younger and his wife Mary, since Penington opened The Grange, his estate in Chalfont St. Peter, to the entertainment of traveling Quaker ministers and also assumed a pastoral care over the new meetings.[20]

The first solid impression of the geography of Quakerism can be gained for the distribution of Quakers about 1662. The Chilterns, Thames Valley, and northeast corner of the county were the strongholds of Quakerism in Buckinghamshire; in Norfolk many of the early Quakers were found in the towns along the Suffolk border and around North Walsham in the northeast. Surprisingly few were to be found in Norwich itself.

I know of no convincing explanation for the distribution within these counties, or for the extent of Quakerism to be found there as compared to elsewhere in England. It has been argued both that Quakers were more likely to be found where there was a long tradition of religious nonconformity — as in the Chilterns or the dales of Yorkshire — and that they were less numerous in areas with a strong Puritan tradition.[21] The

19. Raunce's signature can be seen among those of the other councillors of High Wycombe in a minute reproduced as the frontispiece to *The First Ledger Book of High Wycombe*, ed. R. W. Greaves (Buckinghamshire Record Society, XI, 1956). For Frances Raunce, see Theophila Townsend, *A Testimony Concerning the Life and Death of Jane Whitehead* (1676), p. 6 and *'The First Publishers of Truth'*, ed. Penney, for Oxfordshire.

20. Though he was one of the deepest Quaker devotional and theological writers, Penington could also write letters of simple and loving care to the humblest of his fellow Friends. Several letters "to Friends about the two Chalfonts" as well as to Bridget Attley of Horton, Martha Grassingham of Chalfont St. Peter, and John Mannock of Amersham may be found in the back of vols. II, III, and IV of *The Works of Isaac Penington* (4th ed.; Sherwoods, N.Y., 1861).

21. See Ronald A. Marchant, *The Puritans and the Church Courts in the Diocese of York, 1560–1642* (London: Longmans, 1960), pp. 39–40, 42.

latter claim has been made in reference to the relatively slow development of Quakerism in Norfolk.[22] It does seem that Norfolk Friends themselves were conscious that Quakerism had not made a strong beginning in their county. On 31 May 1662 two of them, William Mowton of Lammas and James King of North Walsham, were presented before the quarter sessions for seditious words; Mowton is supposed to have said that if the repressive legislation against Nonconformists known as the Clarendon Code were put in execution, "rather then wee will be undone by Fynes or sent away at the kings pleasure wee will fight for it," and James King chimed in: "though there be but few hereabouts yet there are great num-

22. Thus Alan Cole writes: "The Yorkshire and West Country textile areas were both Quaker strongholds, but Presbyterian Manchester and prosperous Puritan East Anglia proved less receptive to the Quaker message. It was at Colchester that James Parnell . . . died in gaol." ("The Quakers and Politics, 1652–1660," unpub. diss., Cambridge University, 1955, p. 5.) Parnell's death was the responsibility of his jailers and does not necessarily mean that there were few Quakers in Colchester, still less that this supposed lack was owing to Puritanism. In fact there seem to have been a great many Quakers in Colchester; there were four meetings (compared to two in Norwich) and Wilson Marriage, calculating from the Quaker registers for Colchester for the period 1665–1726, estimates that there were one thousand Friends out of a total population of about eight thousand. See E. Alec Blaxill, *The Nonconformist Churches of Colchester* (Colchester, Eng.: Colchester Borough Council, 1948), pp. 7–8.

Hugh Barbour argues in *The Quakers in Puritan England* (New Haven: Yale University Press, 1964) that "The areas which the Civil War demonstrated to be the real heartland of Puritanism were even more cold to Quaker preachers: Norfolk, Suffolk, Essex, Cambridge, and, except for London, the rest of the Southeast" (p. 42). He goes on to suggest that "The general coldness of the eastern counties to Quakerism was related to the strength of puritan parishes. Local factors must have been involved in the growth of the strongholds at Norwich, Coggeshall, and Colchester" (p. 86). Since no "local factors" are specified, and since Norwich, Coggeshall, and Colchester also possessed strong Puritan parishes, it is by no means clear why Barbour considers them exceptional. Furthermore, the impression that most of the southeast was "cold" to Quakerism rests on some statistical calculations in which I find myself unable to put great confidence. I have attempted to calculate from the rosters of ejected clergy and from Archbishop Sheldon's census of Dissent a geographical distribution for Puritanism, and find no significant underrepresentation of Quakerism in strongly Puritan areas.

bers in other places that will joyne with them And wee doe believe they durst not put that Act in Execucon . . . but if they doe they [Friends] will be as bould as Lyons in opposinge." King lived in the thickest Quaker settlement in the county, and yet apparently felt in an uncomfortable local minority.

The lack of success in Norwich must have been even more disheartening, if not altogether surprising. The city had been the target of what might properly be called a campaign, beginning when James Lancaster "did in the publique markett place . . . gather together a great company of rude and idle people to the disturbance of the peace." [23] George Whitehead and Thomas Symonds entered the churches of St. Peter Mancroft and St. Lawrence to speak, as was still lawful, after the sermon had been completed. Another ministering Friend, Christopher Atkinson, went to church with the same intention, but could not contain himself during the sermon of William Stinnott, and burst out: "leave off thou hypocrite; thou deceive the people." [24] For this he was committed to prison, while Lancaster and Whitehead were banished from Norwich. Whitehead however soon returned, to be joined by even more of his North Country brethren. As William Caton wrote: "*The Word of the Lord* grew mightily in that City, *and many were added to the Faith*; and many *Steeple-houses*, and the most of the *Meetings* in the City were visited by some of the Brethren; for at one time there was Ten or Twelve of us (the Ministring Brethren) in the City that were most of us come out of the *North*." [25]

Another report, from Richard Hubberthorne, was not so optimistic; he wrote on 1 February 1655 that several who had been Ranters and astrologers were converted, and on 25 March he declared that the Lord was gathering a people to

23. Norwich Quarter Sessions Minute Book, vol. X, 1 January 1654/5.
24. Norwich Quarter Sessions Indictments, vol. LXIII, January 1654/5.
25. *A Journal of the Life of William Caton* (1689), p. 13.

Himself, although the people of Norwich "generally is the most wrangling, mischievous, envious, malicious people that ever I came amongst, who are wholly bent to devise mischief one against another, to destroy all the appearances of righteousness in anywhere it appears." [26] No doubt this judgment is partly explained by Hubberthorne's countryman's distaste for urban sophistication; it is very like Francis Howgill's report on London: "here are the highest and the subtellist that we have to deal with . . . that ever was in any age. It is for none to come here but hath a sharp sword and well skilled to handle it." [27]

Despite this promising beginning, the work in Norwich was soon blighted, and it seems reasonably clear that the instability of Christopher Atkinson, who had remained in prison after Whitehead and Lancaster were released, was in part responsible. Atkinson succumbed to temptation with a woman and was disowned by Friends as a "filthy spirit." He also — though this is never mentioned in Quaker records — renounced Quakerism in open court, acknowledging his repentance for disturbing Stinnott's sermon, and saying that he "erred whilst he was in the waye of quakerisme & doth resolve to forsake that Course professinge he was deluded therin & that he hath the foundation of his religion yet to laye & he shall desire god to setle him in the truth." [28]

A few years later the Quaker community in Bristol suffered a severe blow in the disgrace of James Nayler following the

26. Swarthmore MSS, I, 346–347, quoted in Arthur Eddington, *The First Fifty Years of Quakerism in Norwich* (London: Friends' Historical Society, 1932), pp. 13–14.

27. Quoted in Elisabeth Brockbank, *Edward Burrough: A Wrestler for Truth* (London: Bannisdale Press, 1949), pp. 57–58.

28. Norwich Quarter Sessions Book, 1 August 1655. Arthur Eddington does not mention Atkinson's disavowal of Quakerism, and perhaps it never became known to Friends; I have not found any reference to it in Quaker sources. Indeed, two weeks later, on 14 August 1655, George Taylor wrote to Margaret Fell that all Friends in Norwich had been released except for Christopher Atkinson (Fox, *Journal*, ed. Penney, II, 329).

ride into Bristol which some overheated Friends attempted to represent as a kind of Triumphal Entry. Though less spectacular, Atkinson's fall and apostasy must have had a similarly deterring effect on conversions to Quakerism in Norwich, and it may have played some part in a change of heart by some already converted. Of the twenty-nine persons said to have been among the first to welcome Friends in Norwich, several evidently quickly repented and are heard of no more; by 1662 the number of Quakers in the city had risen only to forty-six. As late as 1725 Quakers in Norfolk, with reference to the prosperity of Truth, recalled that there were "in Early days Stumbling Blocks and Stones of Offence." [29]

Thus far our history of the establishment of Quakerism in the two counties of Norfolk and Buckinghamshire has suggested some necessary, though not sufficient conditions: that is, that there be a nucleus of men with some experience of travel who possessed the right mixture of religious zeal and dissatisfaction. I have suggested that such men would be more likely to be found among the hangers-on, if not the actual membership, of some of the "gathered churches." To relate the founding of Quakerism county by county would be a tedious task. No county is "typical," but the patterns we have seen in Buckinghamshire and Norfolk recur. It is more useful not to continue a county by county survey, but to turn instead to a new kind of evidence, which provides a deeper insight into the inner dynamics of early Quakerism: the spiritual autobiographies left by the first Quakers.

Puritan Roots of Quakerism

The spiritual autobiographies of the seventeenth century afford a neat example of the relationship between Puritanism and Quakerism. Friends shared the Puritan impulse to

29. Epistle of Norfolk Quarterly Meeting to London Yearly Meeting, in London Yearly Meeting Minutes, V, 277. The list of the first to receive Friends in Norwich is in " 'First Publishers of Truth' in Norwich," *J.F.H.S.*, 18 (1921), 25.

self-examination; the Puritans, ever in the great Taskmaster's eye, often resorted to keeping a sort of devotional diary or spiritual account book in which they could record their spiritual credits and — more often — debits.[30] The habit of introspection was naturally heightened in the spiritual crisis which had overtaken many during the Civil Wars. The Puritan thus kept accounts of his soul, but did not publish them. At most the spiritual diary might provide the material for a "lean-to," or biographical sketch which was often appended to the collected sermons and writings of a Puritan divine. Only the sectarians of the English Civil War published their own spiritual autobiographies. The reason was often that which William Haller attributes to Milton, who described his religious experiences as his "certification of the spirit for his right to challenge the prelates and to instruct parliament and people in their duties and responsibilities." [31] Even the self-revelations of a Milton or a Bunyan were isolated in comparison to the torrent flowing from Quaker presses. In the first two generations of the movement no fewer than seventy Quakers published some account of the Lord's dealings with them.

Often these accounts — especially the earliest ones — were written as pure evangelical tracts.[32] Some of them were journals of ancient and weighty Friends, published after their deaths for the common edification and smoothed out by the unconscious editing of memory, not to mention the occasional prudent emendation of the Morning Meeting of Ministers.[33] Sometimes a Quaker wrote no consecutive ac-

30. Good examples may be found in *Two Elizabethan Puritan Diaries*, ed. Marshal M. Knappen (Chicago: University of Chicago Press, 1933).
31. William Haller, *The Rise of Puritanism* (New York: Columbia University Press, 1938), p. 115. I have drawn heavily on Haller's admirable discussion of seventeenth-century spiritual biographies and autobiographies.
32. A point made by Owen Watkins in "Spiritual Autobiography from 1649 to 1660," unpub. diss., University of London, 1952.
33. See Appendix.

count of his early life and conversion, but made so many allusions to it that much of the story can be reconstructed. Though there is considerable variation in the time which elapsed between conversion and publication, an evangelical intent can be discerned even in the most sedate. It is obvious in the very titles of the earlier ones; thus Edward Burrough describes his spiritual pilgrimage in *A Warning from the Lord to the Inhabitants of Underbarrow, and so to all the Inhabitants in England* (1654). Charles Bailey delivers his in *A True and Faithful Warning unto the People and Inhabitants of Bristol* (1663); Humphrey Bache recounts his conversion in *A Few Words in true love written to the old long-sitting Parliament* (1659). It is clear from the way these documents were being used that they were inspired by a divine self-confidence which is quite unlike the emotional tone of the unpublished Puritan diaries. As the editor of two manuscript Elizabethan Puritan diaries remarks, the chief concern of the Puritan writers was to analyze satisfactory spiritual states so as to be able to reproduce them and to have a regular opportunity to accuse themselves of various sins and shortcomings. How far such self-indictments as that of the Reverend Samuel Ward were from the triumphant histories of the Quakers will soon become apparent.

Since I have already briefly mentioned the role of Isaac Penington the younger in Buckinghamshire, it might be appropriate to start with him, especially since his life recapitulated so many of the religious changes of his times. His father, the future Lord Mayor of London, was a staunch Puritan. As soon as he had bought the estate of The Grange he became a local celebrity by "violently importuning" the incumbent clergyman at Chalfont St. Peter to give lectures on the scriptures in supplement to his probably inadequate sermons; he also demonstrated his piety by refusing to bow at the name of Jesus in the Creed. This was speedily reported to Archbishop Laud, but there was little the prelate could do. As Laud's informant reported, the vicar of Chalfont St. Peter had agreed to lecture because he was "wonderful timorous . . . as all the rest of the clergy in these parts are, because they are overawed by the justices and lay gentry." [34]

The religious upbringing that such a paragon of Puritanism would give young Isaac can readily be imagined. He soon found himself, as he later put it, "exceedingly entangled about election and reprobation (having drunk in that doctrine, according as it was then held forth by the strictest of those that were termed Puritans)." He prayed much, conned sermons, and awaited some incursion of grace. Eventually "light and mercy sprang upon him" and dragged him out of the doctrinal morass. He "fell a helping to build up an Independent congregation, wherein the savour of life and the presence of God was fresh with me." [35] It was while he was in this dispensation that he married Mary Springett, the widow of a colonel in the parliamentary army.

Mary Springett had been left a widow with an infant daughter when she was barely twenty. She tells us she had grown up in the household of "a kind of loose Protestants." It was a description which might have fitted a large part of the gentry of England, for her guardians seem to have done nothing more debauched than hear common prayer and celebrate such superstitious feasts as Christmas. (Her father and mother had both died when she was three). Braving the displeasure of her guardians, Mary went to Puritan sermons; finally she abandoned common-prayer services altogether and was married without psalm or wedding ring, in harmony with the strictest Puritan practice. While Isaac, though he "never had thoughts of rending" from the Independents, was "forc-

---

34. Charlotte Fell-Smith, "Sir Isaac Penington," in *Dictionary of National Biography*; Hill, *Society and Puritanism*, p. 116.
35. Isaac Penington, *Works*, III, 90–91, 545.

ibly taken by the hand of the Lord" out of their society, Mary Springett and her first husband were also passing through outward religious forms. As she put it: "We were also brought off from bread and wine and baptism with water, we having looked into the independent way, saw death there . . . and looking into the baptism with water, found it not to answer the cry of our hearts." [36] Colonel Springett died before he could have encountered Quakerism, but Mary and Isaac, soon after their marriage, came into touch with James Nayler and then with George Fox. Isaac, in particular, had a hard struggle to win through the last of his reservations, but by the end of 1658 — at the age of forty-two — he was fixed in that serene faith which was to sustain him the rest of his life.

A very similar note was sounded by Edward Burrough as he looked back over the "seven years since the Lord raised us up in the North of *England*": "what we were before in our Religion, Profession, and Practices is well known to that part of the Country, how generally we were men of the strictest Sect, and of the greatest Zeal in the Performance of outward righteousness; and went through, and tried all sorts of Teachers, and run from Mountain to Mountain, and from one Form to another." [37] The young Burrough himself had sought out a Presbyterian "priest" and so "got up to be a Presbyterian, and followed the highest Priests and Professors of that form." When these proved inadequate, he "followed only to hear the highest Notionists" and even preached in their meetings.[38]

Thomas Briggs had "run up and down among those People called Ministers, twenty years together in a Profession that was called *Puritans*." Before he was "convinced of Gods blessed Truth" he was "in the Notion of outward Profession

---

36. Mary Penington, *A Brief Account of My Exercises from Childhood* (Philadelphia, 1848), 5; Isaac Penington, *Works*, III, 545.

37. "An Epistle to the Reader" (unpaginated), prefaced to *The Memorable Works of a Son of Tunder and Consolation* (1672).

38. "Warning to the Inhabitants of Underbarrow," pp. 14–17, in *The Memorable Works*.

amongst the Presbiterians and Independents without life and Power." [39] Similarly when Richard Farnworth began about the age of sixteen to have serious doubts about his salvation, he first frequented the religious exercises of the Puritans. Three or four years later he broke with them and joined a group of Independents. At the same age Thomas Forster felt compelled to pray extempore and to hear and write sermons "after the Presbyterian way, whom I then conceived were the most *Orthodox*." But this was only the starting of his journey from Egypt to Canaan, for he followed successively Independents, Baptists, "Notionists," and then "wandered up and down from one tree of knowledge to another . . . *seeking for rest, but found none*." [40] Thomas Symonds of Norwich had also joined with some Anabaptists, but, seeing the "emptiness and huskiness" of water-baptism, had sought out some Antinomian sect; it was while still associated with this group that he was led to visit Anne Blaykling in prison." [41]

A similar tale of "passing through all professions" was told, though in less detail, by John Beevan, Stephen Crisp, John Crook, William Dewsbury, Francis Howgill, and John Story. Besides these, Thomas Aldam, John Audland, William Bennitt, John Camm, Clement Lake, Thomas Laythes, John Lilburne, Thomas Markham, James Nayler, Thomas Stordy, and John Wilkinson either joined or attended Independent meetings before being called out from them by the preaching of Truth.[42] As might be guessed from Friends' efforts to

39. *An Account of Some of the Travels and Sufferings of Thomas Briggs* (1685), pp. 3, 19.
40. Richard Farnworth, *The Heart Opened by Christ* (1654); Thomas Forster, *A Guide to the Blind Pointed to, or a True Testimony to the Light Within* (1659), preface.
41. Symonds, *The Voyce of the Just*, p. 3.
42. See J[ohn] Beevan, *A Loving Salutation to all People Who have any desires after the Living God, but especially to the people called Free-Will Anabaptists* (1660), p. 4; *A Memorable Account of the Christian Experiences of Stephen Crisp* (1694); *A Short History of the Life of John Crook* (1706), pp. 3–19; *The Faithful Testimony of William Dewsbery* (1689), pp. 44–48; Francis Howgill, *The Inheritance of Jacob*

289.6 V334ᴡ
c./

preach at Baptist meetings, the Baptists also provided a large number of converts to Quakerism. As early as 1644 George Fox had encountered a "tender" Baptist congregation in London, and some of his earliest followers came from a company of "shattered *Baptists*" in Nottinghamshire. One of these was probably Elizabeth Hooton; she was certainly a Baptist before she and most of her meeting turned to Quakerism. Luke Howard, one of the earliest Friends in Kent, had been "as it were, received as a member" of a Congregational Society in London and then became a Particular Baptist, at a time when there were in Kent only "Seven or Eight Dipped-Persons, and they all but new Dipped, too." [43] In addition to those already mentioned, William Ames, William Bailey, Edward and Elizabeth Chester, Solomon Eccles, Samuel Fisher, Thomas Green, Anthony Mellidge, and Rebecca Travers were Baptists at the time of their conversion to Quakerism. Most of them, like Luke Howard, had previously been Independents. [44]

Discovered (1655), in *The Dawnings of the Gospel Day* (1676), p. 41; *The Memory of John Story Revived* (1683), p. 4; *A Short Testimony concerning Thomas Aldam* (1690); for Audland, see Sewel, *History of the Quakers*, I, 111; William Bennitt, *The Work and Mercy of God or a Demonstration of the Visitation of Gods Love to my Soul in the dayes of my Youth* (1669); John Whiting, *Persecution Expos'd* (1715), p. 112; *Something by Way of Testimony Concerning Clement Lake* (1692), p. 17; Thomas Laythes, *Something Concerning my Convincement of God's Truth* (n.p., n.d. [1686?]); Pauline Gregg, *Free-Born John* (1961), p. 116; and *An Account of the Life and Death of Thomas Markham* (1695), p. 3.

   James Nayler was a member of the Independent church at Woodchurch (West Ardsley) in Workshire; see "Examination of James Nayler, upon an indictment of blasphemy, at the sessions at Appleby, in January, 1652," in George Fox, *The Great Mistery of the Great Whore* in *Works* (1810), III, 610. For Stordy, *The Memory of Thomas Stordy Revived* (1692), p. 3; and for Wilkinson, see William Penn's preface to *A Journal of the Life of John Banks* (2nd ed.; 1798).

   43. Fox, *Journal* (1694), pp. 3, 17; see also a letter of Elizabeth Hooton's son Oliver, quoted in Emily Manners, *Elizabeth Hooton: First Quaker Woman Preacher* (London: Headley Brothers, 1914), p. 4. Luke Howard is quoted in Hodgkin, *Shoemaker*, p. 13.

   44. Information about Ames, Bailey, and Eccles comes from Sewel, *History of the Quakers*, II, 59, 244, 317. See also Elizabeth Chester, *A Narrative of the Life and Death of Edward Chester* (1709); for Fisher,

To the outward eye most of these enthusiastic sectaries must have seemed confirmed in their faith, for many of them were "teachers" among their flocks. Such were John Audland, Edward Burrough, Stephen Crisp, Josiah Coale, Francis Howgill, Richard Hubberthorne, James Nayler, John Story, and John Wilkinson; Thomas Markham and Thomas Stordy among the Independents, and William Ames, William Bailey, and Samuel Fisher (who had also been an Anglican priest) among the Baptists.[45] But their ministry was flawed by inner uncertainty. Many could have said, with Richard Hubberthorne, "I was a minister of the letter before I knew the power of the word of God." [46]

It seems overwhelmingly clear from these spiritual auto-biographies that their authors shared a style of religious experience: the scheme of repentance and conversion which had been worked out in English Puritanism. The great majority of the writers — both the leaders and the obscure Friends — had grown up in Puritan households and had passed into one or more of the gathered churches. This phenomenon of passing through a succession of outward professions was perfectly familiar to the early Friends themselves. Isaac Penington put it into a cosmic context. On the one hand, it represented the successive shifts and snares of Satan; yet on the other, perhaps, a progressive attempt of spiritual religion to free itself from the deadness of outworn forms. When there was a stirring against Popery, he wrote, Satan "tempted aside into Episcopacy; when that would hold no

---

see Caton, *Journal*, 176; Thomas Green, *A Declaration to the World of my Travel and Journey out of AEgypt into Canaan* (1659), p. 5; *A True Relation of the Former Faithful and long service, with the present most unjust Imprisonment of Anthony Mellidge* (n.p., n.d. [1657?]); for Rebecca Travers, see Whiting, *Persecution Expos'd*, p. 176.

45. For Josiah Coale, see William Crouch, *Posthuma Christiana* (1712), p. 141; for Markham and Stordy, see Whiting, *Persecution Expos'd*, pp. 121, 235–237 (besides works already cited).

46. Quoted in Elisabeth Brockbank, *Richard Hubberthorne of Yealand* (London: Friends' Book Centre, 1929), pp. 94–95.

longer, then to Presbytery: when that will not serve, into Independency: when that will not keep quiet, but still there are searchings further, into Anabaptism: if that will not do, into a way of Seeking and Waiting: if this will not satisfy, they shall have high notions, yea most pleasant notions concerning the Spirit, and concerning the life, if they will but be satisfied without the life." [47] Still, he acknowledged that "there was, some years ago, an honest zeal and true simplicity stirring in the Puritans (especially among the Nonconformists of them), which was of the Lord," and if the Puritans had remained in it, they might have been opened to further leadings of God's spirit. Instead they departed from that "into some form or other . . . [and] this is our lamentation, that forms and ways of worship abound: but the Puritan principle, the Puritan spirit is lost and drowned in them all." [48]

Several conclusions may be drawn from the transitory associations which so many early Friends had made with Presbyterian, Independent, and Baptist groups. The Quakers were thoroughly within the Puritan tradition in their early consciousness of their own unworthiness. The Puritan saint in the making was expected to feel the stings of conscience and to agonize over his own unworthiness. When John Gratton, who was converted to Quakerism a few years later, was about ten or eleven, he began to repent of "my vain Life and Way I lived in, being much given to Play amongst vain Boys, and took great Delight in playing at Cards, and in shooting at Butts, and ringing of Bells." He went to tell part of his condition to the Presbyterians, whom he now joined with, but they returned the orthodox answer that "It was a good Condition." [49] The virtue of it was that it led to the absolute

47. Isaac Penington, "A Brief History of the State of the Church since the Days of the Apostles, with the Living Seal to it," in *Works* (4th ed.), I, 332–333.

48. Isaac Penington, "An Answer to that Common Objection against the Quakers, that They Condemn All but Themselves," in *ibid.*, II, 138–140.

49. *A Journal of the Life of John Gratton* (1720), pp. 2–7.

dependency on God's mercy which was prerequisite to and close precursor of the seizure by grace. Such a state of repentance, as a wiser pastor like Richard Baxter would have said, ought not to be interminably protracted nor indulged in to the point of physical or psychic breakdown. Yet it was just this sort of overcharged soul which was drawn to Quakerism. Time and time again the early Friends speak of the length of their spiritual struggles (doubtless one of the explanations for the wide range of ages among the early converts, discussed in the next chapter, is that so many found their faith only after years of questing). There were, to be sure, intermissions associated with the semblance of a conversion experience and the joining of a new, purer religious group; but the very fact that the sense of assurance turned out not to be lasting and the new group less holy than its pretentions renewed the spiritual struggle in a yet more intense fashion.

In some, the intensity of the inward conflict brought on the symptoms of physical disorder. Before the age of ten, Elizabeth Stirredge was already "surprized with inward fear what would become of me when I should die." She was not even able to indulge in the depravities of card-playing and bell-ringing which weighed so heavily on the conscience of John Gratton, being "so filled with fears and doubts, that I could take no delight in any thing of this World." She dreaded even to pass by swearers or drunken men, and every thunderstorm drove her to the "privatest" part of the house to mourn for the Lord's vengeance on the wicked. So much did she read and mourn that her mother feared she was "going into a Consumption." [50] George Fox was actually given physic for the maladies of his soul, but when the attempt was made to let blood, "they could not get one *drop* of *Blood* from me, either in *Arms* or *Head* (though they endeavoured it) my

50. *Strength in Weakness Manifest: in the Life, Various Trials, and Christian Testimony of Elizabeth Stirredge* (1711), pp. 2–7.

Body being, as it were, dried up with Sorrows, Grief and troubles." [51] In much the same way William Dewsbury's life was despaired of after he fell under a weight of sin which made his childhood dolorous even for a Puritan. As he writes, "I was conceived in Sin, and brought forth in Iniquity, and in that state lived and delighted in pride and pleasures, lightness and vanity, as all do in that nature, untill I was about eight Years of Age." [52] We may wonder into what depths of worldliness a boy might sink by the age of eight. From our point of view there seems a ludicrous disproportion between childish offense and mature repentance, and we easily weary of so many tales of petty depravity recalled in tranquillity. But this is because our own age understands childhood far differently than did Dewsbury's contemporaries; we must make a real effort of understanding to see how the memory of his childhood misdemeanors oppressed him so sorely that his master feared that the young apprentice was fatally stricken. At the same time, it is probably justifiable to hear a note of exaggeration, even by the standards of their contemporaries, in these Quaker autobiographies.

In fact it is important to recall something which was never far from Fox's mind: that such dark trials of the spirit might drive men mad. Fox's skill at "discerning of spirits" and many of his rebukes to "airy notionists" were employed to draw a line — not always easy to maintain — between justifiable enthusiasm in the Truth and mental illness. The story of one who was for a time drawn into Quakerism illustrates the dangers to sanity inherent in unrelieved introspection. John Toldervy, of London, attracted by the unity of Quaker testimonies and the purity of their manners, joined himself to Friends about 1654, but such light as he had within him became darkened. In his garden a fly flew into his face, and he became convinced that it was a messenger sent from God.

51. Fox, *Journal*, p. 5.
52. *Faithful Testimony*, p. 44.

From that time on he was "guided by Flyes in many things; being very certain, that they were moved by God in them, to make known what was his will to me." One night after disturbing dreams and visions he saw a fly near the fire and felt compelled to hold his leg exactly as near the flames. After twenty minutes he had received a burn which required three months to heal. He preached a sermon informing his auditors that it was God's will that they stack separately the stones, sticks, leaves, and bricks in their gardens. When he encountered two white stones in his path, it was revealed to him that these represented Esau and Jacob, and he threw away Esau, the larger one. The smaller "did not onely signifie Iacob, but the white Stone spoken of in the *Revelations*, which was sent as a token from Christ in Heaven to me; and so long as I kept that stone I had unity with God; but if lost, I should be disunited." [53]

To enemies of Quakerism, of course, such delusions were not surprising. Richard Baxter recognized that the dizzy alternation of "outward professions" and the extremity of spiritual unrest were partly cause, partly symptom of Quakerism. "No person more fit for a Quaker, a Papist, or any sectary to work upon, than a troubled mind," he wrote. He had heard of "very few experienced, humble, sober Christians" who had become Quakers. In an address to Anabaptists and Separated People he attacks them for propagating the errors which had prepared the way for Quakerism: "I have heard yet from the severall parts of the Land, but of very few that have drunk in this venome of the Ranters or Quakers, but such as have first been of your opinions, and gone out at that door." [54] In

---

53. John Toldervy, *The Foot out of the Snare Being a Brief Declaration of his Entrance into that Sect Called Quakers* (1656), pp. 3, 32–42. George Fox tells of being confronted by a woman in a Friends' meeting whom he clearly regarded as demented, though his adversaries said "there was witchcraft amongst us" (*The Short Journal and the Itinerary Journals of George Fox*, ed. Norman Penney [Cambridge, Eng.: Cambridge University Press, 1925], p. 2).

54. Richard Baxter, *Works*, ed. W. Orme (1830), XII, 500, quoted

much the same vein (Baxter had listed Anne Hutchinson as one of the progenitors of Quakerism) the American Puritan divine Cotton Mather claimed that "the first Quakers that ever were in the world were certain fanaticks here in our town of Salem." [55]

Such perceptions of Quakers by Puritans suggest that Quakerism is a kind of "wild Puritanism." The Puritans would have thought the future Quaker quite correct to feel contrition for his sins, but tainted with "enthusiasm" if he went through years of anguish over them. One decisive conversion experience, conveying the sense of regeneration, was the supreme gift of God; several of them made mockery of God's saving power. Therefore, despite the abundant evidence that most of the leaders and many of the followers among early Friends had come to Quakerism through sectarian Puritanism — a fact that, especially since the work of Geoffrey Nuttall, now seems so clear that one wonders why it was overlooked before — we should not confuse Puritan roots with fruits.[56] Bunyan, Baxter, and the other polemicists

---

in Geoffrey Nuttall, "Law and Liberty in Puritanism," *Congregational Quarterly*, 29 (1951), 26 (reprinted in Nuttall, *The Puritan Spirit: Essays and Addresses* [London: Epworth Press, 1967]); Baxter, *One Sheet Against the Quakers* (1657), p. 11; and Baxter, *The Quakers Catechism, or, the Quakers Questioned, their Questions Answered, and Both Published* (1655), sig. B. This last pamphlet contains many assertions that the Quakers were being recruited entirely from these sects.

It will be obvious how much this chapter owes to the writings of Geoffrey Nuttall, especially *The Holy Spirit in Puritan Faith and Experience* (Oxford: B. Blackwell, 1946). There is also an illuminating discussion of the effects of prolonged uncertainty over salvation (*Erschütterung der Heilsgewissheit*) in Theodor Sippell, *Werdendes Quäkertum* (Stuttgart: W. Kohlhammer, 1937).

55. *Magnalia Christi Americana* (Hartford, Conn., 1853), II, 523, quoted in James Fulton Maclear, " 'The Heart of New England Rent': The Mystical Element in Early Puritan History," *Mississippi Valley Historical Review* 42 (1956), 647; see also 630. I am informed by David Swift that Mather's reference is probably to the Separatist Congregationalists who supported Roger Williams before the latter was exiled.

56. Rufus Jones, in his first two volumes of the standard Rowntree history of Quakerism, made comparatively little of Friends' Puritan antecedents and much of the supposed influence of Jacob Boehme and

quoted in this chapter were acutely aware of how much they differed from Friends, not only in doctrine but also in style of religious life. To the Puritans, the Bible was the inerrant Word of God; to the Quakers, a record (more or less corrupted by the errors of copyists and binders) of what the Spirit of God had told earlier writers and would say again. The Puritans believed, with most Christians, in the unique importance of the historical life and death of Christ; they thought that the Quakers disparaged this when they distinguished between the man who died outside Jerusalem and the living Christ who dwelt within them. The Puritans, as their self-accusatory diaries make plain, believed that no soul, even though redeemed, could be free of sin in this life; to Friends this belief was a miserable "pleading for sin" and a gross denial of the palpable operations of the Spirit which they felt. To us these quarrels between Quakers and Puritans may have some of the intimacy, as well as the intensity, of family feuds; but we should not forget that in both doctrine and experience Friends had been prepared to see conversion quite differently from the Puritans with whom they had once walked in fellowship.

The Quaker Mode of Conversion

Distinctive Quaker thinking about conversion starts from the fact that the Quakers had resolved their spiritual struggles in a way quite unlike the Puritans. Too many of them had already had one, or several, conversion experiences which had turned out to be deceptive; too many dreaded the consciousness of sin which the Puritans considered wholesome and necessary. They therefore sought a communion with God so deep that it might be called "continuous conversion"; and

---

other continental mystics. Jones, living in an era of religious liberalism, felt liberated by an interpretation of Quakerism as "a mighty spiritual movement rather than . . . a peculiar and provincial sect." We should remember that we in turn have been directed to the Puritan roots of Quakerism in a theological climate of revived Calvinism.

they rejected the Baptist or Independent claim to find assurance of salvation in a single influx of grace which could be precisely dated and described for the edification and discernment of other Christians.

This unique and "objective" experience made the form of the church much different for the Baptists or Independents. It made possible the membership lists and the "in-churching" of Independent meeting or qualified the candidate for baptism in a Baptist one. In the Bedford meeting of which John Bunyan was the pastor, the procedure for receiving new members seems to have been as follows: the meeting first propounded a candidate, whose life was scrutinized by the members. The candidate was then invited to come to meeting and "give in his experiences"; following this he was admitted to communion. If someone objected to the candidate at first propounding, he was not allowed to make his public declaration. Thus on 28 March 1713 four persons "having been long propounded for Communion, & not permitted to give in their experiences" were to be visited by the members who objected to them, so that they might "receive satisfaction or els bring their objections to the Church to be considered by them." Clearly this sequence was regarded as an ordinance of the church, since any exceptions to it were carefully specified not to be precedents. Alice Clark "was propounded & received into our Fellowship both at the same meeting not as A president for others but because she feared she might be hindred her duty if her Husband heard it." The requirement for public confession of faith was especially important, as seen in the treatment of a Mrs. Freeman, who was "allowed to have Libertie to speake her experience to some Brethren in private, she not being able to speake before the Church by reason of her fitts. but not as A president for future practices." [57]

57. *The Church Book of Bunyan Meeting, 1650–1821*, ed. G. B. Harrison (London: J. M. Dent and Sons, 1928), pp. 17, 85, 95. Geoffrey

Even if not mandatory, this public confession was considered edifying, as was shown when Norwich Old Meeting on 2 June 1650 "resolved upon the question That it is not necessary for everyone that desireth to joyne to the Church, to render an account of the hope that is in them for salvation, in publike before the Church nor to give in publike the reasons of their desires to joyne themselves to the Church; seeing many are soe week as they cannot speake before a publike congregation; but it were much to be desired That all could & would (at their joyning to the Church) speake something tending to edification." I have come across one instance in which a convert to Quakerism made a statement of this kind. Wells Monthly Meeting on 5 March 1729 notes: "Whereas William Goat of Holt, having Joined himself with us as a Society of People, have found himself Concerned to deliver in a paper to this Meeting, setting forth the Causes & motive thereto, which was read, and well received by the meeting, and is ordered to be kept in the monthly meeting bags." But this was clearly William Goat's concern, not that of the meeting, and one might speculate that he had come to Friends from one of the Separated Churches where such things were regularly done.

It is in fact surprisingly difficult to discover what Friends' procedure was to accept or test converts. The minute books are silent; it is not until the 1760's that explicit minutes about converts appear. On 6 November 1771 Hogsty End Monthly

---

Nuttall argues in *Visible Saints* (Oxford: B. Blackwell, 1956), p. 112 that the requirement of a profession of faith was a preservative of the Separated Churches against the incursions of Unitarianism, which soon overcame English Presbyterians. Some substantiation of this can be found in the experience of the New England churches, which began to drop the required confession of faith from the propounded member in the early eighteenth century. No confession was required in Cambridge from 1797, in Medford from 1714, and in Natick from 1730. In Hull in 1734 it was made a matter of indifference whether such professions were made. Eastern Massachusetts was subsequently the stronghold of Unitarianism. See Emil Oberholzer, *Delinquent Saints* (New York: Columbia University Press, 1956), p. 23.

Meeting recorded that "Mary Hart and Catherine Peel do believe that [they] are Convinced of the Truth we Profess and are accordingly admitted as members." After several visits to Susanna Rose and Lydia Ward, the Upperside Monthly Meeting on 1 June 1772 found them "worthy to be taken as Friends." Less fortunate was a would-be Friend of Bedfordshire; the Friends who visited John Cheshire reported to Market Street Monthly Meeting on 12 October 1764 that they "did not find him Sufficiently convinced of Friends Principles so as to be admitted a Member of the Society at Present" (since on 13 September 1765 he was reported to have married a woman Friend, it is probable that his love of Truth was found to be not altogether disinterested). In general, it seems that Friends did not take it upon themselves to judge the reality of the conversion experience. It was noted that Mary Hart and Catherine Peel believed they were convinced, not that the Meeting believed so.[58]

In fact, the idea of requiring a public confession of faith, to be judged by the elders or by the whole meeting, was rejected when proposed by George Keith, the Friend of Scottish Presbyterian origins who eventually left Quakerism to become one of the first missionaries for the Society for the Propagation of the Gospel. During a visit to Pennsylvania in the early 1690's, Keith became much exercised by the multitudes who he felt "are crept into the form & profession of Friends' way, who are not realy friends of Truth and have taken up the said outward profession not from any true inward Convincement . . . but [from] some worldly interest or advantage &c." He therefore advocated some "outward Separation as well as an inward to be made . . . betwixt

58. In the words of Robert Barclay of Reigate, "The 'outward profession of, and belief in, Jesus Christ, and those holy truths delivered by His Spirit in the Scriptures' [a phrase from Barclay's *Apology*] was . . . *evinced* to the officers of the church, and, as far as we can learn, not *openly professed* before the congregation" (*The Inner Life of the Religious Societies of the Commonwealth* [1876], p. 326). There is however no evidence of any formal judgment made by the "officers of the church."

faithfull friends of Truth and all such hypocrites & empty & formal professors." The primitive church, he argued, had bestowed baptism only after "some open declaration & profession of their faith in the most principal and necessary Doctrines of Christian religion either before the Church, or some faithfull Witnesses." Though there was no "need nor service" to renew outward baptism, the open declaration ought to be insisted upon; indeed, all Friends ought to confess their faith regularly, and none should be "newly received into the number and Society of Friends untill they give some open confession and declaration of their real convincement of the Truth." If Friends were satisfied with this declaration and had "a Spirituall discerning of their sincerity in any measure though never so small," they should extend their hands in token of acceptance into the society. Keith went on to argue that Friends should keep lists of "all true and faithfull Friends belonging to every Meeting who are received into the number of Friends of that meeting by the comon consent of Friends." It is instructive to follow his reasoning, since it throws into relief the opposite principles embraced by orthodox Friends. Keith pointed out that some who had departed from Truth, when disciplined, excused themselves by denying they were ever "in the same profession with Friends"; but "their names standing on record by their own consent or by their own Subscription would witness against them" (Friends' practice was simply to take no further notice of anybody who was publicly known not to be a Friend). Again, Keith asked: "seeing Friends think convenient to insert the names of their Childrens outward birth and the time thereof in a Booke, is it not of greater weight and as tending more to the comfort both Parents and Children that the day of their Spiritual Birth be recorded in Friends book." [59] Such a practice would have brought Quakers into harmony with the Baptists and Independents. It is significant that Keith, on the verge of his decisive rupture with Friends,

59. "Gospel Order and Discipline," *J.F.H.S.*, 10 (1913), 70–75.

should have propounded these suggestions in criticism of them, and that they should have repudiated them and him.

Fortunately we are not entirely dependent on negative evidence, such as that provided by George Keith, for a picture of the nature of conversion to Quakerism. Though there is little in the minutes of business meetings, Friends' other writings do allow us to construct a schematic picture of the Quaker idea of conversion and to compare it with that held by other Dissenters.

It is certainly true that no believer in instantaneous conversion could have wished for more spectacular psychic disturbances than those which often characterized the early Quaker evangelism. As Charles Marshall describes the first preaching of Audland and Camm at Bristol: "Ah! the seizings of Souls, and prickings at heart, which attended that season; some fell on the Ground, others crying out under the sence of opening their States, which indeed gave experimental knowledge of what is recorded, acts 2.37." Samuel Fothergill of Scarborough was probably correct in claiming that George Fox was more like Peter Cartwright, the evangelist of the Northwest Territory, than the Friends of Victorian England.[60] Some lives were so remarkably changed that witchcraft or magic seemed the only rational explanation. George Keith, by now controverting Quakerism as an Anglican missionary, resolved the whole matter, on the best scientific principles, "into a natural enthusiasm, or a sort of natural magic or magnetism, by a certain efflux or effluvium of certain animal volatile spirits, mightily invigorated by exalted imagination, in Quakers, that flow from their bodies by the command of their will into the bodies of these new proselytes, that produce the like imagination in their credulous admirers." [61] Elizabeth Bathurst complains that many had been frightened

60. Samuel Fothergill of Scarborough, *Essay on the Society of Friends: Being an Inquiry into the Causes of their Diminished Influence and Numbers* (1859), p. 131.
61. George Keith, *The Magick of Quakerism* (1707), p. 51, quoted in Braithwaite, *Second Period* (2nd ed.), p. 527, n. 1.

away, as by "a *Scare-Crow*, or *Ghostly Apparition*" by the explanation of witchcraft or "Diabolical Inchantment" proposed by some "not knowing the Way of the Spirit in themselves, and yet seeing the evident Change which hath been wrought upon others, by Vertue of the powerful Operation of this spiritual Principle or Power of God in their Consciences." [62]

Friends also believed as emphatically as the Puritans in the absolute necessity of conversion. "Though you have the name of Christians," thundered Edward Burrough to the "outward Professors" of his time, "yet you were not made so, nor received that name by being first converted and changed, and translated from Death to Life, and from being the Children of disobedience, to be the Children of God, through the work and operation of the Spirit of God in you." Instead, those outward professors relied on "tradition, or natural education . . . being sprinkled with a little water upon the face, being Infants, or by a bare confession and profession of the Name of Christ in words . . . without any real change from darkness to Light." [63] Along the same lines Robert Barclay the Apologist attacked the Church of England because it baptized infants and thus incorporated them into its membership without requiring them to be converted. "As to the nature and constitution of a Church . . . the Protestants, as in practice, so in principles, differ not from Papists, for they engross within the compass of their Church whole Nations, making their infants members of it, by sprinkling a little water upon them, so that there is none so wicked or profane, who is not a fellow-member, no evidence of holiness being required to constitute a member of the Church." [64]

---

62. *Truth Vindicated by the Faithful Testimony and Writings of Elizabeth Bathurst* (1691), p. 132.
63. Burrough, "The True State of Christianity" (1658), in *The Memorable Works*, p. 422.
64. Robert Barclay, *Apology for the True Christian Divinity* (1678), proposition 10, section 5.

Friends characteristically took the position, typical of the sects which demanded conversion of all members, that no minister could be effective unless he himself had been converted. As William Penn said, ministers needed to be "changed men themselves before they went about to change others"; or as George Fox put it: "He that is unsanctified is out of the power of God, and the word of God abides not in him, and he runs, and is not sent, and it is not possible that such can convert sinners, who are themselves unconverted from their iniquities." [65] Richard Claridge warned that preaching the gospel was more than discoursing of Christ's life in a "Scholastick or Historical Way"; it was necessary to "preach Christ in his Inward and Spiritual Appearance also, (yea, and more especially) . . . from a Measure of the same Spirit of Revelation which the Apostles had." [66]

Nevertheless Friends drew a distinction which carried them away from Puritan practice. When the necessary "work of conversion" commenced, a man was said to be "convinced." Occasionally the early Friends used "convinced" as if it were merely a synonym for "converted," as George Fox seems to have done; but in general "convincement" was taken to be

65. George Fox, *The Great Mistery of the Great Whore*, in *Works* (1831 ed.), III, 572. The quotation from William Penn is made in Robert Barclay of Reigate, *Inner Life*, p. 255. Barclay adduces a considerable number of other quotations to show that the early Friends believed in the necessity of conversion both for ministers and for ordinary members. Richard Baxter, on the contrary, upholds the traditional Catholic position; he writes that a man "may perform the office of a minister to the benefit of the Church, though he have *no saving grace at all*" (quoted in *Inner Life*, 255). An Anglican writer, Patrick Smith, while not denying that "Grace or real Holiness, is indispensibly necessary to the being of a faithful Minister, and to a Minister's own Salvation" claims that it is not "so indispensibly necessary to the very Being of a Minister, as if without it, all his Work and Labour in the Ministry would be wholly ineffectual. For then, we could never know who are true Ministers." For the same reason he denies that grace is necessary to belonging to the church, for otherwise there could be no visible church (*A Preservative against Quakerism* [1732], pp. 94–96).

66. *The Life and Posthumous Works of Richard Claridge*, ed. Joseph Besse (1726), p. 467.

only the first step toward conversion. Thus John Banks addressed Friends: "because you are *Convinced* of the *Truth*, and because you know the *Truth* and *Way* of *God*, what it is, and so make a *Profession* thereof; think not that this *Knowledge* will serve your turn to justifie you in the sight of God, short of *Obedience*." Those who are obedient "come to know not only a *Convinced Estate*, but a *Conversion* in their Hearts and Souls." The others, unwilling to bear their daily crosses, "yet can satisfie your selves in *coming as the People come, and sit as God's People sit* in their Meetings and Assemblies, *and like to hear thy Words* (as the Lord said by the Prophet) *but will not do them*." [67]

In the same vein Elizabeth Bathurst wrote: " 'tis not a bare Convincement of the Truth in our Understandings, which may produce a change in the Judgment, Opinion and Profession, that will serve our turn, without a change of the Old Nature, without there be a change wrought in the Inward, as well as the Outward Man, whereby the Heart may be thoroughly Sanctified and made Clean, else there can be no real Conversion." [68] Richard Samble exhorted Friends to "a farther work than a Convincement, or a Profession of the Truth: And therefore all must come to the Power, to the Ax that's laid to the Root of the evil Tree, that the Ground may be changed, that the Lusts may be destroyed, that there may not be in any of you a Lustful Heart after any Iniquity . . . otherwise you will come short of the Kingdom, although you may be one in Profession with us." [69] A man unconverted yet convinced, wrote Francis Howgill, is still in darkness, and that which convinces him is the Light. George Whitehead and Robert Barclay the Apologist also distinguished between the converted and the merely convinced.[70] The same distinc-

67. John Banks, *An Epistle to Friends Shewing the great Difference Between a Convinced and a Converted Estate* (1692), pp. 3–6.
68. Bathurst, *Truth Vindicated*, p. 145.
69. *A Handful after the Harvest-Man: being a Collection of Several Epistles and Testimonies of Richard Samble* (1684), pp. 33–34.
70. Francis Howgill, "Some of the Mysteries of God's Kingdom De-

tion also occurs in records of the business meetings, as in the meeting in Norwich for young and convinced persons, or in the minute of Upperside Monthly Meeting on 22 July 1672 deputing some Friends to meet with "the friends & convinced people of Wooburn, Brookend, Koockam & thereabouts, to stir them up to diligence & faithfulnes in waiting upon the Lord." So well known was the distinction, in fact, that it achieved the distinction of being parodied by the Reverend Charles Leslie.[71]

Robert Barclay of Reigate argued that the "convinced" were always and only those who formed a kind of "outside membership" in early Quakerism, enjoying the right to be relieved in necessity, while the "converted" had, besides the privileges of membership, the right of sitting in the business meetings. There can certainly be no doubt that Friends would not grant even the most routine privileges of membership until newcomers had proved their fidelity for a considerable time. In this they followed the experience of John Banks, who "was not made a Quaker in a day" and the opinion of Elizabeth Bathurst, who "would have none mistake, so as to think, that conversion is wrought in an instant, for it is a gradual Work, carried on by degrees in the Soul."[72] After

clared" (1658), in *Dawnings of the Gospel-Day*, p. 121; George White-head, *Memoirs* (1832), p. 37; and Robert Barclay, *Apology*, proposition 11, section 7. The last two are quoted in Howard H. Brinton, "Stages in Spiritual Development as Exemplified in Quaker Journals," in *Children of Light: Essays in Honor of Rufus M. Jones* (New York: Macmillan Company, 1938), pp. 392–393.

71. In the title of *The Present State of Quakerism in England, Wherein Is Shew'd, That the Greatest Part of the Quakers in England are so far Converted, as to be Convinced* (1701). Naturally, he gave the words his own meanings: those "convinced" had at least, unlike the earliest Friends, become Christians, while those "converted" – "a number daily increasing in both town and country" – had renounced Quakerism altogether and undergone Anglican baptism.

72. Banks estimated: "about Six Years after I had Received the Truth . . . through Great Exercise and Godly Sorrow, I came to be setled in the Power of God, and made Weighty in my Spirit thereby" (*Journal* [1712], p. 9). See also Bathurst, *Truth Vindicated*, p. 145.

the Upperside Monthly Meeting had dealt with a wearisome number of young couples, one or both of whom were "raw in the Truth," it advised on 2 September 1695 "that Friends in their respective Meetings would be wary and carefull not to give any encouragement to young-convinced People, to let out their affections one towards another, or seek marriage, in their entrance (as it were) into the Profession of Truth, & before they are come to know in some good measure, a growth & establishment therin." It was in fact proposals of marriage, far more than applications for relief, which forced a Meeting to decide on the reality of conversion. In the latter part of the seventeenth century there were no less than ten persons (most of them men) who appeared before the Upperside Monthly Meeting to obtain permission to be married, although they had "come but little among Friends" or were "but lately convinced."

In such cases the Meeting was careful first to discern whether a real action of the Spirit had begun, or whether the prospective bridegroom, like William Barton of Chesham, had been drawn to meetings "at first . . . by desire of having her to wife." [73] Resorting to Friends' meetings in hopes of marriage was discouraged; thus William Pain the younger, tailor of Chesham, saw his proposed marriage to Jane Mun quashed in April 1698, because "he had come but little among Friends, and that mostly since he had an Eye towards her." And, lest we suppose that it was only marriage which required a considerable period of attendance by both parties, we must reckon with the treatment given John Brooker of Chalfont Meeting, who desired a "certificate" to move from one Monthly Meeting area to another. He had lived for more than a year in a Friend's house (probably as a servant). He had "since his abode there received a convincement of Truth and had made profession thereof for about a year past: and he now intending to return into America" asked for a certificate. But those appointed to

73. Upperside Monthly Meeting, minute of 4 October 1697.

inquire into the matter reported that they "found a dissatisfaction in the minds of some Friends in giving a Certificate, considering his late convincement"; and the request was declined. There may have been other grounds of objection, but this is unlikely, since when others existed, they were regularly specified. Anthony Kibble, laborer of Chalfont St. Giles, had to delay his marriage proposed 3 November 1690, not only because he was "very raw & unsettled as to Truth" but also because "since he came to meetings & was by the world accounted a Quaker, he had been guilty of some scandalous Carriages not yet cleared."

John Brooker's difficulties occurred in the eighteenth century (1 February 1720) and conceivably an earlier generation of Friends would not have deemed a convincement a year prior as "late." Yet the tendency of this evidence is clear; from the time of receiving a "convincement" of truth, one had still to establish, by several months at least of faithful attendance and obedience to the Quaker testimonies, that he was in truth converted. It was for this reason that Friends, in dealing with the newly convinced, often quoted the New Testament injunction to "lay hands on no man suddenly."

We have two glimpses of Friends' procedure in the reception of new converts during the first century of Quakerism. One must be to some extent discounted, since it comes from a hostile source; still, like good caricature, it probably catches a bit of the truth as a basis for its exaggerations. Nathaniel Smith, a Friend who had been disowned in 1668, wrote as the last part of a self-justifying pamphlet "A Few Words of Instruction, to all those that are desirous to come into the Society of the Quakers; and to be Received of them." Smith announces that his instructions will hold good for all sorts of people, whether moved in conscience or not — "they shall all be Received, although it be only for Preferment, and in time be taken for the Faithful." He recommends that the aspiring Quaker make it a point to attend meetings regularly and to praise and flatter Friends whenever possible, taking care to use only the plain speech — for in it "is wrapt up a great Mine, or a great Mystery of Godliness: therefore be sure that thou have this *little Knack*, or else thou dost nothing."

"After thou hast been a constant Goer to the Meeting about a Quarter of a Year," he continues, "then some of the Heads will come to Visit thee . . . give them more kind Entertainment then thou wouldest do to thy Father and Mother . . . Then they will report it to their Minister, what a good Friend there is lately come into the Truth; and then in a short time thou shalt have him come and give thee a visit." [74] After more entertainment, Friends will take the candidate as one of them; the advantage to him is an enhanced possibility of trade. The details about Friends' "ministers," their susceptibility to flattery, and the resort of the greedy to their meetings for the purpose of increasing their trade are doubtless inventions; but the visits, the delay before full acceptance, and the emphasis on the plain speech ring true.

Some fifty years later, two Frenchmen presented themselves to the Quaker Richard Claridge, asking "what Methods they must take to be admitted into the Society of the People called *Quakers*." Claridge answered "that the *Quakers* had no External Forms or Rites of Admission, but as Persons came to be Joyned or United to Christ in Spirit, by the Sanctifying and Purging Operation of the Spirit of God in their Hearts, so they came to be One and the same Holy Society or Communion in the Lord." He further advised the Frenchmen to wait on the Lord, to practice silence, and "to frequent Friends Meetings, and give some Evidence by good Fruits, of their Convincement of the Truth." [75]

This period of gradually bringing the will under the complete domination of God — or adjusting the behavior to the norms imposed by the group — was in fact the Quaker version of the "novitiate" which Max Weber recognized as a

74. Nathanael Smith, *The Quakers Spiritual Court Proclaimed* (1669), pp. 33–35.
75. Claridge, *Works*, pp. 312–314.

characteristic of all the sects. "The sect discipline," he wrote, "is also analogous to monastic discipline in that it established the principle of the novitiate . . . In all probability among all sects there existed a period of probation." [76] In this period (which of course had no formal status or specified length) some wrought in themselves the changes which Friends expected, bringing forth the fruits of their convincement. But inevitably, those fruits had to be such as could be publicly manifested and — at least informally — judged. This meant that while a conversion experience could not be tested, conduct could, and must be. By entrusting the evaluation of conduct to their meetings for church business, Friends set a value on conformity of behavior which was to have momentous and not completely foreseen consequences.

The Quaker emphasis on a sustained process of conversion is probably related to the wandering from teacher to teacher and church to church which so many had done. Furthermore, in their discrimination between convincement and conversion, Friends showed a shrewd knowledge of the psychology of religious movements. No stable or continuing religious group could have been formed from men who might be described, in Cromwell's words, as happy Seekers — that is, men who could not move past the psychic disturbances and excitements of conversion into the more routine course of mature religious life. Those who attached themselves to Friends but could not overcome their fixation on conversion and pass on to the state of happy finders almost always withdrew from Friends and all organized religion, claiming that Quakerism had degenerated into a new formal system.[77] An

76. "The Protestant Sects and the Spirit of Capitalism," in *From Max Weber: Essays in Sociology*, trans. and ed. by H. H. Gerth and C. Wright Mills (New York: Oxford University Press, 1946), p. 317; see also pp. 320–322. Weber instanced only the Methodist probationary period of six months.

77. See Chapter III. It was very rare for anyone to return from Quakerism to one of the gathered churches. So few were relapses back

acute student of modern sects has noted that the atmosphere of evangelical meetings tends to be "interdenominational" and that a further conversion is necessary before the person converted at a revival becomes part of a stable church congregation.[78] Such a statement might have been written in explanation of Friends' distinction between convincement and conversion.

There is of course a great difference between the way that conversion might occur in the first generation of Friends and in subsequent generations. Growing up in a Puritan household just before the Civil War produced a kind of religious tension that would not necessarily be replicated in the Quaker families of more tranquil times. At first Friends were heedless of this; in the first raptures of their communion with God, they were certain that the whole of mankind would be caught up in the same encounter. But the apocalypse, as usual, failed to occur, and Quakerism, as it established itself in English society, had to work out the discipline and polity implied in its vision of God. Conversion had to be passed on to subsequent generations of Friends as a more nearly standardized — perhaps even stereotyped — mode of experience. Here as in other aspects of the Quaker life, forms of some kind were bound to reappear; whether they could be filled with the Spirit was the question that the next two generations of Friends had to answer.

---

into Independency that they were greeted (by the Independents) with inordinate joy. As the pastor of a meeting in Hertford wrote, "Whereas we had mourned that some had gone out from our Meetings to them, in this one instance the Lord hath abundantly made it up to us . . . [for] instances of this nature are so famous and rare, viz. For any to be recovered from this Bewitching" (W[illiam] D[imsdale], *The Quaker Converted, or the Experimental Knowledge of Jesus Christ Crucified, in Opposition to the Principles of the Quakers, declared: In a Narrative of the Conversion of one in Hartfordshire, who was for some years of their Faith and Principle* [1690], p. iii.

78. Brian R. Wilson, *Sects and Society: A Sociological Study of Three Religious Groups in Britain* (Berkeley: University of California Press, 1961), p. 63.

II   *The Social Context of Quakerism*

The early Friends wrote the history of their movement; the sociology of it was written by their enemies. The lives of the first Quakers were transformed by the intense personality of their new relationship to the transcendant God, and they naturally emphasized, in the flood of spiritual autobiographies which poured forth, how solitary had been their path towards conversion. Later historians have been tempted to follow the bias of this evidence and make the history of Quakerism into an amalgam of individual salvation histories. But to the Puritan clergyman who beheld the rise of Quakerism with undisguised horror, a sociological explanation for it was more congenial. England had become a forcing house for the varieties of religious experience, and when Pagitt's *Heresiography* described the Quakers as "an upstart branch of the Anabaptists, lately sprung up but thickest set in the North parts" and with the bulk of their adherents "composed and made up out of the dregs of the common people" it was an attempt, however biased, to relate Quakerism to the social history of the times.[1]

The bigotry of comments such as this may strike us as fit only for Milton's superb scorn; yet it is of obvious importance to establish the social bearings of Quakerism, even though the

1. Ephraim Pagitt, *Heresiography* (5th ed.; 1654), p. 136.

first Friends were predisposed not to see them and though
the evidence is tedious to compile and difficult to interpret.
To investigate the common factors in the social background
of the early Friends, I propose to concentrate upon two elite
groups and three larger samples of the whole movement. The
elites are that group of the most important traveling Quaker
evangelists whom Ernest E. Taylor defined as "the valiant
sixty" and the somewhat larger group of early Friends, many
of them ordinary rank-and-file Quakers, who left some autobiographical account of their entrance into Quakerism.[2] As
for the larger samples, I have compiled from the Quaker
registers the names of all the Friends in Buckinghamshire
and Norfolk (including Norwich, which was in fact administered as a separate county) over the period from 1654 to
1740, arranging them in the appropriate family by the
method of family reconstitution. (I have established the fact
and date of their becoming Friends largely from a collation
of names in the registers of births, marriages, and deaths,
supplemented where possible by other evidence, particularly
the records of meetings for business, wills, and quarter sessions and ecclesiastical records.) Between five and six percent
of the Friends in England during the first century of Quakerism lived in Buckinghamshire and Norfolk.[3] These sources
taken together give us much data not only on the occupational
backgrounds from which the early Friends came, but also

2. A few names are found both on Taylor's list (*The Valiant Sixty*
[2nd ed.; London: Bannisdale Press, 1951]) and on my bibliographical
list of authors of spiritual autobiographies.

3. This estimate is based on the fact that between 1650 and 1749
there were 372 marriages registered in the Buckinghamshire Quarterly
Meeting books and 573 in those of Norfolk and Norwich Quarterly
Meeting, amounting to 5.3 percent of the 17,814 registered throughout
England. See the statistics compiled by John Stephenson Rowntree,
*Quakerism, Past and Present: being an Inquiry into the Causes of its
Decline in Great Britain and Ireland* (1859), p. 86. Both in Buckinghamshire and in Norfolk registration of marriages became more and more
careless in the early eighteenth century, but it is not known how much
more remiss, if any, the clerks of those meetings were than those in the
rest of England.

such valuable demographic information as their ages, position in the family, and geographical mobility — information which, I shall suggest, is even more suggestive than the evidence of Friends' occupations.

The Occupational Background of the Earliest Friends

It is commonly thought that Quakerism began as a sect appealing chiefly to the poor — "dregs of the common people," in *Heresiography*'s social categories — but that Quakers became steadily richer throughout their history. As Frederick Tolles puts it, more generally, recruitment of members from the less prosperous classes is one of the distinctive marks of the sect, and the "institutionalization" of the Quaker movement during its first half-century saw, among other things, a "rise from lower-middle-class obscurity into upper-middle-class respectability." [4] Almost all writers dealing with the earliest period of Quakerism have emphasized the relative poverty of most of the early Friends. Margaret James deems it "significant that Quakerism appealed to the lowest classes more than any other variety of Puritanism." To James F. Maclear, Friends' longing for social justice was entirely natural, for Quakerism "was recruited from the lower classes, the agrarian and 'mechanick' poor." Alan Cole, who unlike these writers had compiled substantial statistical evidence, concluded from it that the early Friends were "mainly drawn from the urban and rural *petite bourgeoisie*." [5]

4. "Introduction," pp. xxx–xxxi, to William C. Braithwaite, *The Second Period of Quakerism*, 2nd ed. prepared by Henry J. Cadbury (Cambridge, Eng.: Cambridge University Press, 1961).

5. Margaret James, *Social Problems and Policy during the Puritan Revolution* (London: G. Routledge and Sons, 1930), p. 19; James F. Maclear, "Quakerism and the End of the Interregnum: A Chapter in the Domestication of Radical Puritanism," *Church History*, 19 (1950), 243; and Alan Cole, "The Social Origins of the Early Friends," *J.F.H.S.*, 48 (1957), 117. In another context Cole states that the majority of urban Friends were "drawn from the class of petty traders and handicraftsmen." See "The Quakers and Politics, 1652–1660," p. 5, unpub. diss., Cambridge University, 1955. A more detailed discussion of Cole's methods

Valuable as it would be to know from what occupational groups and social milieu Friends came, both in the beginning and as the movement progressed, it is extremely difficult to evaluate the conclusions quoted in the previous paragraph. My own data suggest an opposite interpretation — that in the beginnings of Quakerism the gentry and wholesale traders were especially drawn to it, and that the tendency was for the social standing of Friends to decline during the first century — but before presenting it I must consider the formidable difficulties of compiling and interpreting evidence on this question.

Since I know of no statistical data about the appeal of Puritanism or the other Puritan sects to various social groups, I consider it impossible to verify James's statement. The claim that Quakerism was drawn mainly from the poor can, on the other hand, be tested. Such a statement would be trivial in one sense; most Englishmen in the seventeenth century were poor and the Anglican and Roman Catholic churches were also recruited mainly from the poor. To know whether the poor were *disproportionately* numerous among Friends, we would have to know something of the occupational distribution of the total population, or at least the ratio of rich to poor. Unfortunately, evidence about this is extremely difficult to come by. The only seventeenth-century source giving the occupational distribution of the population in an area larger than a single parish is a muster roll from Gloucestershire for the year 1608. Our best idea of the proportions of rich and poor comes from the "political arithmetic" of Gregory King — calculations made in 1696 for the year 1688.[6] There are

---

and findings may be found in my article "Quakerism and the Social Structure in the Interregnum," *Past and Present*, 44 (August 1969).

6. A. J. Tawney and R. H. Tawney, "An Occupational Census of the Seventeenth Century," *Economic History Review*, 5 (1934), 25–64; Gregory King, "Natural and Political Observations and Conclusions upon the State and Condition of England," first printed in *Two Tracts*, ed. George E. Barnett (Baltimore: Johns Hopkins Press, 1936), p. 31.

in addition local occupational surveys from Buckinghamshire and Norwich which are of some use in establishing regional economic patterns in the areas I have especially studied.[7]

Gregory King's "Scheme of the Income and Expense of the several families of England Calculated for the Year 1688" is an estimate of the income of all heads of households in that year. It is epitomized in Table 1.

Table 1. King's estimate of the expenses and incomes of English families in 1688.

Occupation or status	Number of heads of households	Total number in category	Pct.
Gentlemen		26,586	2.0
Peers, baronets, and knights	1,586		
Esquires	3,000		
Gentlemen	12,000		
Office-holders			
(£240 annual income)	5,000		
Office-holders			
(£120 annual income)	5,000		
Merchants and traders by sea		10,000	0.7
£400 annual income	2,000		
£200 annual income	8,000		
Lawyers		10,000	0.7
Clergymen		10,000	0.7
£60 annual income	2,000		
£45 annual income	8,000		
"Persons in sciences and liberal arts"		16,000	1.2
Military and naval officers		9,000	0.7
Total of these		81,586	6.0
Freeholders		180,000	13.2
£84 annual income	40,000		
£50 annual income	140,000		
Farmers		150,000	11.0
Total of these		330,000	24.3

7. See Table 6.

Table 1 (*Continued*)

Occupation or status	Number of heads of households	Total number in category	Pct.
Shopkeepers and tradesmen		40,000	2.9
Artisans and handicrafts workers		60,000	4.4
Total of these		100,000	7.3
Total of all those "increasing the wealth of England"		511,586	37.6
Common soldiers and seamen		85,000	
Laboring people and out-servants		364,000	
Cottagers and paupers		400,000	
Total of all those "decreasing the wealth of England"		849,000	62.4
Total heads of households		1,360,586	

King's notion that laboring people "decrease the wealth of England" is curious, and his distinction between greater and lesser office-holders, clergymen, merchants, and freeholders (apparently grouped by average income) needs further justification. There is a further difficulty in comparing with it the statistics from the Gloucestershire muster roll of 1608, not merely because the roll covers only one county almost a century earlier, but also because it was a legal enrollment of the men of the county liable to military service, and not an occupational census. Its value to us lies in the fact that 88 per cent of the men's names are followed by what look like occupational or status descriptions: "gentleman," "yeoman," "husbandman," "draper," and the like. These names technically are called "additions": words indicating "Estate, Degree, or Mystery" — that is, social status or occupation. They had been added to personal names in indictments since 1413 (1 Hen. 5, c. 5), and are found in most legal documents in the seventeenth century. In all probability Friends' registers decided to imitate these legal forms by including "additions" of fathers and bridegrooms in some of their registers, since the registers themselves were apparently intended to be analogues of the parish registers, where "additions" are sometimes found.

Most of the evidence about the occupations of seventeenth-century men must be drawn from the "additions" found in contemporary records, but it is wise not to assume that they are altogether unambiguous. In particular, as we shall see, the names "yeoman" and "husbandman" may be deceptive. Bearing this in mind, we may now summarize in Table 2 the Gloucestershire muster roll figures:

Table 2. "Additions" on the Gloucestershire muster roll, 1608.

Occupation or status	Number of persons	Total number in category	Pct.
Gentry, professional, and official		519	3.0
Knights, gentlemen, esquires [a]	457		2.7
Professional [a] (includes 5 surgeons, 2 physicians, 6 schoolmasters, 3 clergymen)	41		
Official	21		
Agricultural		7,883	46.2
Yeomen [a]	1,071		6.3
Husbandmen [a]	3,999		23.5
Laborers [a]	1,841		10.8
Servants to men in agriculture	828		4.9
Textiles		2,637	15.5
Clothiers [a]	232		1.4
Weavers [a] (includes 262 broad-weavers)	1,765		10.4
Leather work		201	1.2
Tanners [a]	114		0.7
Making articles of dress		1,261	7.4
Tailors [a]	674		4.0
Shoemakers [a]	342		2.0
Wood work		675	4.0
Carpenters and joiners [a]	420		2.5

Table 2 (*Continued*)

Occupation or status	Number of persons	Total number in category	Pct.
Building and construction		346	2.0
Masons and freemasons [a]	205		1.2
Making food and drink		383	2.2
Millers [a]	151		0.9
Maltsters [a]	74		0.4
Bakers [a]	106		0.6
Dealing and retail trade		715	4.2
Drapers	30		0.2
Mercers [a]	114		0.7
Butchers [a]	259		1.5
Others		2,426	14.2
Servants and non-agricultural laborers	1,329		7.8
		17,046	

[a] Includes men listed as sons or brothers of men of this occupation.

These figures are not comparable with those of King, who was interested in income distribution — or in his terms, income creation — and was not particularly interested in the numbers engaged in different occupations. However, the two sets of statistics are consonant. King's category of "laboring people and out-servants" must include both agricultural and urban laborers, but his total of farmers and freeholders comes to 24.3 percent of the whole, as compared to the yeomen and husbandmen who taken together amount to 29.8 percent of the Gloucestershire figures. King's estimates would suggest that the percentage of gentlemen lay between two and six. "Gentleman" was not an occupational term; it was applied in Gloucestershire to clothiers and was also used in the latter seventeenth century of yeomen, physicians, merchants, worsted weavers, woolcombers, and even tanners.[8] We may as-

8. Many tanners in Somerset — one of whom was the grandfather of the philosopher John Locke — were "of the smaller gentry." See Maurice Cranston, *John Locke: A Biography* (London: Macmillan and Company, 1957), p. 5. Philip Styles has suggested that the term "gentleman" was used more loosely in the latter seventeenth century; often the line be-

sume that a good many in the learned professions and some
army and navy officers and merchants counted themselves
gentlemen also.

Now with this rough idea of the occupational structure of
seventeenth-century English society, we may turn first to the
social background of the Quaker leaders, the "valiant sixty"
as established by Ernest E. Taylor. Their occupations are
summarized in Table 3.

Table 3. Men with known occupations among the "valiant sixty."

Occupation or status	No.	Pct.	Occupation or status	No.	Pct.
Gentlemen	6	11.1	Agriculture	36	66.7
Professional	8	14.8	Gentlemen	5	9.3
Schoolmasters	6	11.1	Yeomen	15	27.8
Secretary, short-			Husbandmen	13	24.1
hand writer	2		Steward, Laborer,		
Soldiers	2	3.7	Shepherd	3	
General Trade	4	7.4	Trade in Food	2	3.7
Drapers	2		(Miller, butcher)		
Fellmonger,			Clothing Production	2	3.7
shopkeeper	2		(Weaver, shoemaker)		

Source: Based on the listing in Ernest E. Taylor, *The Valiant Sixty*
(2nd ed.; London: Bannisdale Press, 1951), pp. 40–42, with amend-
ments discussed more fully in my "Quakerism and the Social Structure,"
Past and Present, 44 (1969). I count Gervase Benson a gentleman, since
as a colonel and a judge he clearly would have been regarded as such.

Percentages of such small numbers do not mean much,
and the findings would fail even a lax significance test, but
since historians are often reduced to working with small
samples and making more or less impressionistic deductions
from them, it would seem that the striking features of this
table are the relatively large number of gentlemen, and even
more professional men; the very strong ties with agriculture;
and the fact that so few came from the "mechanic trades."

tween yeoman and gentleman was blurred. See "The Heralds' Visitation
of Warwickshire, 1682–1683," *Birmingham Archaeological Society
Transactions*, 71 (1953), 122.

Considering the two "gentlewomen," Elizabeth Fletcher and Margaret Fell, as well as the six gentlemen, eight out of the fifty-five families represented in the "valiant sixty" come from the gentry. The number of schoolmasters is especially remarkable when we recall that the same number, six, were enrolled out of seventeen thousand men in Gloucestershire.[9] Although the dales of Yorkshire and the northwest corner of England were probably more completely devoted to agriculture and pasturage than most of the rest of England, and thus the "valiant sixty," who mostly came from this area, could be expected to be predominantly agricultural, the number of substantial freeholders or allodial tenants (called "statesmen" in the northwest of England) is high. These "statesmen," included among the yeomen in Table 3, were among the most important leaders of the early Quakers. Richard Hubberthorne, for example, had been a captain in the parliamentary cavalry — an office often held by gentlemen, which paid eight shillings a day salary, and for which he might have had to spend as much as £140 to purchase the necessary equipment.[10] John Camm and John Audland had also fought, mostly at their own expense, in the wars. Thomas Aldam sustained losses of £42 and Robert Widders of more than £100 in grain in a single year.[11] More tangible evidence

9. The professions were obviously under-reported in the Gloucestershire muster roll. Schoolmasters, clergy, and medical men, of whom there were only six, three, and seven, respectively, enrolled, would have been about twenty times more numerous if the percentage for Gloucestershire were the same as that in King's estimates. This under-reporting of the professions further suggests that the true percentage of gentlemen was a bit higher than three.

10. Elisabeth Brockbank, *Richard Hubberthorne of Yealand* (London: Friends' Book Centre, 1929), p. 24, and C. H. Firth, assisted by Godfrey Davies, *The Regimental History of Cromwell's Army* (Oxford: Clarendon Press, 1940), I, 19.

11. George Bishop and others, *The Cry of Blood and Herod, Pontius Pilate, and the Jewes, reconciled, and in conspiracy with the Dragon, to devour the Manchild* (1656), p. 69; *A Short Testimony Concerning Thomas Aldam* (1690); *The Life of Robert Widders* (1688); *Persecution Expos'd in Some Memoirs Relating to the Sufferings of John Whiting* (1715), pp. 168–171.

survives in the substantial houses owned by Camm, John Blaykling, and Francis Howgill. Despite this, Camm, Blaykling, and Widders were at times referred to as "husbandmen," which can scarcely have had any more specific meaning than "one engaged in agriculture." For that matter, Edward Burrough, though Friends suggested that he had an estate great enough to be a justice of the peace, and Colonel Gervase Benson, who was a justice, were also called husbandmen.[12] Thus we certainly cannot assume that the so-called husbandmen were all menial hodges.

Only four of the "valiant sixty" can be regarded as exercising "mechanic trades": John Scaife, a day-laborer; William Dewsbury, a shepherd; James Nayler, a butcher; and Thomas Holme, a weaver. Although George Fox's occupation is usually given as "shoemaker," he can scarcely have been dependent on day-labor of any kind, and consistently showed a rather cavalier attitude towards money. On one occasion, for example, having silver in his pocket, he was moved to throw it out among the people in the street. His will bequeathed considerable property, and one of his adversaries, Francis Bugg, in the course of a typically perverse effort to prove that Friends were enriching themselves through their public ministry, said that Fox, though "a poor Journey-Man Shoe-maker, died worth abundance, and lived in as much Plenty as most Knights of England." [13]

12. William C. Braithwaite, *The Beginnings of Quakerism* (Cambridge, Eng.: Cambridge University Press, 1955), p. 92, for Benson; *Extracts from State Papers Relating to Friends, 1654 to 1672*, ed. Norman Penney (London: Headley Brothers, 1913), p. 111, for the proposal that Burrough be put in commission of the peace.

13. Francis Bugg, *The Pilgrim's Progress, from Quakerism, to Christianity* (1698), p. 112. Since there is no reason to believe that Fox reaped any rewards from preaching, it is reasonable to assume he must always have had some independent income. Possibly this was augmented by some of the Fell estate. Fox's finances are discussed by F. Aydelotte, *Bulletin of the Friends' Historical Association*, 13 (1924), 72–73, and by A. Neave Brayshaw, *The Personality of George Fox* (2nd ed.; London: Headley Brothers, 1933), pp. 29–31.

The stereotype of the Quaker "mechanic preacher" owes most to the malice of such Christian controversialists as Bugg and Pagitt, but the prominence within Quakerism of such men as Dewsbury and Nayler is the grain of truth which they lavishly elaborated. Nayler in particular came from a poor family; a hostile source says that he and his father were sow-gelders. We happen to know the size of his estate at the time of his death: £86 12s. plus £32 in desperate debts, against which were charged debts and burial expenses of £17 14s.[14] But men of such humble backgrounds were still sufficiently uncommon to arouse alarm as well as contempt. That the unlearned and meanly born should preach at all was outrageous to "shallow Edwards and Scotch what-d' ye call," Milton's "new forcers of conscience"; [15] but we should not let the indignation of the Presbyterians persuade us that most of the "first publishers of Truth" were mere mechanicals or tub-preachers. Ernest E. Taylor was nearer the truth when he pointed out that "the early Quaker leaders were substantial men," more than half of whom had "a good material position in life, a superior education, and widespread influence in the districts in which they lived." [16] What little we can make of the statistics suggests that the preponderance of gentlemen, schoolmasters, and substantial yeomen, and the relative absence of poor men is the impressive fact about the "valiant sixty." And indeed this is what one might have expected.

14. John Deacon, *An Exact History of the Life of James Naylor with his Birth, Education, Profession, Actions, & Blaspheemies* (1657), p. 4. His son's inventory of Nayler's estate is printed in M. R. Brailsford, *A Quaker from Cromwell's Army: James Nayler* (London: Swarthmore Press, 1927), pp. 197–198. On Dewsbury, see *The Faithful Testimony of William Dewsbury* (1689), pp. 44–48.

15. Men whose Life, Learning, Faith and pure intent
     Would have been held in high esteem with *Paul*
     Must now be nam'd and printed Hereticks
     By shallow *Edwards* and Scotch what d' ye call.
     ("On the new forcers of Conscience under the Long
                                    PARLIAMENT")

16. Ernest E. Taylor, "The First Publishers of Truth: A Study," *J.F.H.S.*, 19 (1922), 76, 81.

There is no conservatism like that of the very poor. Men whose income and social rank afforded them some measure of independence were both more likely to seize upon religious novelties and to take the lead in propagating them.

Although the "valiant sixty" seem to have been of relatively high social rank, this does not mean that the rank and file of early Friends were necessarily so. One might expect economic independence, and its attendant habit of command, to go with leadership, but an alienation from society, rooted in poverty or the fear of it, might have predisposed the mass of followers to accept their message. A considerably more ambitious study than this would be necessary to discover with any pretense to certainty whether this was so; but my evidence for the years before 1663, when persecution began in earnest, is found in Table 4.[17]

Table 4. Occupations of men known to have been Quakers before January 1663.

Occupation or status	Buckinghamshire		Norfolk		Norwich	
	No.	% Range [a]	No.	% Range [a]	No.	% Range [a]
Gentlemen	4	4.0– 7.3	4	3.3– 7.4	1	4.3– 6.3
Agriculture	25	25.3–45.5	19	15.7–35.2		
Gentlemen	2	2.0– 3.6	2	1.7– 3.7		
Yeomen (at least						
20-acre						
freehold)	15	15.2–27.3	11	9.1–20.4		
Farmers	3	3.0– 5.5				
Husbandmen	1	1.0– 1.8	3	2.5– 5.6		
Laborers	4	4.0– 7.3	3	2.5– 5.6		
Professional	2	2.0– 3.6	1	0.8– 1.9		
Physicians	1		1			
Tutor and						
Secretary	1					
Wholesale traders	14	14.1–25.5	10	8.3–18.5	2	8.7–12.5
6 maltsters;						

17. The Appendix has a fuller account of how these statistics were compiled.

Table 4 (*Continued*)

Occupation or status	Buckinghamshire			Norfolk			Norwich		
	No.	%	Range [a]	No.	%	Range [a]	No.	%	Range [a]
3 mealmen; 3 drapers or mercers; 3 merchants or shipmasters; 3 grocers; 4 tanners; 2 millers; bone-lace seller; fellmonger									
Retail traders	9		9.1–16.4	6		5.0–11.1	3		13.0–18.8
6 tailors; 5 shoemakers; 3 bakers; butcher; salter; haberdasher; ironmonger									
Worsted weavers				8		6.6–14.8	2		8.7–12.5
Woolcombers				1		0.8– 1.9	5		21.7–31.3
Artisans and laborers	5		5.1– 9.1	9		7.4–16.7	3		13.0–18.8
2 wheelwrights; 2 carpenters; 2 combmakers; bodice-maker; cloth-worker; plowright; currier, blacksmith; chair maker; sawyer; bricklayer; hempdresser; linen-weaver; laborer									
Unknown	44	44.4		47	38.8		7	30.4	
"Yeoman" on indictment				20	16.5				
Total	99			121			23		

[a] The first percentage is of the total; the second is of those whose occupations are known (excluding those in Norfolk for whom the only information is the "addition" of yeoman on an indictment).

It would be wrong to take these numbers at full value. Anything which purports to be statistics from the seventeenth century must come well guarded with qualifications and interpretations, if it is not to be properly considered the dullest kind of historical fiction. In Table 4 the following are the principal difficulties: (1) whether the "unknowns" are likely to be distributed in the same way as the known occupations; (2) what criteria were used to determine gentlemen, yeomen, and husbandmen; (3) whether the distinction made between wholesale and petty or retail trades is a significant one; and (4) what position in the social scale to assign worsted weavers and woolcombers.

I doubt that the occupations which are known are randomly distributed. A good deal of the evidence came from the registers of births, marriages, and deaths, and my impression is that the clerks had some propensity to include the "additions" of prosperous and prominent Friends more frequently. Also, the other main source of evidence for this early period is the records of sufferings, and since these were often for tithes, we are likely to hear of almost every landed Friend. The true percentage of landed Friends is probably near the smaller figure in the percentage range, but for the others nearer or possibly even in excess of the larger one.

The problem of distinguishing gentlemen, yeomen, and husbandmen is one of the nicest with which I had to deal. Since the gentlemen were not a legally defined class, there is some warrant for simply saying that they were men who gave themselves, or who were given by their contemporaries, the "addition" of gentlemen. I have generally classed as gentlemen those who have this "addition" in more than one source; those holding the office of mayor, common councillor, or justice of the peace; university graduates; or those with a rank in the army above that of captain. (The old equation of officer and gentleman had yielded to Cromwell's preference for "a plain russet-coated captain that knows what he fights for, and loves what he knows" rather than "that which you call a gentleman, and is nothing else.").

In Table 4 the distinction was not difficult to make; most of the men listed as gentlemen are referred to as such consistently in the sources. In Buckinghamshire I have listed as gentlemen Isaac Penington the younger, son of the regicide lord mayor of London; Thomas Ellwood, son of a justice of the peace in Oxfordshire; John Raunce, a common councillor of High Wycombe; and William Russell, whose son was a justice of the peace.[18] In Norwich I have counted Colonel Thomas Deney; and in Norfolk, John Lawrence and William Barber, both former captains in the parliamentary army; Edmund Peckover, the founder of a famous Quaker family; and Henry Kittle, Sr., who had been a justice of the peace and the mayor of Thetford.[19]

Thus the percentage of gentlemen among the first Quaker communities in these counties is up to twice that in the population as a whole; but it remains to be demonstrated more precisely what their social station was, for there were sharp social distinctions within the gentry. County society in Somerset has recently been analyzed by Thomas G. Barnes.[20] At the top of the gentry in Somerset were some twenty-five families, who consistently held seats in parliament, deputy lieutenancies of the country, and the office of sheriff as well as that of justice of the peace. Below these in social rank came

18. *History of the Life of Thomas Ellwood* (1714), pp. 13, 58. The restored rector of Amersham wrote in the parish register that William Russell's son Francis was "one of Oliver's Justices, and a fit man for the times."

19. *The Christian Progress of George Whitehead* (1725), pp. 244–252. Peckover served in Fleetwood's regiment, but apparently not as an officer. His grandson Edmund Peckover was one of the more notable eighteenth-century Friends, and the family was eventually to receive the title of barons Peckover of Wisbech. See R. W. Ketton-Cremer, *Norfolk Assembly* (London: Faber & Faber, 1957), p. 106.

20. *Somerset 1625–1640: A County's Government During the 'Personal Rule'* (Cambridge, Mass.: Harvard University Press, 1961), pp. 11–12.

about seventy-five families, from whom the majority of the justices of the peace were drawn. Then came many families of the lesser gentry, most of whom had substantial estates and were lords of manors, but lacked the wealth and influence to be named in commissions of the peace.

Almost all the gentlemen who became Quakers appear to have come from the lesser gentry rather than the older and more established families. Their occasional appearance during the Interregnum as justices of the peace — it has been estimated that there were no less than twelve justices among the early Friends — appears to be explained by a pattern of local history peculiar to the English Revolution. As Christopher Hill summarizes it, most of the old county families which were favorable to the parliamentary cause nevertheless were unwilling to see a parliamentary victory purchased at the cost of extensive fighting in their own counties. This halfheartedness often led to their being forced out of local power by a "win-the-war" faction, often led by men from old families but drawing most of its support from men of lower social origins. This faction advocated a more aggressive military strategy.[21] John Raunce of High Wycombe and John Crook, a justice of the peace and designate for the Nominated Parliament from Bedfordshire, do seem to have come to power as the result of some such struggle, and it would not be surprising to find this true of other Friends as well — especially in royalist counties, where, as Hugh Barbour points out, "Cromwell often had to reach far down among the ranks of gentry . . . to find Puritans to serve as his justices."[22]

Distinguishing "yeomen" from "husbandmen" also pre-

21. Christopher Hill, "Recent Interpretations of the Civil War" in *Puritanism and Revolution* (London: Secker and Warburg, 1958), pp. 21–23.

22. *The Quakers in Puritan England* (New Haven: Yale University Press, 1964), p. 91. Seventeen of the twenty justices of the peace who served in Warwickshire from 1645 to 1660 seem never to have been in the commission before; see A. L. Beier, "Poor Relief in Warwickshire 1630–1660," *Past and Present*, 35 (1966), 93 n. 50.

sents difficulties, because it is by no means clear what these words meant in seventeenth-century usage. We have already encountered sizable landowners among the "valiant sixty" who were referred to as "husbandmen." The later of two village surveys in Warwickshire in the late seventeenth century showed a remarkable increase in the number of "yeomen" and a decrease in the "husbandmen"; but this does not mean there was a Rise of the Yeoman. It was only a nomenclatural revolution; the term "husbandman" was dying out.[23] It was not uncommon for men to be called both yeoman and husbandman, even at approximately the same time (as was true of four among the "valiant sixty"). An extreme example is Edward Lered or Learhead of Amersham in Buckinghamshire, who within five years was described in the Buckinghamshire registers as a laborer, husbandman, yeoman, farmer, and cheesemonger. As this suggests, there is not even any absolute assurance that a man described as a yeoman in legal documents made his living primarily from the land. In Norfolk almost everyone indicted by the quarter sessions is called a yeoman (which is why I have treated these descriptions with skepticism); in Bristol, Friends presented before the quarter sessions were uniformly described as "laborers." The use of the word is variable even in wills, for a study of wills in Yorkshire during this period reveals that the word yeoman "was often only an alias for clothier." [24]

I have therefore decided to pay no attention to the inconsistently used words "yeoman" and "husbandman" as they appear in Friends' registers beyond assuming that Quakers so described did have some connection with agriculture; in other sources, not even that assumption has been made. Wills

23. Philip Styles, "A Census of a Warwickshire Village in 1698," *University of Birmingham Historical Journal*, 3 (1951–1952), 42.

24. Russell Mortimer, "Quakerism in Seventeenth Century Bristol," unpub. Master's thesis, Bristol University, 1946, p. 515; Herbert Heaton, *The Yorkshire Woollen and Worsted Industries from the Earliest Times up to the Industrial Revolution* (Oxford: Oxford University Press, 1920), p. 93.

and records of the sufferings of landed Friends are sufficiently informative to reveal the true economic situation of most of them. I have therefore restricted the word "yeoman" to a man who made his principal living from working his own land. Where the evidence is that the man rented or leased land for his principal livelihood, I have described him as a "farmer." Everyone else, unless there is evidence of renting or owning land, appears in my tables as husbandman.

My definition of a yeoman entails a further difficulty: how does one decide whether a man owned enough land to make his principal living from working it? Here I have descended to guesswork, proposing as the lower limits for the class of yeoman ownership of at least twenty acres of land (as revealed in wills) or incurring tithes of at least £4 annually. But though these are guesses, they are not purely arbitrary. There is no contemporary evidence indicating how much land was owned by the "average" yeoman in Buckinghamshire or Norfolk, but in Lancashire, where conditions favored the small holder, the great majority of holdings were said to be less than thirty acres, if not less than fifteen.[25] In 1624 a book called *A Plaine Path-way to Plantations*, in an attempt to promote emigration by "those of a degree next unto Gentlemen, that is Yeoman and Yeoman-like men" promised as an inducement estates of fifty acres with socage tenure in America. This must indicate that a good many "yeoman-like men" had smaller holdings than this in England.[26] As for the tithe, it is unfortunately impossible to guess at annual income from annual tithes, though there is obviously some connection. In both Buckinghamshire and Nor-

25. Alfred P. Wadsworth and Julia de Lacy Mann, *The Cotton Trade and Industrial Lancashire 1600–1780* (Manchester, Eng.: University of Manchester Press, 1931), pp. 26–27.

26. Mildred Campbell, *The English Yeoman under Elizabeth and the Early Stuarts* (New Haven: Yale University Press, 1942), p. 279. This book discusses the meaning of the "addition" of yeoman on pages 26–32, taking it as a good deal more reliable an indicator of social status than I have felt able to do.

folk, £4 seemed to represent the boundary of a class, since smaller demands were usually much smaller — not more than thirty shillings at most.

In fact, there were comparatively few difficult decisions about classing men as yeomen rather than husbandmen. In the records of sufferings there is a marked distinction both in the amount and in the manner of the sufferings of the more substantial landowners as compared to those who had only a little land. Particularly in Buckinghamshire, most of the yeomen were clearly prosperous. The southern part or "upperside" of the county (so called because of the altitude of the Chilterns) had been substantially enclosed for provision of grain demanded by the great growth of London. Many of the early Friends in Buckinghamshire were engaged in agriculture on a fairly large scale, as can be seen from their wills and sufferings. Robert Charsley and Ralph Trumper left estates of around £1,000.[27] Edward Rose was lord of Grenville's manor in Haddenham and Henry Child was lord of Coleshill manor in Amersham. Child's sufferings for tithes were usually between £7 and £13 a year, while Trumper's tithes were assessed as high as £28 10s. for a single year. John White of Meadle lost annually from £8 10s. to £14 16s. and John Brown of Weston Turville from £10 to £15, sustaining in some years exceptional losses of £50 or even £92.[28]

27. Wills cited in this chapter may be found in the following collections: John Aggs, Norfolk Archdeaconry Court, 1771; Robert Charsley (1705), Jeremiah Stevens (1688), Joseph Stevens (1713), Joseph Stevens (1775), and Ralph Trumper (1692), all in Buckinghamshire Archdeaconry Court; Henry Lombe, "Irby" 219 (1695) in the Prerogative Court of Canterbury; James Frary and Richard Wright, Norwich Consistory Court, 1771 and 1733 respectively. There is a copy of the will of James Byer in the manuscripts of Arthur Eddington in Norwich.

28. John Brown lost £50 in 1674 and George Salter of Hedgerley Dean lost £50 in 1665; John White lost £92 in 1667. Accounts of sufferings, arranged by years, can be found in "A Memorial of the Sufferings of the people of God called Quakers, in the County of Bucks, and parts adjacent, for their Testimony of Truth," a volume of 450 pages kept by Buckinghamshire Quarterly Meeting and now deposited in

The demands of London for food were also spreading capitalistic agriculture into Norfolk.[29] This must have led to sharper class lines in agriculture, with the poorer peasants being forced off the land altogether or depressed into servants in husbandry. But few of these victims of agrarian progress seem to have been attracted to Quakerism, as the figures in Table 4 show.

Just as yeomen predominated among landed Friends, so wholesale traders were more numerous than retailers, whereas the reverse must have been true in the general population. This a fact of considerable significance. In the first place, the social prestige of the wholesale trades was greater. Men still endorsed the opinion of Cicero's *De Officiis*: "Low . . . are the trades of those who buy from merchants in order to sell immediately at a profit . . . For trade is certainly paltry and low when it is mean and done on a small scale." [30] Merchants and shipmasters, as Gregory King's figures show, enjoyed the greatest income and prestige, but drapers and clothiers were not far behind; even tanners and maltsters

---

Friends' House Library in London. For Edward Rose and Henry Child as lords of manors, see *The Victoria History of the County of Buckingham*, ed. William Page, II (1908), 284 and III (1925), 151. There is another reference to Rose in Robert Gibbs, "Jordans," *Records of Buckinghamshire* (Aylesbury, 1887?), VI, 126.

29. N. S. B. Gras, *The Evolution of the English Corn Market* (Cambridge, Mass.: Harvard University Press, 1915); F. J. Fisher, "The Development of the London Food Market, 1540-1640," *Economic History Review*, 5 (1935), 46-64; M. W. Beresford, "Glebe Terriers and Open Field Buckinghamshire: Part II," *Records of Buckinghamshire*, XVI, part 1 (1953-1954), 5-28.

30. This was quoted by a Florentine humanist of the fifteenth century, Matteo Palmieri, in his work *Della vita civile* (1438-1439). See Lauro Martines, *The Social World of the Florentine Humanists, 1390-1460* (Princeton: Princeton University Press, 1963), p. 31. Jacques Savary, *Le parfait negociant* (2nd ed.: Paris, 1679), and Malachy Postlethwayt, *The Universal Dictionary of Trade and Commerce* (2 vols.; 1751) indicate that the higher reputation of wholesale traders persisted into the eighteenth century, as demonstrated by Ray B. Westerfield, "Middlemen in English Business, Particularly Between 1660 and 1760," *Transactions of the Connecticut Academy of Arts and Sciences*, 19 (1915), 401.

might be considered gentlemen. As one would expect, social prestige attended wealth; an examination of one hundred wills left by Friends in wholesale and retail trade in the seventeenth and eighteenth centuries shows that the wholesale traders consistently had considerably larger estates. Merchants and shipmasters, again, tended to be the richest, along with some drapers and clothiers. In the Thames valley, some of the mealmen and millers who engaged in the London corn trade were driving a flourishing trade, while the grocers — the name still retained some of the connotations of "dealing in gross" and was not confined to the food trade — were also substantial men. Tanners and maltsters, though appreciably better off than retail tradesmen, were probably the least wealthy of the wholesalers.

As a general rule, the less perishable the goods traded, the larger the scale of trade and the higher the capital requirement for entering. This accounts for the consistently greater wealth of millers than bakers and of tanners than butchers. In the eighteenth century it was reckoned that a graduate apprentice needed from £1,000 to £5,000 to set up as a draper, £1,000 to £10,000 as a mercer, £2,000 to £10,000 as a brewer, but only £20 to £100 as a butcher.[31] It follows that the wealthier the trader, the greater the distance he regularly traversed to do his business. Just as the merchants engaged in the overseas trade were the aristocracy of the trading classes, so the drapers and clothiers, whose businesses generally spread across several counties, were the richest of domestic traders. The same connection can be found in agriculture, where it was probably the substantial yeomen who were more likely to move about.[32]

For the most part the categories of petty tradesmen, artisans, and laborers are self-explanatory; but the same cannot be said of worsted weavers and woolcombers. It might be

31. Westerfield, 375.
32. Styles, "A Census of a Warwickshire Village," pp. 45–46.

thought that they should be counted as laborers, but it is difficult to determine their social and economic positions merely from their occupational names. The organization of the East Anglian worsted industry in the period before the Industrial Revolution is obscure. It appears that the differentiation of weaver, clothier, and merchant was less complete than in others parts of the country. Thus we find that some people called worsted weavers were undoubtedly wage-laborers; on the other hand there were endowments to lend them capital for a start in the trade, and we read of their being bankrupt. Laws were made to limit the number of looms and apprentices which worsted weavers might have, and even though these were often violated, the legislative ideal must have been the household production unit selling direct to the public.[33]

"Combing" the wool was an intermediary stage in worsted weaving, so that woolcombers, it seems, were more generally wage-laborers. In the 1740's they even had a national union. Because of the strength and skill necessary, they received high wages even though the equipment required was not expensive. Spinning was done by women and by the most poorly paid male workers.[34]

The clarity of this picture is somewhat spoiled by an analysis of the wills of worsted weavers and woolcombers.

33. Arthur Young in his *The Farmer's Tour through the East of England* (1771), II, 74–82, gives a schedule of wages according to which worsted weavers and woolcombers received seven shillings a week, dyers and hotpressers fifteen shillings. On the other hand, Quaker records of sufferings speak of finished cloth being taken from the "shops" of worsted weavers. Francis Blomefield, *An Essay towards a Topographical History of the County of Norfolk* (1806), III, 355, 422, gives examples of endowment to lend capital to poor worsted weavers.

34. John James, *History of the Worsted Manufacture in England from the Earliest Times* (1857), pp. 249–250, gives the best description of combing wool. See also Heaton, *Yorkshire Woollen*, pp. 259–263, 312, 320, 333. An act of 1547 recalls how "the greatest and almost the whole number of the poor inhabitants of the county of *Norfolk*, and the city of Norwich . . . have been . . . for a great time maintained . . . by spinning." Quoted in Blomefield, *County of Norfolk*, III, 220.

It is clear from these that some men calling themselves worsted weavers and woolcombers were not only masters, but masters of many workmen. This was particularly true in Norwich, where the legendarily rich Gurneys were describing themselves as worsted weavers until the latter part of the eighteenth century. Of the twenty-seven wills of Quaker worsted weavers which I examined, only six left more than £300 in specified bequests; however, Henry Lombe of Norwich left at least £1,212 in 1695 and Richard Wright of Norwich bequeathed in 1733 the great sum of £5,200, plus land in nine different parishes. Estates of woolcombers seemed to be a bit larger, to judge from twenty surviving wills. The majority were still below £300, but James Frary of Norwich bequeathed £1,200 in 1771 and James Byer, also reputed a gentleman though calling himself a woolcomber in his will, left in 1716 no less than £4,315 plus a provision of £400 for annuities. Another estate of more than £4,000 was left by a woolcomber named James Aggs in 1770. At the wage rate of seven shillings per day which Arthur Young tells us was paid woolcombers in that year, Aggs would have had to save every penny of wages for more than forty years to accumulate such an estate. It is thus impossible to relegate all the woolcombers and worsted weavers to the industrial proletariat. There is even an occasional anomaly in the clearly "mechanic" occupations; John Gurney the elder, the founder of the great Norwich Quaker dynasty, was still described as a shoemaker at his death, but he left an estate of £2,410.

After this extensive tour of the pitfalls in generalizing from occupational distribution, it may be worthwhile to attempt a comparison of the social composition of the early Friends with that of Gloucestershire men as shown on the muster roll of 1608. This is done in Table 5. Table 6 compares Friends' occupations with occupations listed in the Chesham parish register from 1558 to 1636; with the occupations of voters in St. Giles parish, Norwich — a constituency famous for the breadth of its franchise and the corruptibility of its electors — and with the "strangers" in Norwich.

Table 5. Occupational distribution of male Friends compared with Gloucestershire muster roll (in percentages of those with known occupations).

Occupation or status	Men, 20–60 in Glocs., 1608	Known Quakers in 1662		
		Bucks	Norfolk	Norwich
Gentry, professional and official	3.0	7.3	7.4	6.3
Professional	0.2	3.6	1.9	—
Agriculture (including laborers)	46.2	45.5	35.2	—
Yeomen	6.3	27.3	20.4	—
Farmers	—	5.5	—	—
Husbandmen	23.5	1.8	5.5	—
Laborers and servants	15.7	7.3	5.5	—
Wholesale Traders [a]	4.2	25.5	18.5	12.5
Retail Traders [b]	10.5	16.4	11.1	18.8
Weavers and woolcombers	13.5	—	16.7	43.8
Artisans, servants, and laborers	22.6	9.1	16.7	18.8

[a] Clothiers, drapers, mercers, merchants, tanners, millers, maltsters, and sons and brothers of men in these occupations.
[b] Retailers and their sons and brothers.

When we survey all this evidence, it is easier to abstain from making confident generalizations. In particular, when we discuss early Friends, we are working with numbers too small for significant statistical correlations. But the evidence we have scarcely suggests that excitement of the corporate aspirations of the petite bourgeoisie had anything to do with the origins of Quakerism. This class, like industrial workers and agricultural laborers, is surprisingly under-represented. The core of support for early Quakerism seems to have been the yeomen and the wholesale traders. These social groups, together with the gentry, seem also to have provided most of

Table 6. Local occupational surveys, compared with occupational distribution of early Friends (percentages of those with known occupations).

Occupation or status	Bucks. Quakers 1662	Chesham parish register 1538–1636	Norwich Quakers 1662	"Strangers" in Norwich 1622	St. Giles Norwich Voters 1734–1735
Gentry, professional, and official	7.3	2.7	6.3	1.7	0.8
Professional	3.6	1.8	—	1.7	0.8
Agriculture (including laborers)	45.5	0.9	—	2.7	—
Wholesale traders	25.5	12.4	12.5	6.0	0.8
Retail traders	16.4	35.0	18.8	16.1	10.7
Worsted weavers	—	—	12.5	34.6	50.4
Woolcombers	—	—	31.3	22.1	6.6
Artisans, laborers, and servants	9.1	49.1	18.8	16.8	17.4
Total Number	55	226	16	233	121

Source: Based on a compilation by J. W. Garrett-Pegge in his edition of A Transcript of the First Volume, 1538–1636, of the Parish Register of Chesham in the County of Buckingham (1904), p. 347; W. J. C. Moens, The Walloons and their Church at Norwich 1565–1832 (Lymington, 1888), p. iii; and Sir Peter Eade, Some Account of the Parish of St. Giles, Norwich (1886), pp. 399–401. Servants and laborers have been eliminated from the Chesham figures by Garrett-Pegge, and to make his figures comparable to mine in concerning only men, I have eliminated the occupations which are presumably those of women (e.g., midwife and "meretrix").

the leadership. Given the fragmentary quality of the evidence, we should not place an exaggerated confidence in the percentage distributions among Friends as compared with the samples of the general population; but it can be said with assurance that Quakerism at the beginning drew adherents from all classes of society except the very highest and the very lowest, ranging from the lesser gentry down to a few totally unskilled laborers.

Religious ideas at first gain adherents from all social classes and make a "vertical cleavage" in society, writes Max Weber. As time goes on, the cross section of society represented by the religious group becomes increasingly "horizontal" — that is, the religious group becomes identified with one class.[35] Weber cites the example of the French Huguenots, who originally came substantially from the nobility and the peasantry, but later were increasingly confined to the mercantile and manufacturing classes. In its beginnings Quakerism seems to have attracted men from a wide social range; it remains to be seen whether it also showed a tendency for this range to contract. The evidence can be found in Table 7.

It is hard to detect any spectacular trends, especially since the data are much less complete after 1700. The clearest trend is the gradual disappearance of landed gentry among Friends. This can be explained by their inability, after about 1670, to attract any further converts from this class. Only three gentlemen — none of them landed — became Friends in Buckinghamshire and Norfolk during the two decades before the Toleration Act of 1689. It is true that in the decade of the 1660's the flow of converts from the landed gentry remained undiminished. William Penn, who had special connections with Buckinghamshire, was not con-

35. Max Weber, "Antikritisches zum 'Geist' des Kapitalismus," *Archiv für Sozialwissenschaft und Sozialpolitik*, 30 (1910), 188, n. 14.

Table 7. Occupations of all male Quakers, 1663–1740.

Occupations, Buckinghamshire	End of 1662 No.	% Range	End of 1672 No.	% Range	End of 1686 No.	% Range	End of 1700 No.	% Range	End of 1720 No.	% Range	End of 1740 No.	% Range
Gentlemen	4	4.0– 7.3	6	3.1– 5.3	7	2.8– 4.4	5	2.0– 3.3	2	0.9– 1.5	1	0.7– 1.1
Professional	2	2.0– 3.6	2	1.0– 1.8	1	0.4– 0.6	1	0.4– 0.7	2	0.9– 1.5	2	1.3– 2.2
Agriculture	25	25.3–45.5	53	27.7–46.5	70	28.1–44.0	61	24.6–40.1	53	24.5–39.8	34	22.4–38.2
Yeomen, farmers, graziers,	20	20.1–36.4	35	18.3–30.7	33	13.3–20.8	31	12.5–20.4	27	12.5–20.3	21	13.8–23.6
Husbandmen and laborers	5	5.1– 9.1	18	9.4–15.8	37	14.9–23.3	30	12.1–19.7	26	12.0–19.5	13	8.6–14.6
Wholesale traders	14	14.1–25.5	26	13.6–22.8	36	14.5–22.6	37	14.9–24.3	28	13.0–21.1	21	13.8–23.6
Retail traders	9	9.1–16.4	22	11.5–19.3	31	12.4–19.5	27	10.9–17.8	27	12.5–20.3	14	9.2–15.7
Artisans and laborers	5	5.1– 9.1	11	5.8– 9.6	21	8.4–13.2	26	10.5–17.1	23	10.6–17.3	18	11.8–20.2
Unknown	44	44.4	77	40.3	90	36.1	96	38.7	83	38.4	63	41.4
Totals	99		191		249		248		216		152	

Occupations, Norwich	End of 1662 No.	% Range	End of 1669 No.	% Range	End of 1678 No.	% Range	End of 1689 No.	% Range	End of 1700 No.	% Range	End of 1720 No.	% Range	End of 1740 No.	% Range
Gentlemen	1	4.3– 6.3	—	—	1	1.2– 1.5	1	0.8– 1.2	2	1.3– 2.2	1	0.5– 1.2	1	0.5– 1.5
Wholesale traders	2	8.7–12.5	1	3.3– 4.8	1	2.4– 3.0	3	2.4– 3.7	2	1.3– 2.2	2	1.0– 2.4	2	1.0– 3.0
Retail traders	3	13.0–18.8	4	13.3–19.0	11	13.1–16.4	12	9.5–14.6	2	1.3– 2.2	3	1.5– 3.7	3	1.5– 4.5
									8	5.1– 8.7	8	4.0– 9.8	3	1.5– 4.5
Worsted weavers	2	8.7–12.5	2	6.7– 9.5	11	13.1–16.4	18	14.3–22.0	29	18.7–31.5	39	19.7–47.6	36	17.6–53.7
Woolcombers	5	21.7–31.3	8	26.7–38.1	26	31.0–38.8	33	26.2–40.2	34	21.5–37.0	21	10.6–25.6	11	5.7–16.4
Artisans and laborers	3	13.0–18.8	5	16.7–23.8	12	14.3–17.9	13	10.3–15.9	15	9.5–16.3	9	4.5–11.0	22	5.9–17.9
Unknown	7	30.4	9	30.0	17	20.2	13	34.9	66	41.8	116	58.6	138	67.3
Totals	23		30 [a]		84 [a]		126 [a]		158 [a]		198		206	

Table 7 (*Continued*)

Occupations, Norfolk	End of 1662 No.	% Range	End of 1669 No.	% Range	End of 1678 No.	% Range	End of 1689 No.	% Range	End of 1700 No.	% Range	End of 1720 No.	% Range	End of 1740 No.	% Range
Gentlemen	4	3.3– 7.4	5	2.2– 5.2	5	1.4– 3.6	3	0.7– 2.0	4	0.7– 2.3	7	1.4– 4.7	9	1.8– 8.2
Professional	1	0.8– 1.9	1	0.4– 1.0	1	0.3– 0.7	—	—	—	—	2	0.3– 1.3	2	0.4– 1.8
Agriculture	19	15.7–35.2	33	14.5–34.4	42	12.0–30.4	52	11.5–34.2	62	10.3–35.3	42	6.6–28.0	34	6.8–31.0
Gentlemen, yeomen	13	10.7–24.1	23	10.1–24.0	26	7.4–18.8	31	6.9–20.4	39	6.5–22.2	33	5.2–22.0	28	5.6–25.5
Husbandmen, laborers	6	5.0–11.1	10	4.4–10.4	16	4.6–11.6	21	4.6–13.8	23	3.8–13.1	9	1.4– 6.0	6	1.2– 5.5
Wholesale traders	10	8.3–18.5	10	4.4–10.4	15	4.3–10.9	17	3.8–11.2	22	3.7–12.5	25	4.0–16.7	25	5.0–22.7
Retail traders	6	5.0–11.1	15	6.6–15.6	18	5.1–13.0	23	5.1–15.1	23	3.8–13.1	21	3.3–14.0	12	2.4–10.9
Worsted weavers	8	6.6–14.8	11	4.8–11.5	20	5.7–14.5	16	3.5–10.5	23	3.8–13.1	15	2.4–10.0	10	2.0– 9.1
Woolcombers	1	0.8– 1.9	3	1.3– 3.1	7	2.0– 5.1	8	1.8– 5.3	13	2.2– 7.4	17	2.7–11.3	13	2.6–11.8
Artisans and laborers	9	7.4–16.7	23	10.1–24.0	35	10.0–25.4	36	8.0–23.7	33	5.5–18.8	28	4.4–18.7	14	2.8–12.7
"Yeoman" (indictment)	20	16.5	36	15.8	37	10.5	35	7.7	24	4.0	4	0.6	—	—
Unknown	47	38.8	96	42.1	176	50.1	265	58.6	402	66.8	476	75.6	391	78.0
Totals	121		228		351		452		602		630		501	

^a Norwich Friends in Agriculture omitted.

verted until 1666.[36] About the same time John Archdale, of High Wycombe, of the family which owned Temple Wycombe manor, joined Friends. Archdale, like Penn, was interested in the American colonies; he was an emissary of Charles II to the part of the Massachusetts Bay Colony which is now Maine, and at one time was governor of North Carolina. He was also the first Friend to be elected a member of parliament, being returned for High Wycombe in 1698, though he was not seated because he refused the oath which was tendered him.[37]

Another convert from one of the most eminent families in Buckinghamshire was Hester Fleetwood, who was married to George (once Sir George) Fleetwood, one of the first to raise a company for the parliamentary cause in the county. He signed Charles I's death warrant, was knighted by Cromwell, and served as a knight of the shire for Buckinghamshire in the Nominated Parliament. He also assisted in the proclaiming of Charles II, but this was judged insufficient amends for his regicide past, and he was sentenced to death. The sentence was not carried out, though he was deprived of the family property of The Vache, the largest manor in Chalfont St. Giles; shortly after the Restoration he died. The baptisms of four children of George and Hester Fleetwood are recorded in the parish register of Chalfont St. Giles, the last being on 6 May 1663, so she must have joined the Friends afterwards.[38] In Norfolk Robert Gawsell, of Shottisham, the son of a justice of the peace during the Interregnum, and James Long, whose daughter married into the

36. Pepys notes in his diary for 29 December 1667 that Penn was "a Quaker again, or some very melancholy thing."

37. The most reliable short biography of Archdale is in the *Dictionary of American Biography*. See also *Victoria History of Buckingham*, III, 121, 125; and *J.F.H.S.*, 8 (1911), 5.

38. *Victoria History of Buckingham*, III, 188. Another "Mrs. Fleetwood," the sister-in-law of Hester, was the chief upholder of the Presbyterian conventicle in Chalfont St. Giles; see G. Lyon Turner, *Original Records of Early Nonconformity under Persecution and Indulgence* (London: T. F. Unwin, 1911), I, 78.

Peckover family, seem to have been landed gentlemen converted during the 1660's, but these were to be the last.

Not only were there no further converts from the ranks of the landed gentry; some of the lesser gentry who had been drawn into Quakerism in the early years left it, and few of them founded families which remained Friends. Of the gentlemen among the earliest converts in Buckinghamshire, only two, William Russell and Isaac Penington, had children who were active in the following generation. None of Mrs. Fleetwood's children became Friends. William Penn and John Archdale moved out of the county; John Raunce adhered to the Separatists; and Thomas Ellwood married a woman too old to have children. In Norfolk the story was similar: with the exception of Edmund Peckover, none of the four gentlemen among the earliest converts had children who were active Friends. Robert Gawsell evidently left Friends after a decade (at any rate nothing further is heard of him). In Norwich, Colonel Thomas Deney, who had been one of the first to receive Truth, fell away by 1662, if not before; James Halls proved imperious and intractable, and had to be disowned; and James Byer, a wealthy woolcomber, had the not uncommon experience (shared by John Bellers in Buckinghamshire) of having his oldest son return to the established church.[39]

No class could be exempt from the sterility or "daughtering out" of its constituent families, so that without continual recruitment the landed gentry among Friends would eventually have been extinguished in any case. Nevertheless its disappearance was much more rapid than could have been produced by mere demographic wastage. Possibly the galling effects of Quaker discipline, particularly as it prohibited much of the life style of the upper classes, alienated some;

39. This had the odd result that Byer is one of the few seventeenth-century Quakers with a monument in a parish church; when his son died both he and his parents were commemorated in St. George Colgate Church, Norwich (Blomefield, *County of Norfolk*, IV, 473.)

but the main explanation probably lies in the unfavorable political climate. The temporal advantages of conformity to the religion by law established often proved attractive to upper-class sons, if not to their fathers. Those who wished for political power had to conform or else limit their sphere to colonial affairs. To this extent, and for much the same reasons, the Quakers conform to the pattern seen by Weber in the defection of the French nobility from Protestantism. It appears that the upper-class adherents to a Protestant religious minority are more susceptible to the threats and especially to the blandishments of the established order than are Catholics, if we contrast the experience of the Quakers and Huguenots to the stubborn persistence of the English recusant Catholic nobility and gentry.

The other obvious tendency in the changing distribution of Quaker occupations is the concentration of the Norwich Quakers in the manufacture of worsted cloth and the increasing numbers of worsted weavers. At first it had been the woolcombers who had been predominant: "I think the combing trade is the nursery for almost all the dissenters from our church," said the mayor of Norwich on 27 February 1676 after interrogating yet another Quaker woolcomber.[40]

It seems clear that the converts made after 1670 were generally of lower social status than the original ones. There were no professional men, and proportionately only half as many wholesale traders, whereas there were more petty tradesmen, artisans, and laborers among the newer converts. In Buckinghamshire, moreover, there was a striking change in the status of converts engaged in agriculture. Yeomen were slightly less prominent among later converts in Norfolk, but they were remarkably less so in Buckinghamshire, where the great majority of the new adherents were husbandmen or laborers.[41] Thus Quakerism, in the areas I have studied,

40. Interrogation of John Fiddeman, Norwich Book of Sufferings.
41. Readers whose appetite for tabulated material has not been

was more nearly a "plebeian" or "petty bourgeois" movement than it had been in 1662, and since the tendency for converts to be of lower social rank than existing members contined until 1740, the social composition of eighteenth-century Quakerism still had a somewhat more "plebeian" cast than that of the earliest Friends.

It is, of course, open to question whether intensive studies of other counties would not show that Buckinghamshire and Norfolk were untypical. Until they are made, we can only guess; but it might be pointed out that the most considerable study yet made, that by Alan Cole, is (as he himself emphasizes) very far from conclusive. In particular it should be emphasized that Cole treats the terms "yeoman" and "husbandman" as really representing a clear social distinction, which in my view is unwarranted; and in order to obtain large enough units for statistical comparison, he has combined the data for occupations of Quakers bridegrooms from all years prior to 1689 — whereas, if my finding of a perceptible lowering of social level between 1662 and 1689 should hold good for other counties, this technique would underestimate the social rank of the early Friends. Most important, Cole's source of evidence, the "additions" of bridegrooms in the Quaker registers, seriously understates the number of gentlemen among the earliest Friends. The registers, though not entirely avoiding the term "gentleman," use it sparingly; and more important, the gentlemen who were drawn to Quakerism in the beginning were almost all already married, and thus not likely to figure in the marriage registers.[42]

---

sated by the ones already given may consult at Widener Library, Harvard University, and Friends' House Library, London, further tables which show the exact occupational distribution among converts from 1662 to 1740.

42. Alan Cole "The Social Origins of the Early Friends," *J.F.H.S.*, 48 (1957), 99–118, and "Quakerism and the Social Structure in the Interregnum," *Past and Present*, 44 (1969). No studies of other localities are nearly so satisfactory as Cole's. Besse, *Sufferings*, I, 68–70

It may be argued that the lack of evidence of changes in the occupational distribution of Friends does not by itself discredit the idea that Quakers grew richer. Though a few more of them may have been artisans or shoemakers, they may have been richer ones. Can statistics, especially somewhat inconclusive ones, overthrow Fox's famous and often-quoted statements that Quaker drapers and grocers were so honest that, after their customers had at first shunned them because of their religion, they later had double the trade of anyone else — or the fact that the wealth of the Gurneys was so proverbial that it was immortalized in a Gilbertian couplet? The best hard evidence we are likely to get about such questions would be a series of wills by the successive generations in a family, but such series are very rare. We can get some idea of the increasing wealth of the Gurneys from their wills, and we can trace a fivefold increase in the size of estates left by heads of the Stevens family, mealmen of Amersham. The grandson of Jeremiah Stevens, the first of the family to become a Friend, had accumulated an estate of over £2,660, plus several tenements. But even wills are often uninformative on such questions, because it became a custom for rich fathers to make settlements on their children before their death. (It is likely also that dependence on wills, in the increasing absence of other evidence of occupations, leads us to overestimate the social standing of eighteenth-century Friends; most of the "gentlemen" who appear in Norfolk in the early eighteenth century were tradesmen who called themselves gentlemen in their wills, and sometimes these

---

gives a list of names and occupations of ninety-two Bristol Friends who were fined £20 per month for absence from Anglican services; of these one was a gentleman, four professional men, twenty-seven wholesale traders, sixteen retail traders, nine textile workers, twenty-three artisans, and twelve laborers. Copies of wills deposited by Westmorland Friends in Kendal seem to reveal that almost all of them were yeomen, but it is hard to know how representative the evidence is; see *Some Westmorland Wills, 1686–1738,* ed. John Somervell (Kendal, Eng.: T. Wilson and Son, 1938).

wills were made well after 1740.) Besides the obviously flourishing families like the Gurneys and the Stevenses there were farmers like Thomas Lane and Abraham Butterfield in Buckinghamshire, who were ruined by annual tithe distraints of as much as £30 a year and finally, at the end of their lives, had to accept help from the monthly meeting. In sum, the evidence for the alleged general enrichment of eighteenth-century Quakers is far from conclusive, and it seems more likely to me that the over-all wealth of the Society of Friends, especially if one excepts those in the largest cities, was not increasing to any great extent, and may well have been diminishing.

Some Demographic Peculiarities of Quakerism

An analysis of occupational distribution by no means exhausts the inquiry into the social context of Quakerism. Indeed, the particular virtue of the method of family reconstitution is that it throws into relief a number of other factors such as age and sex distribution and geographical mobility. Sometimes the evidence for these is even more fragmentary than for occupational distribution, and our conclusions consequently even more speculative; but these factors have been so generally neglected that even raw speculation may be something of an advance.

A precursor here too is Richard Baxter, who claimed that the majority of early Friends were "young raw professors, and women, and ignorant ungrounded people." [43] Archbishop Sheldon's informants for the census of Dissent in 1669 appear to have believed that a good many Quaker meetings were largely composed of women, and the Quaker view of women, including the scandalous license of allowing them to preach, perhaps should have attracted them in unusual numbers. [44] In many of the "gathered churches" there was a

43. Richard Baxter, *One Sheet Against the Quakers* (1657), p. 11.
44. Excerpts from the censuses are printed in G. Lyon Turner, *Original Records of Early Nonconformity.*

considerable preponderance of women; but, as Table 8 shows, for some reason this does not seem true of Quakerism.

Table 8. Sex distribution in the sects.

Meeting	Date	Total members	Pct. women
Quakers			
Buckinghamshire	1662	185	44.9
Norwich	1662	46	50.0
Norfolk	1662	196	43.3
"Gathered Churches"			
Bedford	at founding	12	66.7
"	later undated	141	68.6
"	" "	135	60.7
"	" "	127	60.0
"	1693	34	75.0
Broadmead	1671	100	73.0
"	15 July 1679	133	72.2
Fenstanton	1658	185	53.7
"	1676	84	58.4
Hexham	10 Jun 1660	46	50.0
Norwich	29 June 1645	114	72.8
"	9 Nov. 1675	185	67.6
Warboys	1660	45	45.4
"	1680	54	45.3

Source: Compiled from *Records of the Churches of Christ, gathered at Fenstanton, Warboys, and Hexham,* ed. Edward Bean Underhill (Hanserd Knollys Society, 1854), 251–254, 283–284, 294–297; *Records of a Church of Christ Meeting in Broadmead, Bristol, 1640–1687,* ed. Edward Bean Underhill (Hanserd Knollys Society, 1847), 135–136; *The Church Book of Bunyan Meeting, 1650–1821,* ed. G. B. Harrison (London: J. M. Dent and Sons, 1928); and "Church Book belonging to a Society of Christians who assemble for divine Worship at the Old Meeting Norwich" (seen by the permission of the pastor and trustees). "The Entire Records of the Congregational Church at Great Yarmouth, 1642–1813," a copy of which I consulted at Dr. Williams' Library, London, also shows a persistent majority of women. These figures confirm for the Independents and Baptists, but not for Friends, the assertion of feminine preponderance made by Keith Thomas in "Women and the Civil War Sects," *Past and Present,* 13 (1958), 45. It is not always easy to tell from the lists of members the sex of some (for example, those

As for the ages of the early Friends at the time of their conversion, many subsequent writers have echoed the opinion that they were "young raw professors"; almost all the writing done by psychologists on the subject of religious conversion has assumed that it most often occurs in adolescence. Elmer T. Clark, striking a note that happily blends the naive and the pompous, assures us that "the first fact established by the science of the psychology of religion was that the dawn of the religious consciousness was almost exclusively a phenomenon of adolescence." So sure was Clark of this scientific fact that he conducted an elaborate questionnaire as to the age of "religious awakening" of 2,174 subjects, only 139 of whom were not still students — thereby deftly eliminating almost everyone over twenty from his investigations.[45] I have been able to establish the age at the time of conversion to Quakerism of about one third of the "valiant sixty," one

---

named "Francis" or "Frances," given the vagaries of seventeenth-century spelling) so I have eliminated these doubtful names from the percentage calculations. My figures for Quakers depend to some extent on records of sufferings (at least for the earliest years) and since sufferings were much more likely to fall upon men, the percentage of women is probably somewhat understated; however I do not believe that in any area at any time before 1760 more than 55 per cent of Friends were women.

45. Elmer T. Clark, *The Psychology of Religious Awakening* (New York: Macmillan Company, 1929), pp. 53, 26. Edwin Starbuck in his book *Psychology of Religion* (1899), still respectfully cited in the literature of the subject, indiscriminately mingled literary accounts of conversions in the past, including that provided in George Fox's *Journal*, with the results of questionnaires circulated to members of evangelical sects, which in the nineteenth century had a traditional expectation of adolescent conversion. Clark seems to consider Starbuck the discoverer of the particular scientific fact that conversion almost always occurs in adolescence. Like most psychologists at the turn of the century, including Freud, Starbuck had had his vocabulary electrified, so that he pictured religious experiences as throwing switches and opening new circuits. Reading work of this sort intensifies one's admiration for William James's *Varieties of Religious Experience* (New York: Longmans, Green, 1902) and makes it somewhat more understandable why after about 1930 most American academic psychologists, finding it difficult to induce religious experience in experimental animals, dismissed the subject as of no further interest.

fifth of the early converts in Norwich, and less than ten per cent of those in Buckinghamshire and Norfolk. These (admittedly very limited) data show clearly that most of these were adults and many were the heads of families.

There appears to be a much sharper difference between the ages of the "first publishers of Truth" and their early converts than the difference in occupational background. The median age at conversion of the "valiant sixty" was twenty-three, about ten years younger than the median age of converts in Buckinghamshire, Norwich, and Norfolk. The average age at conversion of the first Quakers in these counties would have been even higher; one in Buckinghamshire was sixty-two and one in Norfolk eighty. Such elevated ages are perhaps a further witness to the protracted spiritual struggles of many of the first Friends, and it is interesting that the little data available on the ages at conversion of later adherents to Quakerism suggest that their median age was no higher than thirty and probably somewhat lower than this. Even so, they were not instances of the supposed first law of the psychology of religion.

Of all the efforts I made to trace the origins of the early Quakers, the most uniformly unsuccessful were attempts to discover in the parish registers the entry relating to the birth of men and women who were subsequently converted to Quakerism while residing in that parish. Part of the difficulty lies in the logistics of research (most parish registers are still kept in the parish itself) and part in the various lacunae in the registers and transcripts. After reading through about half of the pertinent parish registers in Buckinghamshire and Norwich, I had finally to limit myself to these and the registers of one or two large towns in Norfolk. Still, the comparatively few cases where I did discover the record of the birth and thus the position of the convert within his family of origin do lend themselves to one generalization: eldest sons were almost never converted to Quakerism. Its appeal was all but entirely limited to the younger children within a family. Given the customs of primogeniture which usually prevailed, particularly with regard to inheritance of land, this meant that the prospective heir had a much greater propensity to remain loyal to the established church — and presumably thus to the religion of his father — whereas those excluded from inheritance of the family land or business were more susceptible to joining a persecuted religious minority.

If this were indeed a general pattern, as I suspect it was, it would help to account for the particular quality of egalitarianism in Quaker attitudes and "public testimonies." Very often, as we shall see in Chapter V, the plainness enjoined upon Friends manifested itself most vexatiously in their behavior within the family, particularly in their not removing their hats in the presence of their fathers and in insisting on addressing parents as "thou," a word usually reserved for servants and other inferiors. Quaker social thought generally accepted the equity of the existing class and social structure, while insisting on just and honest behavior on the part of all men and deprecating the elaborate gradations of respect and courtesy which were conveyed by the contemporary conventions of politeness. The little that we know about how often Friends were younger children, together with the somewhat greater evidence that we have about their occupational background, is certainly consonant with this radical rejection of manners combined with general acceptance of the legitimacy of the social structure.

Although it is dangerous to draw conclusions from the silence of the parish registers, the very low percentage of Friends whose births can be traced in the parish registers of the towns in which they were living at the time of their conversion suggests that the mobile population had a greater propensity to embrace Quakerism. It is true that there was a high degree of mobility in the general population during the latter seventeenth century, particularly since young people were very often put out to service in a different parish. Two censuses of the parish of Clayworth in Bedfordshire for 1676 and 1688 reveal that sixty per cent of the people living there in 1676 — including sixty-six out of the sixty-seven domestic servants — had moved away by 1688.[46] Perhaps, therefore, the fact that more than ninety per cent of the converts to Quakerism were not living in the parish in which they were born is not too significant, particularly since it would have been the younger children in a family who would have been more likely to have to establish themselves in a different location.

The experience of moving from parish to parish no doubt enhanced the force of the metaphor of pilgrimage which is so often found in Quaker spiritual autobiographies; and it may be that the mobile part of the population was more able to make sense of life through the mode of the conversion experience rather than the more orthodox Anglican or Catholic pattern of religious nurture. A man who could expect to succeed his father in the same station in life could more easily visualize his religious life as the smooth and steady acquisition of proper attitudes and behavior than one who had to set forth by faith to improvise his life.

These speculations are designed to do no more than suggest some other aspects of the social background of Quakerism which may have influenced its development, especially since my findings failed to confirm most of the existing theories which purport to explain either the social bearings of Quakerism specifically, or of religious experience generally. I am aware of having suggested no solutions, having confined myself to the safer task of pointing out additional complexities to the problem. Nevertheless, what we have to account for

46. Peter Laslett and John Harrison, "Clayworth and Cogenhoe," *Historical Essays, 1600–1750, Presented to David Ogg,* ed. H. E. Bell and R. L. Ollard (New York: Barnes & Noble, 1963), pp. 174, 179.

is a great ingathering in which a nation was shaken. As John Crook put it, Truth brought "the Honourable of the Earth, in that day, to deny their Titles and Attendants; some from the Judgment-Seat, and others from their great Gains, in their needless Trafficks . . . the Wise and Learned, and Men of all Professions, Religions and Opinions, that were gathered in from all Quarters of the Land." [47] It would have been convenient if Crook had thought to specify exactly how many were called from the judgment seat, or just how great were the gains from "needless Trafficks"; but the quotation reminds us that our explanations will have to have an amplitude commensurate with the movement itself, and beyond the reach of mere statistical rigor.

47. *The Design of Christianity Testified, in the Books, Epistles, and Manuscripts of John Crook* (1699), p. 264.

III   Persecution and Organization

To some Englishmen, the Restoration of Charles II in 1660 was the awakening of England from a nightmare of civil war and upstart rule; to Milton and others it was more like a dog returning to its vomit. To almost all, it was the end (or beginning) of an epoch.

Quakers were denied the luxury of simple judgments about the moral worth of the Restoration. Edward Burrough gave early voice to Friends' ambivalent attitude towards the returning king: *"Charles Stuart* must either be Converted to God, and ruled by him, or else he can never rightly Rule for God in this Nation; though this I believe it is not impossible but that he may be a Rod upon them that once smote him." [1] Whatever optimism might have existed about the likelihood of his conversion must soon have been dissipated, but his prospects as a rod were considerably more promising. The collapse of hopes for a comprehensive church settlement and the expulsion of the Presbyterian ministers from their parishes inevitably struck Friends as a delicious stroke of divine justice. The "eminent Leaders, overseers, and tall Cedars

1. Edward Burrough, *A Visitation of Love unto the King, and Those call'd Royallists* (1660), pp. 4–5, quoted in W. A. Cole, "The Quakers and Politics, 1652–1660," unpub. diss., Cambridge University, 1955, p. 220.

amongst the outside and formall professors of our times" had been brought low, and Quakers could not forget that "they were the highest and most contentious against us, where the Truth, and power of God first appeared amongst us." [2] Samuel Fisher took the opportunity to taunt the eminent Independent John Owen, now "deprived of thy dainty *Deanery* [Christ Church, Oxford]" and reminded him that "Even ye, and all sectaries that side not, or ride not with them back to *Rome*, are branded by that same Name *Fanaticks* of thy own *faining*, which is become the common *Characteristical* of all, but either *Romish* or *Canterburian* Catholicks." [3]

But there was only bitter comfort in seeing their erstwhile persecutors brought down, for it soon became apparent that none of the "fanatics" were to be left at ease. The Restoration marks a sort of epoch in Quaker history not because of the restored monarch but because of the restored parliament. The Cavalier Parliament, which sat until 1679, combined a much greater antipathy towards religious dissent than Charles II entertained with a greater power of repressing it than Charles I had exercised. During the Protectorate there had been local outbreaks of persecution of Friends by mobs, priests, and justices of the peace, and such parliaments as had sat had manifested (as by their savage punishment of James Nayler on the charge of blasphemy after his unfortunate "triumphant entry" into Bristol) the desire if not the ability to extirpate Quakerism. The Cavalier Parliament had the same desires, but Charles II was much less able to hold them in check.

2. "To the Reader," by G[eorge?] W[hitehead?], the preface to *A Collection of the Several Books and Writings of Richard Hubberthorn* (1663).

3. "Rusticus ad Academicos or The Rustick's Alarm to the Rabbies Or, the Country Correcting the University and Clergy" (1660) in *The Testimony of Truth Exalted by the Collected Labours of Samuel Fisher* (1679), p. 216.

Not content with the expulsion from their benefices of those who would not subscribe the Thirty-Nine Articles (an expulsion nicely timed to deprive them of their Michaelmas tithes), parliament attempted to make illegal the propagation, if not the very exercise, of every religion but that of the reestablished church. Meetings for worship (stigmatized as "conventicles") were forbidden except where the liturgy of the Church of England was read. The expelled ministers were not allowed to come within five miles of the towns. The laws passed in Elizabeth's reign against Roman Catholics, which required men to attend Anglican services, were now put in execution against Protestants, who faced equally ruinous fines for having religious services in their own houses or for absenting themselves from their parish churches.

Even in the common persecution the Quakers fared the worst. They were the only ones to be specifically named (in the "Quaker Act") and they suffered from scruples which went beyond those entertained by other Christians. In particular their refusal to swear judicial oaths exposed them to the extremes of fear or malice of the magistracy. Oaths had been the immemorial core and sanction of English jurisprudence, and Friends' disposition to take literally the injunction "Swear not at all" smacked of Popery.[4] When Quakers shared a scruple with other Nonconformists — and none of theirs were entirely original — they pursued it with unique tenacity. Though others objected to tithes — especially when

4. Oaths were devised primarily to detect and inhibit Roman Catholics. Christopher Hill, *Society and Puritanism in Pre-Revolutionary England* (London: Secker and Warburg, 1964), pp. 382–419, provides a political and social context for Friends' testimony against them. Russell Mortimer in "Quakerism in Seventeenth Century Bristol," unpub. master's thesis, Bristol University, 1946, pp. 358–359, gives several examples of the widespread and not altogether absurd suspicion that traveling Friends were Jesuits or some species of crypto-Papist. The Anabaptists had also taught that Christians should never swear under any circumstances, but usually did not pursue this precept to inconvenient lengths; see Robert Barclay (of Reigate), *The Inner Life of the Religious Societies of the Commonwealth* (1876), p. 114.

they were no longer receiving them — Quakers would spend years in prison rather than pay. A good many met their deaths on this account. Similarly, it was not difficult to avoid the clutches of the conventicle act if services were held in private houses and adjourned to secluded meadows; it was the Quaker insistence on keeping up their public meetings that inspired Pepys' wish that they would conform, "or else be more wise, and not be catched!" [5]

It was not only its unparalleled severity which made persecution pose a special problem for Friends. In 1660 they had neither any established organization for resisting persecution nor any source of ideas as to how to get one. All their assaults on the "hireling" clergy and their "formal" mode of worship arose from a desire to let ministry be purely spontaneous, sustained only by the continued inspiration of God which it could mediate to the group. As we have seen, the leadership of the earliest Quaker groups came entirely from Friends "traveling in the ministry," almost all of them communicating with Swarthmoor Hall. But the first two years of Charles II's power had taken a large toll of the "valiant sixty." By the spring of 1663 Thomas Aldam, John Audland, Edward Burrough, John Camm, Richard Hubberthorne, and James Nayler were dead, to be followed soon after by William Caton and Richard Farnworth. Francis Howgill, William Dewsbury, George Fox, and hundreds of other Friends were in prison. The network of traveling Friends was disrupted almost beyond repair, and the survival of the movement required some sort of organization to sustain suffering Friends, secure what legal relief was available, and provide for local leadership. Thus the reality, and perhaps even more the omnipresent threat, of persecution gave a distinctive cast to Quaker discipline and institutions, as we are reminded by the fact that the leading agency of community will and common concern is called to this day the Meeting for Sufferings.

5. *Memoirs of Samuel Pepys* (1825), 7 August 1664.

The Seed of the Church

The laws against Nonconformity, like most of the laws of England, were largely what the justices of the peace wished to make of them. It would be wrong to suppose that the magistrates showed an unrelieved hostility to Quakers or other Dissenters. The peaks of persecution roughly coincide with periods of general political tension. In Leicestershire, for example, the penal laws were briskly enforced in 1660 and 1661, from 1670 until 1672 and from 1675 until 1677, and, most severely, between 1680 and 1686.[6] The same years were also remarkable for persecution in Buckinghamshire and Norfolk. It is clear that the most severe executions of the law followed the forfeiture of borough charters and the widespread overthrow of Whig town officials in the last two years of the reign of Charles II. In Norwich, where in 1683 and 1684 almost all male Quakers were imprisoned, the newly installed justices also secured the indictment of their predecessors, Hugh Bokenham (the former mayor), John Riches, Henry Crow, and John Man, for not suppressing conventicles, refusing to issue warrants to search for them, issuing blank warrants, and for other such defaults of justice.[7] Persecution, except for tithes and "church rates" (an urban tax payable to the established church) all but stopped with the accession of James II.

By then, however, it had done its work. It had not, of course, accomplished what its authors intended. Quakerism, far from being rooted out, spread with even greater vigor; in fact, no such growth over a similar span of years would ever again come to it. Despite the disadvantage of a more hostile political environment, traveling ministers visited "Germany, America, and many other islands and places, as

6. R. H. Evans, "The Quakers of Leicestershire, 1660–1714," *Transactions of the Leicestershire Archaeological Society*, 28 (1952), 80.

7. Norwich Quarter Sessions Indictments, vol. LXXXII, for offenses committed 23 April 1682, 29 January 1681/2, 12 February 1681/2, 5 March 1681/2, 2 April 1682, and 26 April 1682.

Florence, Mantua, Palatine, Tuscany, Italy, Rome, Turkey, Jerusalem, France, Geneva, Norway, Barbados, Antigua, Jamaica, Surinam, Newfoundland." [8] Some Friends made an attempt to convert the Pope; others addressed themselves to the Great Turk. Nor did they neglect the cultivation of more accessible and likely prospects. The result was an ingathering as great as that of the first few years in Buckinghamshire. In Norfolk, where the early years had been difficult, the years of persecution were the years of solid establishment. If, as has recently been argued, "the Restoration was aimed against the missionary work of Quakers and others who were extending radical sectarian ideas into the countryside," [9] the statistics in Table 9 make plain its failure.

Table 9. The growth of Quakerism, 1662–1689.

	Number of adult Friends, end of:						Percentage increase		
	1662	1669	1672	1678	1683	1689	1662–1669	1669–1678	1678–1689
Bucks.	176	267		458		543	51.7	71.5	18.6
Norfolk	217	398		645		831	83.4	62.1	28.8
Norwich	41	65	104	166	240	254	58.5	155.4	52.4

	Number of adults appearing for the first time as Friends during various intervals						
	1663–1669	1670–1672	1673–1678	1670–1678	1679–1683	1684–1689	1679–1689
Bucks.	142			187			223
Norfolk	220			280			260
Norwich	34	48	84	132	87	57	144

8. Quoted in William C. Braithwaite, *The Beginnings of Quakerism* (Cambridge, Eng.: Cambridge University Press, 1955), p. 337.

9. Hill, *Society and Puritanism*, p. 499. Hill speculates that the Clarendon Code and the Act of Settlement of 1662 perhaps were responsible for "saving the countryside" — as distinct from the towns — from nonconformity. (500)

To all appearances, then, persecution was utterly ineffective in deterring conversions to Quakerism; if anything, it seems to have been a stimulant. But perhaps appearances deceive; obviously we must ask whether many persons could have been associated with Friends for several or even many years before they happened to be mentioned in the registers of births (as parents) or marriages, in the records of sufferings, or in ecclesiastical or quarter sessions records. It is true that the peaks in Table 9 coincide with the peaks of persecution, not because the more intense the persecution, the more were converted, but because records of persecutions are one of the best sources for the composition of Quaker communities.

Since there were not only no membership lists but also no formal procedure for receiving converts, it is only from the parish registers that we can sometimes date a conversion to Quakerism with any accuracy. This would normally be by the entry of a marriage or baptism shortly before the bridegroom or parent appears in Friends' records — though sometimes the vicar took it upon himself to comment on the births and marriages of Dissenters in the parish.[10] This kind of evidence is unfortunately very rare.

Despite these difficulties in interpretation of data, there is good reason to believe that it would be unlikely that men could join Friends and yet for years not show up in any of the evidence — at least in those areas where sufferings were fairly copiously reported and attenders of business meetings noted. One estimate of the size of the Quaker community in Buckinghamshire in 1661 was made by Thomas Ellwood. He was imprisoned in that year along with sixty or seventy other Quaker men, whom he reckoned to be almost all the

10. For example, this entry in the Wavendon parish register for 26 November 1655: "The first sonne of Joseph Brinkloe and Olive his wife was borne and with out being Baptized is named (as they say) Joseph & was buried the 21st May following." Brinkloe was one of the first Quakers in Buckinghamshire.

male Friends in the county at that time.[11] This is very close to the number who had appeared in Friends' records in Buckinghamshire by the end of that year; so in that county the appearance of numerous conversions during the period of persecutions is no illusion, and the evidence that great growth was achieved in Norfolk at the same time seems to me even stronger.

To historians of liberal bent this has often seemed the only effect of persecution worth bothering about. Many have been delighted to conclude, with G. Lyon Turner, that the "history of persecution seems to show that only its severest forms have any real efficiency. Wholesale massacres may effect their diabolical purpose. Yet even capital punishment — unless inflicted wholesale — does little more than winnow the chaff from the wheat . . . anything less than the extremest measures universally applied is invariably useless. Penalties less than capital, such as imprisonment, fine, and social or ecclesiastical excommunication, usually multiply the numbers, and serve only to purify and intensify the religious zeal, of those who have to suffer 'for conscience' sake." [12] A conclusion so pleasing to our notions of divine justice ought to receive more diligent scrutiny than it usually gets. One may even wonder whether multiplication of numbers and intensification of religious zeal are necessarily concomitant phenomena. Without denying the seminal properties of the blood of martyrs and the incomparable stubbornness of early Friends — especially when confronted by the cumbersome and inefficient machinery of terror of the early modern state — we may legitimately ask what would have happened had the institutions of Quakerism been allowed to develop under more genial auspices. As we shall see, the threat of persecution caused serious disagreement and even schism

---

11. *History of the Life of Thomas Ellwood* (1714), p. 108.
12. G. Lyon Turner, *Original Records of Early Non-Conformity under Persecution and Indulgence* (London: T. F. Unwin, 1914), III, 40.

among Friends, imparted a certain premature rigidity to their meetings for church business, and made their discipline more censorious than it otherwise might have been.

The Provision of Ministry

One of the first effects of persecution was the breakdown of the network of traveling ministers, most of whom were confined to prison for considerable periods. Without their efforts, meetings for worship were likely to be altogether silent, sometimes for months on end. Elizabeth Chester, an early Bedfordshire Quaker, has left a description of the first days of their meeting, when they sat in silence "not having a word spoken among us for some months together" until the visit of a ministering Friend with a "living Testimony." [13] Speaking in meeting was an awesome matter for the early Friends. While in theory God might entrust a message to any worshipper, He was thought to prefer certain customary vessels. To devise a church order which would allow the more gifted preachers to operate effectively while at the same time preserving the "freedom" of the ministry was one of the most delicate tasks facing the early Friends.

Quakers desired to maintain a "free" ministry both in the sense that it was to be unsalaried and in the sense that there were to be no formal prerequisites for men and women to assume it. Robert Barclay's *Apology* had stated clearly: "That which we oppose, is the distinction of *Laity* and *Clergy,* (which in the scripture is not to be found) whereby none are admitted unto the work of the ministry but such as are instructed in *Logick* and *Philosophy,* &c. And so are at their Apprenticeship to learn the *Art* and *Trade of Preaching,* even as a man learns any other *art,* whereby all other honest *mechanick* men, who have not got this *heathenish art,* are

13. Elizabeth Chester, *A Narrative of the Life and Death of Edward Chester* (1709), p. 10.

excluded from having this privilege." [14] It was this conception of the ministry which underlay Friends' tenacious resistance to tithes. As Richard Hubberthorne put it, "every one that will minister, must do it freely, and . . . no profession of people may maintain anothers Minister; but that there may be a free preaching, and a free hearing among all people, that so it may be a free Nation; and they that will have Teachers according to their own lusts and judgments, they to maintain them . . . and maintain their poor which are crying at their Meeting-house doors." [15]

A curious confirmation of Friends' belief that the church was organized as a guild to protect and perpetuate the trade of preaching comes from a statement drawn up by some Anglican laymen in 1681. After commending Friends as "very good Christians" who preached true doctrine, these laymen proposed that the Church of England institute a voluntary ministry, not only to preach to "poor people in poor tabernacles, who cannot pay anything sufficiently to maintain a ministry, nor yet get pews in their parish churches," but also to inspire the learned clergy to be more sober and studious. In the great parishes these "poor tabernacles" with lay prophets would carry the gospel to the poor, while the regular church and its clergy would serve those who could afford pew-rents.[16] The scheme was not adopted.

No doubt the free traveling ministry of Friends was able to reach some who were excluded by pew-rents and other financial burdens from the services of the established church. And it was characteristic of the desire of Friends to make opportunities for a ministry which might be chosen by God rather than men that they undertook to gather a "stock" at

14. *Apology for the True Christian Divinity* (1678), proposition 10, section 26.

15. "The Real Cause of the Nations Bondage and Slavery, here Demonstrated," in *A Collection of the Several Books and Writings of Richard Hubberthorn* (1663), pp. 218–219.

16. Quoted in Robert Barclay of Reigate, *Inner Life*, p. 531.

Swarthmoor Hall (and later at other places) for the support of those early preachers who could not otherwise sustain themselves.[17] Though the expenses of travel might be defrayed for those otherwise too poor to bear them, it was still necessary to have at least some leisure to pursue an active ministry; and inevitably the great majority of ministers were men who could afford to live from their own resources. Indeed, it is almost impossible to imagine a testimony against a hireling ministry sustained without the institution of the independent income. Though Robert Barclay might deplore the exclusion of "other honest mechanick men" from the Anglican ministry, they were not very numerous even among Friends; at least three quarters of the recognized male ministers, or "Public Friends," as they were called, in Norfolk and Buckinghamshire were gentlemen, professional men, wholesale traders, or the wealthier yeomen and farmers.

Contemporaries associated material success with the "public ministry." Francis Bugg pictures the traveling ministers as "spreading ourselves in the Country, into great Acquaintance" and thereby receiving orders for parcels from "the best of the Country Trades-men." [18] Nor was this identification made only by the enemies of Truth. David Hall, writing in 1758 to encourage young apprentices, remarked that many such "though but very poor as to this World, and even of mean Capacities too . . . have made notable Improvements in their own natural Parts, and in the Arts and Mysteries that they were bound Apprentices to learn, have been wonderfully bless'd by divine Providence . . . becoming in due Time honourable Tradesmen upon their own Bottom, yea many have risen (thro' God's Blessing on their honest

17. Traveling Friends did not receive any offering collected on the spot at meetings which they might attend; as far as I can determine there was no collection of money at any meeting for worship in the seventeenth and eighteenth centuries.

18. Francis Bugg, *The Pilgrim's Progress, from Quakerism to Christianity* (1698), p. 112.

Endeavours) from poor laborious Apprentices to prosperous, rich, and honourable Masters, and often even have been anointed for the Ministration of the glorious Gospel." In a remarkable letter written twenty years earlier, Hall unselfconsciously mingled shrewd judgments of the trading capacities of Public Friends with reports of their services as ministers. With no sense of incongruity he wrote: "We find, Dear Friend, there's some stirings & revivings of Trade amongst the Young People & Elders in London, in this Country there is a Brave appearance of the Young Generals, I hope many may be made willing in Time to take up the Cross Daily, & follow the Captain of our Salvation." [19]

"Anointing" for the ministration of the Gospel was of course purely spiritual; any might speak in his own meeting who felt inspired to do so. This does not mean, however, that everything said in meetings was taken as a direct communication from God. When Voltaire visited a Friends' meeting during his first stay in England, he heard a torrent of nonsense which, he was told, was not a unique event.[20] It was not uncommon for meetings to censure "unprofitable ministry," as Norwich Monthly Meeting did on 1 June 1687 and again on 9 June 1690, when a man and his wife were admonished not to "burden the meeting with words that are not Sound." Wells Monthly Meeting on 6 September 1699 went to the extreme of disowning Elizabeth Dapelin as an unprofitable minister. Meetings might also control the quality of the ministry offered when it came to issuing the "certificate" which was required from the home meeting before a minister might travel. Sometimes these certificates were long delayed or flatly denied. Elizabeth Haycock asked the Wells Monthly Meeting on 4 August 1731 for a "certificate" to travel in the

19. *Some Brief Memoirs of the Life of David Hall* (1758), p. 120; the letter of David Hall, to James Wilson of Kendal, is printed *J.F.H.S.*, 18 (1921), 26–27. William C. Braithwaite, *ibid.*, 110, contends that throughout the letter "trade" is a metaphor for the Quaker ministry.

20. *Letters concerning the English Nation* (1733), chap. 2.

ministry to London, which was refused. In July 1736 she was reproved by the meeting for appearing in a public testimony. Finally on 2 April 1740 the meeting gave her the desired certificate, describing her as a "very sober Religious Woman, and Exemplary in her Conversation" and adding, no doubt with real conviction, "we desire the Lord may make her Ministry serviceable among you."

As such quotations suggest, the status of "Public Friends" was not given lightly. As soon as Friends built their own meeting houses, they recognized the special status of ministers by giving them a sort of architectural ordination. A "gallery" — ordinarily two raised fixed seats running across one end or side of the room — was reserved for them. Although this could be justified on practical grounds — those most likely to speak being placed where they were most likely to be heard — the "gallery" did give the early Quaker meeting-house an appearance not unlike those of the Baptists, who had a "hireling" ministry and prepared sermons. Referring to these "galleries," George Keith gibed that the Quaker preachers and elders had mounted up into "the chief places in the Synagogues . . . beyond I think what is to be seen in other Congregations." [21] By the middle of the nineteenth century, when it was still assumed that a meeting without a recorded minister would be silent, Samuel Fothergill of Scarborough described meetings as a "spectacle of the whole waiting in silence, and depending as completely on the one or two 'acknowledged' ministers, as other denominations do on the regularly appointed preacher." [22]

We do not know how ministers were designated in the very earliest periods of Quakerism. No doubt a very serious self-examination was required before men or women undertook to speak; and probably even from the beginning other Friends

21. H. G. Arnold, "Early Meeting Houses," pp. iii–iv, 17.
22. Samuel Fothergill (of Scarborough), *Essay on the Society of Friends: Being an Inquiry into the Causes of their Diminished Influence and Numbers* (1859), pp. 44, 66.

were willing to rise in meeting and "testify against" unsound doctrine. In general, it seems that ordinary Friends rose to the challenge presented by the arrest of so many of their leaders, and the institution of "Public Friends" was well suited to the open and flexible texture of early Quakerism.

Governing the Church

The great pioneers of spirituality in the Anglo-Saxon world have often — and justly — been admired for their superior achievements in ecclesiastical organization. The very name of the Methodists is a tribute to the discipline imposed by their system of classes. In some ways the structure of meetings in the Society of Friends, which must be credited to George Fox, is an equally impressive accomplishment.

Quaker meetings for worship were in every sense public meetings, open to all who cared or dared to come. No lists of members were kept, nor were there any external ways in which membership could be acknowledged. Growing out of these were meetings which, besides worshipping, had to deal with the practical concerns of Friends. The most influential was the Meeting for Sufferings, in London, with its network of correspondents in each county to mobilize the whole resources of the group against persecution. Similarly, the morning meeting of ministers in London kept a vigilant eye on the morals and doctrine of traveling ministers — and of their books. The great annual forum for Friends was the London Yearly Meeting, assembling every Whitsuntide, from which the common concerns of the society emerged.

Some of these concerns found expression in the queries directed by the London Yearly Meeting to each quarterly meeting (covering one or two counties) and in turn to every local or preparative meeting. Preparative meetings sent their answers to these queries (which concerned their spiritual state, the progress of "Truth" in their area, and their freedom from certain specified sins such as vanity in speech or dress, or smuggling) to the monthly meetings, which were by far the most important body as far as the life of the ordinary Quaker was concerned. Monthly meetings, generally covering a substantial part of a county, had responsibility for the relief of the poor, the authorization of marriages, registration of births and deaths, and the disciplining of errant members — duties which are discussed in detail in Chapter IV.[23] In theory there was a parallel structure of women's meetings, helping in the relief of poor women and judging fitness of marriages.

Monthly and quarterly meetings were established in 1667 and 1668 after a remarkable tour of the country by George Fox. Women's meetings were established in some though not all areas about a decade later. Preparative meetings do not appear until the end of the seventeenth century, and then only in the north of England. All of these meetings, it must be emphasized, were meetings for worship, but with regular administrative responsibilities attached. Therefore they could not, for obvious reasons, be quite like the open public meetings for worship. The establishment of meetings for church government (as Friends called them) for the first time gave some Quakers institutional power over others. The introduction of such power was bound to change the character of Quakerism.

Some Friends were altogether opposed to the permanent establishment of such meetings, at least in the form that George Fox projected. It is true that from the beginning Friends had felt the obligation to relieve the needs of their poor and to discipline their disorderly members; but the meetings which were charged with these responsibilities had, as William C. Braithwaite notes, only a "subordinate, and almost accidental place" in the life of the Quaker com-

23. Sometimes monthly meetings might cover a smaller area (there was one just for the city of Norwich) and there were comparable organizations which met more frequently, as Bristol Two Weeks' Meeting.

munity. They "in no sense superseded the individual or the particular congregation. They did not assume any control over the ministers who exercised spiritual leadership in the Church." [24] Braithwaite went on to speculate how Quakerism would have been affected if these "almost accidental" meetings had been allowed a gradual and more natural development, instead of withering under the first blasts of persecution. As it was, the national "settling" of meetings by Fox in 1667 and 1668 cost Quakerism its only really sizable schism. The schism is usually called the "Wilkinson-Story" movement, and its adherents are referred to as Separatists.

It is not easy to discover the issues which led to this separation. The orthodox party charged that the Separatists were less staunch under persecution, meeting in fields rather than in their accustomed places and paying, or conniving at the payment of, tithes. This the Separatists denied in the course of exchanging abuse with the "Foxonian" party. The growing influence of Fox within the Quaker movement and simple reaction against his masterful personality doubtless account for some of this violent outburst. But wherever the schism made headway, the chief grievance was the composition of the business meetings. The Separatists objected particularly to the establishment of women's meetings for church business. All Friends were supposed to apply first to the women's meeting if they wished permission to be married, which meant that men were subjected to the power of women. This was scandalous to some; one dissident Friend described it as "a thing never heard of, but of late Years, except the Government of the *Amazons,* who were not so Censorious upon the account of marriage." [25] The Separatists proved themselves adept at invoking the old slogans of Quakerism against the innovations in discipline and organization; thus

24. *Beginnings of Quakerism,* p. 339.
25. William Mather, *A Novelty: Or, a Government of Women, Distinct from Men, Erected amongst some of the People call'd Quakers, Detected* (n.d.), p. 4.

W. Mucklow, in *The Spirit of the Hat* (1673) charged that "Foxonion-unity" was calculated to "deprive us of the Law of the Spirit and to bring in a tyrannical Government." [26] Fox's lavishly offered advice (some of which was, indeed, given in a rather peremptory fashion) was described as "canons" and "decretals."

A large number of the early and most influential Friends sympathized with Wilkinson and Story, which may be some indication that jealousy of Fox was one of the underlying causes of the schism. In Bristol it seems that the majority of the earliest converts sided with the Separatists. In Berkshire three fourths of the trustees of Reading meeting house, who would have been the weightiest Friends, joined with the schismatics, who for a time kept the monthly meeting books and registers.[27] They also enlisted the support of a good many Friends in Buckinghamshire, including such influential men as John Raunce and his son-in-law, Charles Harris. Significantly, there is not a trace of the schism in Norwich or the rest of Norfolk — where there is also no evidence of women's business meetings in the seventeenth century.[28]

It is also probable that the establishment of business meetings provided the occasion for those who had not been able to find complete satisfaction in Quakerism to resume their search for the pure and perfect religious expression. Whatever the reason, it seems clear that there was a substantial discontinuity between the leading Friends of the first ten years of the movement and those who came forward to take up the leading positions in the Quaker organization which dates from 1667. This discontinuity is very marked in Buck-

26. Quoted in Geoffrey Nuttall, *The Holy Spirit in Puritan Faith and Experience* (Oxford: B. Blackwell, 1946), p. 46.

27. Mortimer, "Quakerism in Bristol," p. 56; Howard R. Smith, "The Wilkinson-Story Controversy in Reading," *J.F.H.S.*, 1 (1904), 57–61.

28. The only reference I have found to a women's meeting in Norfolk is a casual reference in response to queries from London Yearly Meeting in 1732 (Yearly Meeting Minutes, VII, 312). There is no indication what this meeting was or how long it had been established.

inghamshire and other counties where the Separatists were strong, but it can also be seen in Norfolk and elsewhere.

A serious problem arose for the majority of Friends who accepted the necessity of continuing business meetings. The power of such meetings had to be exercised by persons who were believed to be unusually responsive to God and responsible in their dealings. How were criteria for membership in business meetings to be established and maintained? If one looks first to the writings of George Fox, an ambiguous answer emerges. In defining and defending the meetings for church government, Fox characteristically could do no less than set forth their place in the entire cosmic order. "Many thousands haveinge received this Gospell: now agane a mens meetinge is sett uppe as was in the days of the Apostles in the power of God & in the holy ghoast," he wrote. "And now the power of God is the authority of both our men & womens meetinges & all the other meetings, which power of God was before the Apostacy was from the Apostles." It was possession of the power of God which qualified members for business meetings, which were to be confined to "the Converted & elect before the worlde began." [29] Since Fox thus identifies the power of these meetings with the power of God, it was natural that he should limit membership to those who shared that power. As he wrote in a letter read to London Yearly Meeting in 1676: "all the faithfull men and women in every Country Citty and Nation whose faith stands in the power of God the Gospell of Christ . . . have all right to the Power of the Meeting . . . Soe here is God's choice and not mans." Fox seems to be saying that all true Friends, but only true Friends — in other words, everyone truly converted (or at least believed to be so) — should have been entitled to sit in such meetings. In this respect they resembled the

29. George Fox, *Journal,* ed. Norman Penney (Cambridge, 1911), II, 344.

"church meetings" of the Baptists and Independents, where everyone who had been truly converted might vote for a new pastor or the reception of new members, just as he might be admitted to communion.

We must therefore reject the contention of John Stephenson Rowntree that only " 'two or three true and faithful Friends' from each particular meeting constituted the monthly meetings." [30] The severe limitation of such meetings to two or three from each particular meeting or to those of unimpeachable character was indeed proposed in the early history of Quakerism, but by the Separatists. In Buckinghamshire the schismatics voiced their desire that "Our Meetings might consist of qualified chosen Friends, from each particular Meeting, and not be filled up with Youths, and Girls, and Strangers from other Countries." Less politely, they charged "that whores & Rogues come to the Men's and women's Meeting." [31] Orthodox Friends attacked this position of the Separatists in the London Yearly Meeting epistle of 1677, which condemned the fact that "none of their owne County are allowed to be of the monthly or quarterly meetings but such as are appointed and Chosen by the particular meetings." Even Public Friends, so the epistle said, were merely allowed to give their messages to the Separatists' meetings and then were required promptly to depart.[32]

30. John Stephenson Rowntree, *Quakerism, Past and Present* (1859) p. 58.
31. Thomas Ellwood, *The Account from Wickham* (*Lately published by John Raunce and Charles Harris*) *Examin'd and found False* (n.p., 1689), p. 11; the comment about whores and rogues was reported in the Upperside Monthly Meeting minutes on 3 July 1682 as having been made at the preceding quarterly meeting by Charles Harris. At the next meeting Harris did qualify his judgment to the extent that "what he did speak was not intended of any Meetings in this Country."
32. Although it seems that the Separatists generally claimed to have the only properly select meetings, John Story, one of their leaders, denied that they intended to restrict them to a few nominees from each particular meeting. He writes: "particular Persons . . . were chosen for that Service of the Poor, &c. out of the particular Meetings held for the

But the choice of members, as Fox wrote, was God's and not man's; and I have argued that Friends, unlike the Baptists or Congregationalists, did not presume to judge the spiritual states of those who resorted to their meetings for worship. Did they make such a judgment before allowing someone to sit in business meetings? Robert Barclay of Reigate believed that just such a formal distinction, based on a decision as to the reality of conversion, was made by early Friends, and that every meeting kept lists of "Members entitled to transact the business of the Church." [33] He cites the survival into the nineteenth century of such lists in Somerset and in London.

This contention, if true, would make a considerable difference in our interpretation of early Quakerism; but the evidence for it seems very inconclusive. If there really had been such lists in every monthly meeting, it seems almost inconceivable that not one of them should still be extant and that there would be no references to them in other records (as for example appointment of Friends to look over them or put them up to date). The only list I have been able to find in England which might have been a list of qualified members of business meetings is from Nottinghamshire. It is headed: "The names of such friends as are appoynted for the service of truth in the monthly & Quarterly Meetings. 1668." It shows no signs of having

---

Worship of God, yet I never understood that any designed to exclude any Member or Members of the Church of Christ, (who had, or might have a Concern upon their Spirits) from Sitting or Acting amongst them, whil'st any such Member or Members (though not chozen) behaved themselves Men of Peace, good Order, and in Unity with the Faithful Friends chozen for the Management of the Affairs of the Truth relating to the Poor, &c. in such Meeting" ("John Story's Epistle to Friends in the North, in which is signified his Desires for true Unity and Reconciliation" [1677] in *The Memory of that Servant of God, John Story, Revived* [1683], p. 41). Since this epistle was designed to show the harmony of the Separatists' practices with those of other Friends, it provides a further indication that business meetings were not intended to be composed only of men nominated by the various meetings for worship.

33. Barclay, *Inner Life*, p. 362.

been kept up to date by interpolations or scoring-out of names. Occasionally minutes in Norfolk, Bedfordshire, and elsewhere are prefaced by the names of members attending that particular meeting, but these clearly are not lists of eligible members.[34] Somerset Friends, as Barclay says, did keep lists in the monthly meeting books, but it is not clear what they were meant to be. On 21 December 1710 the question arose in Somerset Quarterly Meeting whether any Friends' names should be recorded in the Monthly Meeting Book except those from each particular meeting "deputed to give account of that to the monthly meeting." Unfortunately for our understanding of the question, it was referred to the next meeting and never taken up. It appears, however, that the names listed were not of all those eligible to attend, but rather of quasi-official messengers to the monthly meeting from the local one.

It is certainly clear that Friends were nominated by local meetings for worship to attend the monthly meeting, and again by the monthly meetings to attend the quarterly meeting; but the critical point is that these meetings were not confined to those nominated, and the nominations were designed

34. The Nottinghamshire list is printed in *J.F.H.S.*, 17 (1920), 46. In front of the first volume of the Upperside Women's Monthly Meeting minutes is a list of "the names of the several meetings belonging to the monthly meeting of the upper side of the County of Bucks & the names of several friends that come to the women's monthly meeting at Larkin's Green." What may have been one of the missing pages in the first volume of the Upperside Men's Monthly Meeting minutes, in the hand of the clerk, Thomas Ellwood, gives a list of Friends attending what may have been its first meeting; it is printed under the title "Friends in Buckinghamshire, 1668," *J.F.H.S.*, 16 (1919), 70. But these lists were obviously not intended to define the composition of the meeting, for those from some meetings (such as Chalfont) trail off in et ceteras. It is more likely that the list of members in the women's book was inserted to muster support and identify opponents. The establishment of this meeting had led to the secession of almost forty Friends, which left its mark in the heavy scoring through of some of the names on the list. Sometimes, as in the front of the second volume of Upperside Men's Monthly Meeting minutes, there is a list of constituent particular meetings of the monthly meeting, but not of individual Friends.

not to limit, but rather to augment the business meetings, since the usual problem was that not enough members attended.[35] The Westminster Monthly Meeting in the 1730's seems to have had the idea of a quorum, for their minutes note that on 3 November 1736 eleven met and waited for a considerable time, but "for Want of one more to make up a Sufficient Number . . . Could not proceed on Buisniss." [36] Several other times in this decade similar minutes appear. In 1721 the Sudbury Friends set up a regular rota to assure representation at the Quarterly Meeting, but presumably this did not conflict with its advice in 1704 that "as many as have freedom" were to attend the quarterly meeting. Similarly on 10 August 1754 when the Upperside Monthly Meeting named several Friends to go to the Quarterly Meeting, it was clearly to assure that some at least would be there, for the minute adds that "This appointment is not in the least to discourage any friends from going who are not in the Nomination."

It thus appears that nothing beyond good character and judgment was required to be a member of a business meeting. But, given the fluidity of the conception of membership, especially among the first generation of Friends, and the fact that business meetings were also meetings for worship, it

35. The only Quaker business meeting which clearly was limited was the London Yearly Meeting. Its epistle of 29 May 1672 outlined the procedure for having Quarterly Meetings selecting members, and requested "all others except such as are nominated appointed and Chosen by the Quarterly Meetings as aforesaid" to refrain from attending Yearly Meetings – though it left open the possibility that after it had come together, the Yearly Meeting might then admit Friends who had not been selected by the Quarterly Meetings. Unlike most quarterly and monthly meetings, London Yearly Meeting did keep an annual list of Friends nominated by the quarterly meetings. Obviously it would have grown to an unmanageable size – especially with the Quaker reliance on consensus – if not limited in some such way.

36. In 1725 the Westminster Monthly Meeting had a group with a quorum of five or seven to consider business arising between the regular sessions of the monthly meeting. How this worked can be seen in their minute of 7 April 1725 when they received news of an appeal against them to Yearly Meeting.

often became necessary to devise some machinery assuring that business meeting members would be "serious well approved Friends," as the first minute of the Wiltshire Quarterly Meeting put it, or "approved good friends in the Truth & such as in the wisedome of god are Fitt to Judge of & order things in the said meetings according to truth," as the Somerset Quarterly Meeting's minute of 23 December 1669 specified.

I have found one instance where there was a scheme of nomination for the purpose of discouraging the attendance of "persons who, though they may go to our publick meetings, are not so settled & grown in Truth, as to be fit members of this Meeting." The Upperside Monthly Meeting, in order to deter persons who were "a Clog to the meeting, bringing weights and burdens on it," sought a remedy in law and history. Some Friends were appointed to look through the old minutes of the meeting, and found one "for remedying the like inconvenience" in the oldest minute book.[37] It recommended that Friends should "send from their respective Meetings, such persons as they know to be faithful to Truth, & fittest to do service for the Lord in the monthly & Quarterly Meetings." Since this practice apparently had lapsed, the meeting agreed that there should be in every particular meeting a regular conference, on the First Day preceding each monthly or quarterly meeting, to choose only "faithful, serviceable & suitable Friends" for the forthcoming meeting. If any others "thrust themselves in," Friends of the meeting "to which such belong" were to "take them out, & better inform them, & tenderly advise them to withdraw & depart."

Some categorical exclusions from business meetings were suggested in 1706 by the London Yearly Meeting. Those who had violated "trueths testemony as to the knowne Branches

37. Upperside Monthly Meeting minute, 1 August 1698. The earlier minute referred to is not in the first volume of minutes; it was probably written on one of the pages which have since been torn out of the front of that volume.

thereof" — especially by paying tithes — were first to be expelled from the business meetings and their collections were not to be received; if they remained obdurate, they were then to be testified against. In Ireland, where Quakerism had a somewhat more moralistic cast, much energy was devoted to excluding the unworthy from business meetings. Those whom Satan had tempted by "the glory & beauty" and the "comelyness & decency of the severall fashions & customs of the world" were naturally unsuitable. William Edmondson, the patriarch of Irish Quakerism, was greatly concerned to limit attendance at business meetings to those of "clean and orderly Conversations" and often spoke in meeting about "the Qualifications necessary to fit Members for such Meetings and Services." [38]

Despite such instances of concern that business meetings should be limited to those of high character and sound judgment, the machinery which might have guaranteed this was intermittent in its operation, and the line separating fit from unfit members was far from being generally understood. There is much evidence that business meetings were even less select in practice than in theory. Sometimes persons who were under censure from Friends nevertheless attended them, like Gregory Darby of Biddlesden who, on attending the Biddlesden Monthly Meeting, was surprised to hear a testimony against him read out.[39] William Mather, who subsequently left the Friends, wrote, "I must confess, I have been at two of these Meetings of Government, but it was accidentally." [40] In Buckinghamshire a Friend called William Eburn

38. Testimony to William Edmondson by Leinster Province Meeting, 8 April 1713, in *A Journal of the Life of William Edmondson* (Dublin, 1715), xxi. See also Half-Year's Meeting Epistles, May and November 1696, May 1698, May 1709; Cork Six Weeks Meeting, 14 October 1682, 16 November 1692, November 1719, May 1720, 22 January 1694. Edmondson even spoke, in a prayer delivered on his death bed, of "All who were admitted into a close Communion, as Members of Men and Women's-Meetings" (*Journal*, p. 276).

39. Buckinghamshire Quarterly Meeting minute, 24 June 1696.
40. Mather, *A Novelty: Or, a Government of Women*, p. 8.

who had committed "a great Miscarriage . . . in carrying away another man's wood in the night time" was to be told by the Upperside Monthly Meeting that it could not "own him as a Member of the body." The Friends who were supposed to deliver this message to him could not find him; but they had their chance a month later, in March 1686, when (as the minutes note without evident surprise) "it so fel out that the said William Eburn came now to this Meeting."

The most remarkable instance of this sort concerns Timothy Child, whose refusal to submit his proposed marriage to the authority of the Women's Monthly Meeting set off the great schism in Buckinghamshire. Although he was not the sort of Friend to commend himself to the orthodox party, he came and sat in their Monthly Meeting, and, as the minutes for 5 February 1683 report:

> The power of the Lord fell upon them in a wonderfull manner . . . But ah alas! he remained hard & obdurate . . . & by the perversness of his Answers did plainly manifest, that he was out of the sense of that divine life, which friends were at that time filled with, & that that overcoming Power, which had melted the hearts of Friends into a tender compassion towards him, had made no impression on himself . . .
>
> At length, (it being late, & other business remaining to be done) he was desired to withdraw, but would not; which occasioned some further discourse with him, wherin it was declared by Friends, that in the State & condition wherin he now stood he had no right to sit among Friends as a Member of the Meeting, but (in refusing to withdraw) was an uncivil Intruder upon the Meeting.

Apparently it was not the irregularity of his coming and sitting among Friends, but the refusal to yield himself to their entreaties and to the extraordinary psychic atmosphere which rendered his "state and condition" unfit for membership in the meeting. It is noteworthy that the meeting could not continue to other business while a single dissentient person remained in it. The constitutional reason for this can be expressed as the requirement that no decision could be reached except by the unanimous sense of the meeting; but this sense had to be reached by the efforts of all to tender themselves to the promptings of God. This feeling that even one person out of harmony with the meeting could prevent it from accomplishing anything doubtless explains the repeatedly expressed concern that members should be properly qualified; but the ease with which unqualified men could wander in seems to show that there was little difference in appearance between a meeting for church affairs and the ordinary meetings for worship.

There even were extreme cases where Friends could only preserve the unity of spirit of their business metings by appointing doorkeepers and authorizing them to use physical force. The Wiltshire Quarterly Meeting appointed two on 8 July 1700 to let in none but those "in unity with the Quarterly Meeting and of good report in their conversation." The Wells Monthly Meeting on 7 May 1707 decided that for the future their meeting must be more select, "for we find to our great grief and exercise that several coming to our said Monthly Meetings on purpose to see and hear what pass and is done at the said Meetings, and so to tell it about in town and country to the enemeys of Truth and Friends." Their remedy was also a doorkeeper "to keep out the rabeley part of People, and all such who comes with an evil intent and purpose."

Force had to be resorted to in Cumberland to deal with the actions of one Isaac Pearson. Pearson, according to hostile sources, used to howl and shout during meetings; he would also embrace his fellow worshippers so ardently that they almost fainted. The Cumberland Quakers finally decided to

deny him the right to sit in business meetings; and then —
in an unprecedented step — since "he appear'd so turbulent
in our Religious meetings, and took up so much time with his
confus'd Ribaldry and Prophesying, we thought it convenient
to keep him out of them likewise." [41] Pearson attacked the
doorkeepers as "luggers" and "trailers," arguing that Friends
ought to depend on miraculous ejection; but the orthodox
party countered by claiming the right, like civil societies, to
maintain themselves by the police power. Besides, they contended, disturbing meetings for worship was contrary to the
principle of religious toleration.[42]

Provision for the recruitment of new members so that the
size of business meetings could be maintained sheds further
light on Friends' attitudes towards church government.
Among Cumberland Friends, the aspiring member himself
took the initiative. This was done in the first instance through
the preparative meetings, which at this time were limited
to the North of England. The Pardshaw Preparative Meeting agreed on 7 February 1708 that young men or others who
had not frequented business meetings should "propose to the
preparative meeting for consent to come" before they were
admitted to sit in such meetings. In the Moorhouse and Sol-
port Preparative Meetings there are minutes from the Quarterly Meeting dated May 1705 which suggest a similar procedure. In order to prevent unsuitable persons from intruding
into quarterly meetings, these minutes prescribed that the
elders of Preparative Meetings should qualify "young Friends
or others" for membership in them. None should "thrust
themselves" into Monthly Meetings without the consent of
the same elders; "and so consequently none who have not the

41. [Thomas Senhouse], *Outragious Apostates Exposed* (n.p., 1718),
p. 31. Pearson's case is put forward in his *The Implacable Cruelty of the
People Call'd Quakers in the County of Cumberland, against Isaac Pearson, One of that Persuasion* (1713).
42. *Outragious Apostates*, pp. 52–56.

privilege of the two Meetings abovesaid may presume themselves as Members of the Quarterly Meetings."

Some minutes show the process of admitting new members to the business meetings. For example, in 1717 the Pardshaw Preparative Meeting considered "a Proposition . . . for admiting John Udall to have the privelidge to sitt in this meeting." It was "defered to see what further Satisfaction friends may have with him, and give him our answer as find freedom therein." Below this is entered a notation that he has freedom to sit.

There were regional variations. The tone of the minute from Cumberland Quarterly Meeting can hardly be said to be cordial to those aspiring to "thrust" or "intrude" themselves into the business meetings (perhaps because of the disturbances raised by the Pearsons at about this time). In other parts of the country Friends were more concerned to stir up laggards to assume their rightful share in the affairs of the church, and consequently could not wait for them to make any application. The London Yearly Meeting recommended generally in 1704 that Friends should take it upon themselves to secure the attendance of young Friends "Worthy to be Esteemed Members" of meetings that they might "come up and stand in the life of righteousness, to be serviceable in the Church, helpful to the ancient Friends, and fitted to supply their places as such shall be removed." Norwich Quakers had already devised a procedure for assuring this. They had a meeting for "younger men and convinced persons," who were not yet thought suitable to serve in the regular monthly meetings.[43] From time to time (as for example on 13 October 1690) two Friends were asked to speak to such young men as they thought fit and invite them to the next monthly meeting.

43. When the first Goats Lane Meeting House was being built, the young and convinced persons' collection was kept separate from that taken by the women's and men's monthly meetings, to mark their separate status.

I know of no other meeting which used this method of initiating the young and new converts into the business meetings. Others tended to rely on hortatory minutes, like the Westminster Monthly Meeting, which on 2 April 1712 asked Friends in their respective neighborhoods to bring in the names of those who were thought fit to frequent the monthly and quarterly meetings. The Wiltshire Quarterly Meeting, in the belief that meetings for business would be improved by the presence of "young well behaved Friends" as well as "such Elders, who thro' disgust have not constantly attended said Meetings," sent to each monthly meeting on 5 July 1736 a minute urging all such to attend in the future.

It might be noted that when early eighteenth-century Quakers speak of "young" men, their standards of youth are not necessarily ours. In those meetings which regularly noted all men attending for a long span of time it is possible to tell the ages at which some men first attended. Eighteen such ages are available in Buckinghamshire, ranging from seventeen to twenty-nine with a median of twenty-three; and nineteen in Norfolk, ranging from seventeen to forty with a median of twenty-five.

To learn how Quaker business meetings actually worked more is needed than the generalized recommendations of various minutes about the qualifications of ideal members. Fortunately we can get a fuller picture by making a statistical analysis of the composition of the Upperside Monthly Meeting from 1668 to 1740 and of the Norfolk Quarterly Meeting from 1709 to 1739. The data are the signatures to the various "certificates" issued by the Upperside Monthly Meeting — two or three a year, on average — and the lists of Friends attending Norfolk Quarterly Meeting (the only long series of such lists that I found).

Though it is impossible to be certain either of the full number who sat in business meetings or of the total number of male Friends at any given time, the evidence suggests that about half of the male Quakers in the area formed by the Upperside Monthly Meeting did at some time sign a "certificate," whereas slightly less than one third of the men in Norfolk attended at least one quarterly meeting. The proportion of attenders in Buckinghamshire remained fairly constant; in the period covered by the first minute book, 1668–1690, there were 204 men aged twenty or over within the compass of the Monthly Meeting, of whom 93 appeared at some time among the signers of the "certificates" which it issued. Of the 111 who did not, 18 either adhered to the Separatists or had been disowned for some moral offense. These could hardly have expected to be members. Of the 94 others who do seem to have been excluded from the business meeting, 14 moved away before 1680 and 21 more before 1690. In the second minute book, covering the years from 1690 to 1713, certificates occur more frequently, averaging almost three a year. Disregarding those who were disowned or moved away in their twenties, there were in the area 220 men old enough to be members, of whom 104 appear in the lists of signatures. In the third book certificates are relatively infrequent, there being on the average not more than three every two years. There were 184 male adults (again disregarding the nine who were disowned) of whom 78 were at some time signers of certificates. Although the percentage of those appearing in business meetings thus slowly declines, this may simply reflect an overestimate of the total of adults, owing to the increasing inadequacy of the records.

Most of those who came to the monthly meetings at all seem to have been fairly regular in attendance. Of the thirty-six certificates in the first minute book, thirty-five were signed by Thomas Ellwood, the clerk, and by Robert Jones, a maltster of Cholesbury. Thomas Dell, a yeoman, signed thirty-four. Another six Friends signed more than two thirds of them, and sixteen signed about half or more. Among the less frequent attenders, fifteen signed about one quarter of the total number of certificates and there were thirteen who signed four or fewer. Most of these thirteen men were not in the county during the whole of this period. In the period covered by the second minute book, there were eleven Friends whose names appear on almost every certificate, seven more who signed more than two thirds of them, seventeen signing one half or more, and sixteen who signed only a few. Thus we can say there that a core of about ten Friends were almost always in attendance at the monthly meetings, and another group of about twenty were usually there. Fairly often some of about forty other Friends would attend, and there were about twenty Friends who seldom came.

In the Norfolk Quarterly Meeting there were, for natural reasons, few Friends who attended with anything like the constancy which might be expected in a monthly meeting. The pattern of attendance suggests that often Friends were in a rota where each attended one quarterly meeting a year. Nevertheless there were a few stalwarts, twelve in all, who attended three quarters or more of the meetings, and another forty-three who attended at least one half. Thirty more attended one quarter or more and these eighty-five constituted the experienced and weighty Friends of the county; they amounted to perhaps eight per cent of the total number of male Friends.

I have already pointed out that since there was no payment for service in the affairs of Truth, most — though not all — of the Quaker ministers would have to be men of considerable if not independent income. The manifold concerns of the Quaker conscience also threw the weight of responsibility for the governance of the church (through the business meetings) upon men who had the leisure and means to take it up. In Buckinghamshire, the most constant attenders were the gentlemen, rich yeomen, and wholesale traders who provided the social and fiscal strength of the Quaker movement. Of the eleven Friends who signed almost every certificate

Table 10. Occupations of members and nonmembers of the Upperside Men's Monthly Meeting and the Norfolk Quarterly Meeting.

Occupation	Upperside, 1669–1690				Upperside, 1690–1713				Upperside, 1713–1740				Norfolk, 1709–1739			
	Members		Nonmembers		Members		Nonmembers		Members		Nonmembers		Members		Nonmembers	
	No.	% Range[a]	No.	% Range	No.	% Range	No.	% Range	No.	% Range	No.	% Range	No.	% Range	No.	% Range
Gentlemen	8	8.6–10.3	—	—	7	6.7–7.4	—	—	2	2.6–3.0	1	0.9–2.0	11	3.4–7.3	4	0.5–3.0
Agriculture	33	35.5–42.3	32	34.4–60.4	36	34.6–37.9	30	25.9–47.6	16	20.5–23.9	26	24.5–51.0	53	16.4–35.1	38	5.0–28.4
Yeomen, farmers, etc.	24	25.8–30.8	28	30.1–52.8	25	24.0–26.3	25	21.6–39.7	14	17.9–20.9	9	8.5–17.6	41	12.7–27.2	21	2.8–15.7
Husbandmen, laborers	9	9.7–11.5	4	4.3–7.5	11	10.6–11.6	5	4.3–7.9	4	5.1–6.0	17	16.0–33.3	12	3.7–7.9	17	2.3–12.7
Professional	2	2.2–2.6	—	—	1	1.0–1.1	—	—	1	1.3–1.5	1	0.9–2.0	3	0.9–2.0	1	0.1–0.7
Wholesalers	18	19.4–23.1	6	6.5–11.3	30	28.8–31.6	10	8.6–15.9	29	37.2–43.3	9	8.5–17.6	33	10.2–21.9	20	2.7–14.9
Retailers	16	17.2–20.5	6	6.5–11.3	15	14.4–15.8	8	6.9–12.7	12	15.4–17.9	3	2.8–5.9	20	6.2–13.2	12	1.6–9.0
Laborers and artisans	9	9.7–11.5	9	9.7–17.0	13	12.5–13.7	15	12.9–23.8	9	11.5–13.4	12	11.3–23.5	15	4.6–9.9	36	4.8–26.9
Worsted weavers	—		—		—		—		—		—		10	3.1–6.6	17	2.3–12.7
Woolcombers	—		—		—		—		—		—		17	5.3–11.3	10	1.3–7.5
"Yeomen" on indictment	—		—		—		—		—		—		6	1.9	9	1.2
Unknown	15	16.1	40	43.0	9	8.7	53	45.7	11	14.1	55	51.9	166	51.4	611	81.0
Totals	93		93		104		116		78		106		323		754	

[a] The first percentage is of the total; the second is of those whose occupations are known.

between 1690 and 1713, three were gentlemen, four yeomen, and four wholesalers. Furthermore, it is clear that there is a considerable difference in wealth and social status between Friends who were and were not judged fit for the responsibilities of business meetings, as can be seen from Table 10. Friends certainly did not believe that their "weighty, seasoned, and faithful members" were necessarily those who were rich; they did not exclude day-laborers, for example, from business meetings. Nevertheless the latter were far less likely to attend; probably they lacked the necessary margin of leisure to absent themselves from their callings and were also restrained by mere diffidence.

What we know of the composition and work of the various business meetings is quite similar to what we can discover about the early ministers. The "power of the meeting" was widely distributed and exercised, just as many believers participated to some extent in the ministry. The absence of membership lists suggests that strict lines of membership for business meetings were not maintained, but the select character of the meetings was often invoked ad hoc when someone took advantage of their quasi-public character to disturb or hinder them. This is similar to the private "eldering" or denial of a certificate to travel for someone whose ministry was not deemed acceptable. Despite their relative freedom and openness, both the public ministry and the meetings for church business made discriminations between Friends which in the very beginning had not existed. The Public Friends seated in their gallery were literally not on the same level as the ordinary worshippers, and inevitably the members of business meetings — "*active Members* in the Church," as the London Yearly Meeting epistle of 1718 called them — formed a sort of elite. Furthermore, it was an elite chosen on grounds of character and common sense; and because of the heavy demands of both the business meetings and the public ministry, the majority of Friends who exercised their gifts in these areas were the wealthier ones.

This was one of the predictable, yet probably unanticipated consequences of the Friends' rejection of a salaried ministry. If they were to do all their business by committee, the more businesslike would naturally assume power. The "bourgeoisi-fication" of the Society of Friends, so much oftener described than proved, does have a certain reality in the growth of the powers of the meetings for church affairs, which had a decidedly more "bourgeois" complexion than the membership as a whole. In giving a cachet, no matter how slight, to pru-dence as a quality requisite for church government, Friends ran the risk of eliminating that eminently Christian type, the holy fool, from the range of religious experience which Quak-erism could encompass.

IV   The Idea of Membership

To trace the conception of membership as a status within the Quaker community is to epitomize the history of the first century of Quakerism. Ideas about membership were most obviously associated with the theory of conversion as a prerequisite to membership; but Friends' ideas about themselves, their religious mission, and "the world" in which they lived all found their focus in the gradual discrimination among those who attended Friends' meetings.

In particular, the working out of the idea of membership throws into relief the tension between the survival of a past that had been suffused with eschatological hopes and the present daily exigencies of administering the affairs of the church. The first Quakers had aspirations too intense for the limits of England and too vaulting for mere denomination as yet another group of "Protestant Dissenters." They had no sectarian notion of membership. As we have seen, the coming together of a group of "saints" to "inchurch themselves" and thus create a new locus of church power; the careful scrutiny of those aspiring brothers and sisters who presented themselves as converts; and the preservation of the purity of the group by casting out all errant members — all typical of the Congregational and Baptist churches — were alien to the original impulse of Quakerism. In fact, so far were they from any such sectarian concept of membership that they really had no coherent theory of religious organization at all; they were animated instead by the conviction that the direct operations of the Spirit of God were to supersede all existing religious institutions. The possibility, almost the imminence, of universal salvation, so long as it was a lively hope, burst the confines of any determinate form of ecclesiastical organization.

This expectation that the whole world would soon be converted accounts for the vehement repudiation by the early Friends of the charge that they were a sect. Called in 1660 "a chiefe upholder of the Quakers sect," George Fox returned the indignant answer: "The Quakers are not A sect, but are in the power of god before sects was." [1] Early Friends were willing to allow that salvation could come to members of all Christian bodies, or even to Moslems, for that matter. Robert Barclay the Apologist defined the church as "no other thing, but the *society, gathering,* or *company of such as God hath called out of the World, and worldly Spirit, to walk in his LIGHT AND LIFE.* The *Church* then so designed is to be considered, as it comprehends all that are thus *called* and *gathered* truly *by God,* both such as are yet in this inferiour World, and such as having already laid down the earthly Tabernacle, are passed into their heavenly Mansions, which together do make up the one Catholick Church." Outside the church as so defined, continued Barclay, "we freely acknowledge there can be no Salvation, because under this Church and its denomination are comprehended all, and as many, of whatsoever Nation, Kindred, Tongue or people they be . . . There may be members therefore of this Catholick Church both among Heathens, Turks, Jews, and all the several sorts of Christians, Men and Women of integrity and simplicity of Heart, who though blinded in something in their understanding, and perhaps burthened with the Super-

1. George Fox, *Journal,* ed. Norman Penney (Cambridge, Eng.: Cambridge University Press, 1911), I, 379.

stitions and formality of the several Sects in which they are ingrossed, yet . . . become true members of this Catholick Church." [2]

Consistent with this avoidance of the sectarian role was the Friends' reluctance to accept a name. "Quaker," of course, has been rubbed smooth in three centuries, so that the sneer in it no longer comes through. But, like Christians and Lollards, Whigs and Tories, Quakers did not name themselves; they were named by their enemies. Justice Gervase Bennet of Derby was the first to apply the name, and Fox denounced him in unusually sulphurous terms for doing so: "A Justice to wrong name people, what may the brutish people doe, if such A one A Justice of peace give names to men, but thou art Lifted upp proud and haughty and soe turnest Against the Just one given upp to misname the saints." Fox trembled at the word of the Lord, but quaking was really more appropriate for Justice Bennet and his ilk, "scoffer mockers proud Earthly ones fatt dronken lust full ones, beastly people that follow pleaswer, headdy high miended and haughty and covitious given upp to Uncleanenes." [3] We must always remember that the name sounded very much like that of the notorious antinomians, the Ranters; in fact it was commonplace to define the Ranter, as the *Heresiography* did, as "an uncleane beast, much of the make with our *Quaker*, of the same puddle, and may keep pace with him; their infidelity,

2. *Apology for the True Christian Divinity* (1678), proposition 10, section 2. The religious status of Turks is made clearer in proposition 5 and section 16 of proposition 6, where Barclay defines the light within and distinguishes it from conscience, which may be corrupted: "As for example, a Turk who hath possessed himself with a false belief, that it is unlawful for him to drink Wine, if he do it, his conscience smites him for it: But though he keep many Concubines, his conscience troubles him not, because that his judgment is already defiled with a false Opinion that [it] is lawful for him to do the one, and unlawful to do the other. Whereas if the Light of Christ in him were minded, it would reprove him, not only for committing Fornication, but also as he became obedient thereunto, inform him that *Mahomet* is an *Impostor*; as well as *Socrates* was informed by it, in his day of the falsity of the Heathens Gods."

3. Fox, *Journal*, ed. Penney, I, 5, 7.

villanies, and debochements, are the same, only the Ranter is more open, and lesse sowre." [4]

Within a century, Friends had traveled a long way from the open-textured, inspired casualness of the early days of the movement, with its reluctance to name itself, its rudimentary theory of organization, and its lack of any clear definition of membership. As L. Hugh Doncaster puts it, in the 1670's: "Anyone associating with Friends might be regarded as a Friend. Those who identified themselves with Quaker testimony were at once recognisable by speech, manner of greeting and fashion of clothing, quite apart from doctrine or other less immediately discernible testimony." [5] Yet even the earliest Friends did use the word "member." The Yearly Meeting epistle of 1659 says that "every member may act in his own freedom"; the epistle of 1666 refers to Friends as "members of the church." And the processes of Quaker history steadily supplied a greater content for the word. In establishing their business meetings, Friends had created self-perpetuating organizations with power and money. Now such organizations, with the function of bringing to bear power and money, were bound to force a sharper definition of what had been — before there was systematic discipline and poor relief — unformed and vague. The way in which Friends, as they were drawn into the common task of overseeing the concerns of the church, established institutions which sharpened their distinction from "the world," will be the theme of this chapter.

Let us begin with the matter of names. Although they almost always referred to themselves as "Friends," it was almost a century and a half before the name "Religious Society of Friends" was adopted as the official collective noun. Throughout the first century — and well beyond — Friends had no

4. *Heresiography* (5th ed.; 1654), p. 143.
5. *Quaker Organisation and Business Meetings* (London: Friends' Home Service Committee, 1958), pp. 15–16.

legal corporate existence. There was no way, for example, to leave money to a Monthly Meeting or to a Friends' charity. This led to such difficulties as that confronting the Westminster Monthly Meeting on 1 May 1728, when it was decided that the best way to proceed was to give a legacy or bequest "Spetial and positive" to someone who was not an executor, with an explicit paper of instructions as to how it was to be used. The problem is further illustrated in a paper dated 30 September 1754 and inserted in the back of the third volume of the Upperside Monthly Meeting Minutes; in it ten Friends specify that if any of them were left a legacy by Mary Olliffe of High Wycombe, they were satisfied "that such Legacy is Wholly Intended for the Use of the Monthly Meeting of the People Called Quakers in the Upper Side of the County of Bucks and not for our own use." [6]

Such necessities of corporate life as getting sufficient legal personality to receive and administer bequests finally impelled Friends to take a corporate name. And just as these administrative problems demanded such a solution, so Friends were drawn into a further degree of self-definition by one of their earliest impulses, to withdraw entirely from the ministrations of the established church, and hence to duplicate its institutions within their community. The most notable example of this is the distinctive Friends' procedure for marriage (discussed in Chapter V), but undoubtedly their thorough registration of births and deaths was intended as an analogue to the parish registers. Friends even collected their wills in an attempt to create their own equivalent of probate registries, although their wills still had to be proved in the church courts.[7] Now as L. Hugh Doncaster remarks, a con-

6. Lack of corporate status meant a wholesale creation of Quaker trustees, and there are many examples of the care which various meetings had to take with them; for example, minutes of Somerset Quarterly Meeting, 22 December 1692; Upperside Monthly Meeting, 7 November 1726; Norfolk Quarterly Meeting, 25 December 1726.

7. This explains why copies of Friends' wills are often found in Monthly Meeting papers. A collection of wills kept in Kendal has been

ception of membership is entailed in these registration procedures, and Friends were careful to assure themselves that they were not used indiscriminately.[8] On several occasions the Norwich Monthly Meeting made a point of inquiring why a father wished to have his child's birth recorded before the entry was made.[9] Sometimes such questions were associated with discipline; for example, the Wells Monthly Meeting, before it would register the birth of a child to Edmund Newbegin, inquired on 7 October 1719 "what the perticular meeting unto which he belong have done in his Cause wether they have given him Gospell order, and how they Find him; he having Some time Since gon From amongst us & taken a wife by the Priest." Finding in the following March that they could not get from him a satisfactory paper of self-condemnation, the meeting did not allow registration of the birth. Generally the births of children born less than nine months after the marriage of their parents were not registered.

A similar care was exercised towards Friends' burying grounds. The Westminster Monthly Meeting on 6 June 1705 took note that burying grounds had been bought for the interment of those who had walked in the Truth and left a good savor behind them. At times, some persons who had requested to be buried therein, and who had manifested in their last illnesses a tenderness towards Truth and Friends, had been allowed to be buried with Friends.[10] But the Meeting could not in good conscience allow the burial in Quaker grounds of those who had not been in such a temper of

---

published: *Some Westmorland Wills, 1686–1738*, ed. John Somervell (Kendal, Eng.: T. Wilson and Son, 1938).

8. Doncaster, *Quaker Organisation*, p. 28, n. 2.

9. See the Norwich Monthly Meeting minute of 14 November 1681 for an example.

10. Clearly a good many persons who were not considered Friends were buried in Quaker burying grounds. On 6 November 1728 the Norwich Monthly Meeting inquired whether Thomas Eldridge was to be considered a member. It was reported that he was not; but his burial is recorded on 12 February 1732.

mind and spirit. Indeed, it decided that Friends who had been testified against could not have their deaths or the births of their children recorded; nor could any members of their families be buried in the burying ground. Furthermore, it provided that those who had asked for burial because they or their parents had paid towards the cost of purchasing the burying ground should instead have the money refunded.

Such decisions give us an occasional insight into the process of self-definition, but they were in a sense peripheral. The most important concerns of the meetings for business, the ones which occupied them month after month, were the disciplining of the unworthy and the dispensing of charity to the "household of faith." These concerns called for the keenest discrimination, and in wrestling with the difficulties which they presented, Friends felt their way towards establishing a coherent and universally accepted theory of membership.

Gospel Order and the Invisible Quaker

One of the earliest concerns of George Fox was that the "people of God" should purge themselves of what he called "disorderly walkers." Any person bearing the name "Friend" who failed to sustain Friends' standards of conduct must be disciplined. Discipline of such sort would serve what sociologists call a "boundary-maintaining" function — that is, it would define and dramatize the distinction between acceptable and deviant behavior. But the logic of this "boundary-maintaining" function ran counter to Robert Barclay's definition of the "true Catholick Church" as invisible, as consisting of members who could be known only to God. How, and against whom, could Friends justify the exercise of discipline? The resolution of this difficulty led Friends to develop a form of discipline different from that practiced by other Dissenters, but in harmony with their distinctive conception of membership.

A few examples of Quaker discipline in action will show that there were superficial resemblances to the punishments and penances inflicted by other churches, but that there were very different principles at work among Friends. When Richard Dell of Chesham was found to have got his third wife with child before their marriage, the couple wrote a long statement or paper condemning their offense. Papers of this sort were invariably sought by Friends; this one was ordered to be copied in the book of the Upperside Monthly Meeting (it was entered 7 August 1693) and to be read out in Chesham meeting for worship, with both offenders being there to acknowledge it. Finally, it was to be kept in Chesham meeting house so that it could be shown to those who reproached Friends in the matter. Similarly, after Peter Gill of Aylsham was found regularly "overtaken with drink," he was directed by the Norwich Monthly Meeting on 14 December 1670 to make public confession to his former pot-companions. Even more thoroughgoing was the treatment of Henry Costard of Owlswick by Upperside Monthly Meeting. Costard, who had been married by a priest to "one of the world," was summoned to meeting on 3 August 1696 and with "a dejected Countenance" and "much brokenness & sobbing" read his paper of self-condemnation. Then he was directed to make several copies, one to be given to the clergyman who had performed the wedding, one to be read out and kept by the Meadle meeting, and — not least — one to be given to the Separatists of the county, "who greatly rejoyced at his Fal."

In all three of these cases, the transgressors wrote the requested paper of self-condemnation. If they had remained impenitent, the monthly meeting would have written a similar paper "disowning" the unrighteous action and given it equivalent publicity. These procedures did resemble some which were exercised by other churches. Public humiliation, degrading as it now seems, had been common even in the Church of England, which Friends generally treated as morally lax because its members, on their own weekly admission, remained "miserable offenders." [11] In the palmy days of the Court of High Commission, transgressors, especially against sexual purity, were required to make a public parade to the pillory, dressed only in a sheet, and to stand therein with a placard announcing for what sin they were being punished. The Church of England also still reserved the pains of excommunication for persistent sinners, although by the middle of the seventeenth century it had become contemptible.[12] The temporal penalty of excommunication was to be shunned by all friends and neighbors; for it to be effective the believer had to be part of a vital community. It is therefore not surprising that the Baptist and Independent meetings made more effective use of the "awfull ordinance" of "casting out" their delinquent brethren. They in fact employed even more severe procedures and language than did Friends. For example, Norwich Old Meeting on 7 January 1655 dealt with Sister Margaret Tompson for telling untruths, levity during meeting, and giving entertainment to a man of evil reputation, culminating in "that she went into the mans company & stayed with him alone in his chamber till he went to bed Contrary to Rom. 13, verse 13." The result was that she was "cut off from the congregation." Although this was the common formula, sometimes the "gathered churches" employed a more severe and strictly biblical one. In January 1668 Abraham Grimly, a dicer and frequenter of alehouses, was "delivered to Satan for the de-

11. Robert Barclay of Reigate, *The Inner Life of the Religious Societies of the Commonwealth* (1876), p. 267.

12. For an account of the High Commissioners as scourges of lechery, see F. D. Price, "The Commission for Ecclesiastical Causes for the Diocese of Bristol and Gloucester, 1574," *Transactions of the Bristol and Gloucestershire Archaeological Society,* 59 (1937), 61–184. The decrepit condition of excommunication is discussed in the same author's article, "The Abuses of Excommunication and the Decline of Ecclesiastical Discipline under Queen Elizabeth," *English Historical Review,* 57 (1942), 106–115; and in Christopher Hill, *Society and Puritanism in Pre-revolutionary England* (London: Secker and Warburg, 1964), pp. 354–381.

struction of the flesh that his spirit might be saved in the day of Christ." Such language indeed proved too full-blooded for some, who protested to the deacons of Fenstanton Church: "For shame! You deliver men to Satan; and the apostles of Christ never delivered any to Satan, unless it were for fornication." [13]

The Quakers delivered nobody to Satan, not even for fornication; nor did they ever use such phrases as "cut off," with its implication of lopping corrupt members off a pure body. In "testifying against" an unrighteous action or even in "disowning" a sinful member, Friends were not excommunicating in the sense that other Christian churches did. Their discipline was criticized in 1693 for lacking "that Ancient Apostolique Authority of Binding or Cutting off a Member off the Church — As the Church of Christ (by his spirit) hath." [14] But this is not what they claimed or wanted to do. "We . . . cast out none, but they cast out themselves through their Wickedness; for we do not receive them in, therefore we cannot cast them out," George Fox is supposed to have said.[15]

It is important to note that if the offender made it sufficiently plain that he made no pretensions to being a Friend, he

13. *Records of the Churches at Fenstanton, Warboys, and Hexham,* ed. Edward Bean Underhill (1854), p. 132. Bedford Meeting in 1679 also used the phrase "deliver . . . up to Sattan" (*Church Book of Bunyan Meeting,* ed. G. B. Harrison [1928], p. 68.)

14. This was said by a Bristol Friend who had been "testified against"; see Russell Mortimer, "Quakerism in Seventeenth Century Bristol," unpub. Master's thesis, Bristol University, 1946, p. 181.

15. The statement is attributed to him in Nathaniel Smith, *The Quakers Spiritual Court Proclaimed, Being an Exact Narrative of two several Tryals had before that New-High-Court of Justice, at the Peele in St. John's Street* (1669), p. 31. Although this is a hostile source — the reference is to the Peel Monthly Meeting in London — the quotation has an authentic ring and is consonant with Friends' attitudes, at least in England. Irish Friends seem here as usual to have been closer to the sectarian ideal. John Burnyeat held it as a defect of the Church of Ireland that there was no "dis-membring" or excluding from church membership of evil-doers (*Truth Exalted in the Writings of John Burnyeat* [1691], p. 226).

did not have to write any paper of self-condemnation, or have the appropriate meeting write one about him. Thus on 25 October 1680 members of the Biddlesden Monthly Meeting visited a man "to know whether he will deny himself to be one of us and if not then to give forth a paper speedily in the denyall of him." Three years later, on 7 May 1683, the Upperside Monthly Meeting did nothing to censure William Fisher of Flanden, Hertfordshire, even though he was reputed to have sired a bastard, since he had "of late sufficiently manifested himself not to be a Quaker, by his going to the Steeple house & receiving the Sacrament, as it is called." In the same spirit the Bristol Meeting on 30 September 1675 heard the report of a visit to "a mann soe much in darkness that wee cannot receive him as a friend of truth. Yet are well satisfied (Since he frequents our meetings) that he had been thus reproved and admonished." The Bristol Meeting also dropped disciplinary actions because the person in question was established not to be a Friend.[16]

Not only did they decline to proceed against persons who had given public notice that they were not Friends; Quakers also, in testifying against persons or their actions, characteristically stated that the offender was at best only "reputed" or "esteemed" to be a Quaker. Their reasoning was that falling away from Truth meant that it had never taken proper root. Wrongdoers were *eo ipso* not Friends. This principle would virtually allow Friends to retain both the power of censure and the belief in an "invisible" membership, since God alone could judge the propensity to sin, though the meeting must judge the actual fruits of the exercise of that propensity. Reasoning along these lines, Friends could keep alive the old dislike for the name "Quaker" and the old hope (or memory of it) that Friends would soon be the new and universal church. They could place the responsibility for

16. These cases are reported in Mortimer, "Quakerism in Bristol," pp. 460–461.

defining Quakers on "the world" and could justify their papers of denial because their objects, "by the world reputed a Quaker," were not so much disowned by the meeting as certified to have detached themselves from it. Of course we never find this said in so many words; but it is the only interpretation which will explain the language of many Quaker disownments. The Somerset Quarterly Meeting, for example, on 22 December 1670 was laboring with a "very contrary and perverse spirit" who, unless he repented, was to be testified against "that he may not under the name of a Quaker deceive the world." On 26 September 1672 another disorderly person, this time with a weakness for women and drink, "hath manifested himselfe as a Branch broken off & out of the fellowship of truth, So that a necessity lyes upon us to give forth this testimony against him, That he is not att all owned by us as one in fellowship with us." A Friend who had made an irregular marriage and committed other sins was said on 25 September 1684 to have "excluded himselfe from the felowship of trueth & them that live in it." These motifs rise to a crescendo in the affair of Samuel Trent, who was dealt with on 18 December 1679 in the following resounding terms: "Samuel Trent . . . hath for severall yeers Last past walked so disorderly & contrary to the truth That he hath by his owne doinge manifested himself that he is not of us . . . And though it be well knowne to many that we had noe fellowship with him, But [he] hath walked Loose off from us for severall yeeres . . . yett now upon the late outrages & wickednesse committed by him, It is unduely reflected upon us & our way . . . It therefore remains with us to lett all people know That we detest & abhorre such wicked & evill practices."

It is not only in Somerset that we find such language. Thomas Ellwood, the first clerk of the Upperside Monthly Meeting, prefaced papers of denial with elaborate disquisitions on the history and problems of God's people, reminiscent of the prologues to Elizabethan statutes. He would begin: "As the Lord in good wil & tender compassion hath been graciously pleased to visit & gather a people in this latter day, after the dark night of Apostacy, & hath called them to the knowledge & obedience of his saving Truth, that they might be saved thereby: So the Adversary of Mankind envying the happines of God's people hath continually opposed this blessed work of the Lord." [17]

In several of these prefaces we find further traces of the "invisible Quaker." For example, the Upperside Meeting had to testify against John Clark and Elizabeth Winkfield, who were living together though she was single and he married to another woman. They were said "by going sometimes to the Meetings of the People called Quakers" to "have procured to themselves amongst some of their Neibours, the name & denomination of Quakers." But, although they had at some times come to meetings (which were "wel known to be publick & open to al") yet they were "never received or owned by us, as living Members of that heavenly body, whereof Christ our Lord is head or as partakers of that immortal Life, in which our unity stands, nor otherwise regarded by us than as such as might possibly gather into their understandings some Notions of Truth to talk of, as too too many do, who notwithstanding are Enemies to the Cross of Christ Jesus." [18]

Similarly, Roland Foster of Aylesbury seemed in 1680 to be a Friend in good standing, for the monthly meeting paid attention to his objection that Joyce Olliffe should not be allowed a certificate to go to America because she was engaged to be married to him. But in February 1684 he failed to get approval of his marriage to Hannah Costard of High Wycombe because of certain "miscarriages." These, it turned

17. Minute of 3 August 1685. Ellwood had been Milton's secretary for a time and claims to have suggested the subject for "Paradise Regained."
18. Minute of 1 August 1677.

out, were mostly instances of drunkenness. Nothing daunted, he tricked the meeting into giving him a certificate for the marriage, and so he was testified against with these words: "Rowland (though he had now and then dropt in at a Meeting) had never really come to a subjection to Truth, nor was a man that was seriously or religiously disposed." James Pickett, too, had come to Wendover from London "under the name & in the appearance of a Quaker." He had "some times, though seldome, gone to some meetings thereabouts" but had "exceeded the bounds of sobriety in drinking & frequently put off his hat in the way and spirit of the world's people." He, too, was testified against in February 1691 as "not really of us" but yet "reputed to be a Quaker." Another Wendover offender given the same sort of treatment was John Robins, a tallow chandler, who in November 1695 was given a certificate by Upperside Monthly Meeting to marry Sarah Clifton of Coventry. The certificate said that the meeting had "no cause to deny . . . his orderly conversation." But on 2 May 1698 he "who bears the name of a Quaker" had "run himself out of his estate . . . been several times arrested for a debt, & [was] much complained of for breaking his word and promises with them he deals with, & owes money to." This led on 5 September 1698 to the usual denouement: "although, since he first came to live in this Country, he was never esteemed by us, as one who had so received the Truth we profess, as to be seasoned and governed thereby, as he ought to have been; yet, inasmuch as he pretended to our Profession & was therupon reputed a Quaker."

By the same reckoning the children of Friends might also fail to come into the proper subjection to Truth. Grace Hawks of Chesham "from a Child had been accustomed to go with her Mother to Meetings." But she "ran out from Truth" in marrying a man of "the world." She was ordered on 1 August 1687 to write a paper condemning her action, because "(although Friends that knew her, seeing her to be a proud vain Lass, did never value her as a friend, yet) by reason of her so going to Meetings, the World's people there do in some measure account her a Quaker."

Even those who had been admitted to sit in the meetings for business might find themselves charged with never having been in the Truth. Edward Lered or Learhead of Amersham on 4 March and 1 July 1689 had set his name to certificates issued by the Upperside Monthly Meeting. Unfortunately, he "let in a Suspicion" that one Emlin Dean of Amersham had bewitched one of his children, and in order to break the spell by drawing her blood, he and the child fell upon her and scratched her face. The monthly meeting understood that this assault was to be tried in the Quarter Sessions; it required "gospel order" not particularly because it violated Friends' teachings against violence, but because Lered had been moved by "Heathenish Superstition." [19] Consequently a paper was issued in October 1690 denying him, with this characteristic preface: "in this day of the Lord's gathering a peculiar People to himself, some persons have sometimes resorted to the meetings of God's people, & made some shews of Profession of the Truth." Such a one was Edward Lered, who had (despite his former service in the meetings for business) taken only the "outward characters of our Profession."

Perhaps none of these examples of the prose of Thomas Ellwood is so striking as one example in Norwich. David Reed, a tailor, was listed in the Norwich return of the "first publishers of Truth" as one of the first to receive Truth and Friends in the city. Apparently he became somewhat more cool towards Friends, since the Norwich Monthly Meeting directed as early as 10 April 1672 that he should be visited for, among other things, attending Anglican services and "complaining against Friends." This visit produced some

19. The Quarter Sessions book, however, does not mention the case.

satisfaction, which seems to have lasted about a decade, but on 16 July 1683 he was disowned, and even though he finds a place in "The First Publishers of Truth," the Norwich Monthly Meeting declared that he was never owned or in any wise countenanced, despite his long attending, but for the sake of his wife!

So pervasive was the idea of "invisible membership" that the offenders themselves sometimes recognized it. This is made clear in the paper that Sarah Russell of Chalfont St. Peter gave to the Upperside Women's Monthly Meeting in January 1683 — a paper which makes clear some of the human cost of Friends' discipline. "Though I walked amongst Friends I was not one of them, for then I had never done this thinge, and had I toke councel of the Lord, or of Friends, I had not done it, and when I have been at the women's meetings and heard marriages spoken too often thought I wont never have him and that I would tel him so for I knew it was contrary to truth but when I came to speake to him I had not corrage. And at the very time I toke him for my husband I had a sence I was doing that I should not and when I saw Friends afterward I was ashamed to look on them." The wretched girl "desired with tears that Friends might not cast her off, for they know not what the Lord may doe for mee."

The idea of a purely invisible membership is one implication of Friends' testimony against outward "signs." Their baptism was by the downrushing of the Holy Spirit, and not by water. They barred none from the communion table, because there was neither bread nor wine to be distributed; and they opened their meetings for worship to whoever wished to come. As the Bristol Friends said, "we dare Not for Conscience Sake, keep any out of our Metinge how profane soever." [20] Their society was gathered by the Holy Spirit,

20. Quoted in Mortimer, "Quakerism in Bristol," p. 107. Bristol

but — as we have seen — since no one could know the spiritual experiences of another, there were no "visible saints" in the Congregational sense.

Just as they imposed no excommunications on the obdurate, so Friends had no penances for the contrite. The papers of self-condemnation to be read out in public meetings or posted in public places were not intended to humble the offender; they were rather designed to show that the evil deed was not in harmony with Friends' principles. The London Yearly Meeting in its epistle of 1673 said that the publicity attached to testimonies against offenses ought not to be greater than that of the offense; nevertheless papers of penitence were useful for the offender to "take away the Scandal in their acknowledgment before all to whose Knowledge it hath come." [21] All these public "papers" were to include an explicit statement that the evil action was not in accordance with Friends' principles. Whenever disciplinary action was begun, an inevitable — and often the only — reason alleged was that the offender must "clear Truth" by making it publicly known that his misdeeds were not taught nor countenanced by Friends. Notably, the reformation of the offender was never stated as a reason for initiating discipline; "clearing Truth" came to be, in the minutes of Friends' meetings, a shorthand designation for all disciplinary matters.

The reason for insisting on a public confession, where obtainable, was that it was more credible and impressive than a statement from the meeting concerned, but there was no pastoral reason to insist on confession.[22] When their disci-

---

Friends did in 1669 forbid one man who had been disowned to come even to meetings for worship (*ibid.*, p. 184). Isaac Pearson was also excluded from meetings for worship.

21. Robert Barclay, *The Anarchy of the Ranters* (1676), p. 47.

22. The nearest approach to a pastoral reason given for the exercise of Quaker discipline that I have found occurs in a minute of the Somerset Quarterly Meeting on 20 March 1684, which directed two Friends to visit a backslider and "lay his iniquity before him That he may be left

pline was challenged, Friends defended it not on pastoral grounds, but because, as Thomas Ellwood put it: "Every Religious Society or Body, hath a certain Power within it self over the particular *Members* that make up, or pretend to be of, that Society or Body; by vertue of which such Society or Body may call to account, deal with, and (if they see cause) deny any such Member as shall walk disorderly, contrary to the Rules, and against the Safety or Honour of the Society." [23]

Because they were concerned to exercise their discipline in behalf of the "safety or honour of the Society," Friends almost never struck at doctrinal errors, but rather at unrighteous actions. "Corrupt opinions," for which the early Quakers had been excommunicated by Baptists or Independent meetings, caused little exercise to Friends, and those who went off to join the Separatists, or fell away from attendance at meetings through ceasing to believe in Quaker teachings, were never pursued with punishments; the monthly meeting was simply relieved of the obligation "to take further notice of them." [24]

The practical necessities of judgment, and the necessary consequences of "clearing Truth" in this way greatly sharpened the image of an ideal Friend. A generation of "gospel order" administered in this spirit inevitably narrowed the range of acceptable conduct by Friends and went far towards replacing the generous early conception of Christian liberty with "the rules of our Society" — a phrase which came into

without Excuse in the day of the Lord when every man shall reape according to what he Sowes." This does not take a very optimistic view of the case.

23. Thomas Ellwood, *An Answer to George Keith's Narrative of His Proceedings at Turners-Hall* (1696), p. 16.

24. The only case I have found resembling a disownment on doctrinal grounds was that of Elizabeth Dapelin, disowned by the Wells Monthly Meeting on 6 September 1699 as an unprofitable minister. Occasionally persons attempted to stand in Friend's meetings and deliver unacceptable testimony; Friends then stood up and "testified against" what had been said, though not necessarily against the speaker.

vogue at the beginning of the eighteenth century.[25] The way that the "Christian and Brotherly Advices," issued in manuscript by the London Yearly Meeting in 1738, was indexed and used betrays its quasi-legal character; and indeed, as early as 2 April 1705, the Wiltshire Quarterly Meeting was deciding on a questionable marriage in the light of "a very pertinent president" from the Friends of the Bradford meeting, which they paid 13s. 8d. to have copied out and sent to them. (Friends of the Upperside Meeting, it will be remembered, sought precedents in deciding how to exclude undesirable persons from business meetings.)

The constant emphasis on preserving the good name of Quakerism and the reputation of Quaker principles, which is found consistently from the earliest disciplinary actions, must be seen in the light of the polemics of the first days of Quakerism, and in particular in light of the excesses of the antinomians and Ranters with whom Friends were often confused. In the much-quoted opinion of Richard Baxter, "the Quakers were but the Ranters turned from horrid profaneness and blasphemy to a life of extreme austerity on the other side. Their doctrines were mostly the same with the Ranters." [26] The unusual severity of Fox's denial that Friends were a sect and of his repudiation of the name "Quaker" shows how sensitive he was to these identifications, and in a sense the whole of the Quaker discipline might be looked at as a gigantic engine to maintain that "life of extreme austerity on the other side."

Finally, the effects of religious persecution and the nature of eventual religious toleration conspired to rivet the idea of group respectability into the structure of Quaker discipline.

25. As in minutes of the Wiltshire Quarterly Meeting and the Westminister Monthly Meeting, 7 October 1730. Irish Friends used the curious phrase "the rules of Truth."

26. *Reliquae Baxterianae* (1696), I, 77, quoted in William C. Braithwaite, *The Beginnings of Quakerism* (Cambridge, Eng.: Cambridge University Press, 1955), p. 22.

Since persecution was so often based on the identification of Friends with such disreputable groups as the Fifth-monarchy men, it became a vital interest of the group to keep its honor and reputation unspotted in the eyes of "the world." Since "the world" persisted in paying such unpleasantly close attention to the affairs of Friends, it is not too surprising that they at times seemed more sensitive to its opinion of them than to the leadings of the spirit within.

Toleration then finished what persecution had begun, for toleration came in the form of an annual exemption from the law, and Friends were acutely conscious that this was a privilege which might be revoked.[27] This entailed an understandable anxiety to protect the legal position granted to them after 1689. For example, their refusal to take judicial oaths unquestionably gave rise to more punishment than anything except their objection to tithes, and the only way to escape the oath was to gain universal agreement that Friends were bound always to speak the truth. Even before the Affirmation Act passed in the reign of William III, Friends were sometimes allowed to testify in court without taking an oath. John Wootton of Chalfont St. Giles in 1690 gave evidence before the Quarter Sessions which was accepted without an oath, because he was a Quaker. Unhappily, when he left the court, he told a bystander that "Truth is not to be spoken at al times, or in al Cases." On 8 June 1691 the Upperside Monthly Meeting ordered that he should be visited by several weighty

27. Russell Mortimer in "Quakerism in Bristol" notes the importance of preserving the good name of the Society in Friends' discipline and believes that this motive became progressively more important as the Society entered the eighteenth century (see p. 459 and elsewhere). I believe that there was an enhanced concern for their reputation in the eighteenth century, owing to the peculiar nature of the religious toleration accorded Friends, which was licensed Nonconformity rather than true religious freedom. On the other hand the same motive is expressed in the earliest papers of disownment, dating from around 1670. A good many of the examples in this chapter are drawn from before 1690, and I did not notice any great change in either the character or the incidence of such considerations from the seventeenth to the early eighteenth centuries.

Friends and brought to a sense of the wrong he had done. They rehearsed the sufferings of Friends on account of their testimony against oaths, and reproached him particularly for having compromised the grounds on which it rested. As usual, he was told to draw up a "paper" confessing his offense, and after a four-month delay for literary assistance (Wootton was illiterate) it was ready for public reading.

Friends' sensitivity on this point is not surprising, but by the early eighteenth century it had developed to the point where the moral precepts of Christianity had almost entirely dwindled into the peculiar rules of the Society. There can be no better illustration than the action of the Somerset Quarterly Meeting when it was informed on 19 December 1723 that someone who was not a Friend had ventured — or "intruded himself," as they put it — to affirm, rather than swearing, in giving evidence before the Quarter Sessions. It was questioned whether such persons ought not to be exposed on the spot, and the meeting decided that Friends present at the Quarter Sessions should immediately declare that they did not recognize any such to be Quakers, "that there may not be Occasion of Reflection from the Bench or Authority on us for sheltering fraudulent or designing persons under our profession." In the days when Friends had sometimes offered up their lives rather than swear, they had held that Christ's commandment to "swear not at all" bound all men; but two generations later, in Somerset at least, anyone unwary enough to obey it found that he incurred the guilt of an apparently greater offense, that of impersonating a Quaker.

The link between suffering, discipline, and reputation can be seen again in the action of Westminster Monthly Meeting on 6 March 1723 towards James Hoskins. He was testified against, as usual, so that it would be clear he was not a Quaker and would not deceive others and do further prejudice towards the Society. The meeting however spoke of itself as "still dreading the Suffering that hee may bring on us by his Still Sheltering himselfe under our name and thereby Obtain the previlidge Intended by the Government to such only who in good Conscience Justice and honesty have Demeaned themselves." A discipline operating in this spirit would conduce in another way to the "dangerous possibility" of respectability which came to Friends with the Toleration Act of 1689.[28]

Relief and the Definition of Membership

Quakerism has contributed the concept of "birthright membership" to the sociology of religion. It is generally used to denote a state in which full religious acceptance is given more or less automatically to children of members of a religious group, without any expectation of conversion. Nineteenth-century Quakers recognized that most of their members were "birthright members" in just this sense; and most of them believed that such members had been recognized in the Society of Friends since membership itself was first formally defined by the London Yearly Meeting in the 1737 rules of settlement. This is a misconception of the rules of settlement and of the whole question of membership and conversion among the early Friends; but since the rules of settlement, which arose from Quaker poor relief, certainly say something about membership, it is necessary to understand the evolution of the Friends' way of caring for their poor.

George Fox insisted that for Friends to minister to the necessities of the "household of faith" was no less important than for them to keep themselves clear of the disorderly. It was one of the primary responsibilities which justified the settling of business meetings in 1667; Robert Barclay the Apologist defends the institution of elders among Friends by saying that "the Care of the Poor, of Widdows and Orphans" was what "gave the first Rise for this Order among the Apostles, and I do verily believe might have been among the first

28. Doncaster, *Quaker Organisation*, p. 21.

Occasions that gave the like among us." [29] Here again, Friends were setting up for themselves institutions analogous to those of the Church of England, since the Poor Law which provided the last remedy against starvation for the general population was administered by the churchwardens of the parish.

The word "members" almost always occurs in local business meeting records in connection with the relief of the poor. It is no doubt this fact which accounts for the general impression among Victorian Friends that "membership" was established by the rules of settlement adopted in 1737. As John Stephenson Rowntree declared in 1872: "The terms members and membership are modern: or at least, they were not in very common use amongst the first generation of Friends." In 1737, he believed, " 'membership' was first recognised by the Yearly Meeting. Previous to that period . . . the only criterion for determining connection with the Society of Friends was habitual attendance at its religious meetings." [30] L. Hugh Doncaster, writing almost a hundred years later, accepts this interpretation of the importance of the 1737 rules of settlement. Not only did the Friends for the first time define the status of membership; they even required a formal admission to it for all future converts. But this new definition involved no new principle and was simply a matter of clarifying procedures which had gradually grown up.[31]

29. *Anarchy of the Ranters* (1676), p. 37.

30. John Stephenson Rowntree, "Membership in the Society of Friends," *Friends' Quarterly Examiner*, 6, no. 22 (1872), 251; John Stephenson Rowntree, *Quakerism, Past and Present* (1859), p. 111.

31. *Quaker Organisation and Business Meetings*, pp. 26 and 28, n.2. Doncaster goes a bit beyond the similar view of the importance of the 1737 rules of settlement taken by Edward Grubb in *The Meaning of Membership in a Christian Society* (London: Headley Brothers, 1910), p. 17, and by Rufus M. Jones in *The Later Periods of Quakerism* (London: Macmillan and Company, 1921), I, 108. The most remarkable account of the reasons for the 1737 rules is that of Walter Joseph Homan in *Children and Quakerism* (Berkeley: University of California Press, 1939), p. 102. Homan attributes the need for a clearer definition of membership to the increase of Friends' numbers, especially because "educational opportunities for children influenced many people to associate

When nineteenth-century Friends reflected on the languishing condition of Quakerism, many of them blamed the rules of settlement for having allowed children who had no real attachment to Friends' principles to remain Quakers, out of mere inertia. However, the way Friends defined "membership" in 1737 had little or nothing to do with conversion or with the expectation that children of Friends should have a vital spiritual experience of their own. The word "members" is certainly used in contexts which have nothing to do with rules of settlement; besides the 1659 and 1666 Yearly Meeting epistles quoted at the beginning of this chapter, the Yearly Meeting of 1728 spoke of "active Members of the Church" — which can only apply to members of the business meetings. Most important, the rules of settlement of 1737 constitute no important advance over other earlier and equally "official" definitions of membership; nor did any of them really touch the critical question of whether or not a person should be regarded as a Friend.

"Rules of settlement" came into being because the burden of the relief of the poor was a heavy one at times, and it chafed especially when those with doubtful association with Friends applied for relief, or when a poor Friend moved into the area of another meeting. Though these might represent roughly equal burdens, they posed two different questions: in the first instance, whether the applicant for relief was enough of a Friend to be entitled to it as a right; in the second, whether the meeting to which the Friend had moved should relieve his necessities, or whether the meeting from which he had moved should bear some or all of the respon-

---

themselves with the Society," to the need to make provision for the children of imprisoned Friends, and to the fact that "in the nation, religious toleration made progress." Since the number of Quakers was probably decreasing and conversions, even for interested motives, were becoming somewhat rarer, and since the problem of imprisoned Friends was somewhat less acute than it had been — owing to the very progress of religious toleration referred to in the next sentence — this explanation is rather unconvincing.

sibility. This distinction must be kept in mind; neglect of it has led to much confusion in the discussion of "membership" as defined by the support in time of need which Friends believed they owed one another.

In the first category of cases, where the issue was whether an applicant was a Friend, judgment was quick and decisive. Meetings were notably (and understandably) careful to avoid relieving someone who might fall permanently on their charge, unless he were an unimpeachable Friend. The Norfolk Quarterly Meeting on 31 December 1714 made a distinction which was generally accepted by all business meetings: "that all such as ar members of us: ought to be relieved by us whenever they shall or may be exercised, with the tryall of poverty, and not by the parrish to which they belong . . . And that such poor as may att times come to our Meeting, on whom we never lay hands, nor Received nor ownd as Members — as well as those who have walked so disorderly, as have Church censure upon them not reversed, be wholy committed to the parrish to be relieved: unto whome they belong; Not hereby excluding any particular Meeting or persons Charity: nor yet bowells of Compassion to receive any such, whenever they shall return by an unfeigned repentance."

To those whose connection with Friends was more dubious, as this minute indicates, mercy was tempered with legal circumspection. The meeting would emphasize that it acted out of mere love. When Sarah Treacher of Prestwood was reported to be ancient and ill, the Upperside Women's Monthly Meeting in February 1689, "having reason to question how far she is really related to Friends in truth, did not think fit to receive her as one who ought to be maintained by Friends. Yet in as much as she had used in the time of health to go some times to meetings, they put a crown into Mary Graveney's hand to help her for the present as an object of common charity." The same discrimination is reflected in the action of the same meeting on 14 April 1731, when they sent ten shillings to a "Widow woman in Wickham she being the Daughter of an honest friend" and five shillings "as a token of Love to a poor Widdow that ust to come to Hungerhill Meeting formerly." The Horsleydown Monthly Meeting sometimes gave relief to persons other than Friends, but never without specifying that they were "necessitous persons, and not a Friend." [32] Bristol Friends also avoided supporting one who was not "soe faithfull a friend as one whom they are obliged to take such care of" but did not object to giving to "as of privet Charety For that friends doe not give him countenance as a friend." [33] The Westminster Monthly Meeting on 1 September 1697 proposed, before extending relief to any in the future, to have some Friends visit them and "inspect their worthinesse." When on 1 December 1708 a Friend under discipline was in need, the meeting declared that because of his offenses Friends could not relieve him as a Friend; but "it was suffered Thatt Divers Particular Friends in the Meeting might bestow something on him out of their owne Pocketts as An Object of Charity." Like other meetings, the Westminster Monthly Meeting often used the phrase "an object of charity" to distinguish those whom it did not feel obliged to support.

Although careful to keep up such distinctions when the need arose, most meetings were never confronted by an applicant for relief whose status as a Friend was doubtful. There is very little evidence to support the frequent assertion that the widespread resorting of such people to Friends for support was an important factor in the final definition of membership (conventionally taken to be the 1737 rules of settlement). In fact this and earlier rules of settlement had nothing

32. Some idea of the care which this meeting took in these matters can be gained from its habit of having frequent reviews of the list of those who were receiving relief. Persons on this list were required to make over all their property to the Monthly Meeting. See T. Frederick Ball and William Beck, *The London Friends' Meetings* (1869), p. 233.

33. Quoted in Mortimer, "Quakerism in Bristol," p. 231.

to do with such people, and there seems from the beginning to have been a clear national consensus about their proper treatment. What was much more troublesome to Friends, and what eventually demanded the quasi-legislative action of the London Yearly Meeting, was the second sort of problem, deciding which monthly meeting should undertake the care of an undoubted Friend who had moved from one area to another.

The laws of England still allowed an Anglican pauper, regardless of sex, to be stripped to the waist, whipped until bloody, and driven out of a parish where he had attempted to "gain a settlement." The quarter sessions books show that this penalty was still sometimes inflicted. Friends' disputes over the "settlement" of their poor are not very edifying, but at least they were bloodless. If a meeting were hard-pressed with its own poor, it generally appealed to the monthly meeting to reduce its regular contribution to the general funds or "stock" of the meeting. If the meeting still had too many responsibilities for its resources, the quarterly meeting might use some of its stock to help the particular meeting relieve the poor. But if someone fell upon Friends' charity who had not been born and raised within the compass of the meeting, it was often contended that the burden properly belonged to the meeting within whose compass the pauper last resided.

Such contentions were common enough in the seventeenth century and were a great staple of Yearly Meeting business in the eighteenth. If the contending meetings were within the same monthly meeting, they generally accepted its adjudication, or at worst appealed to the quarterly meeting. For example, in 1704 Mary Littlepage, a servant living in Chalfont St. Giles, applied to the Upperside Monthly Meeting, claiming that Chalfont Meeting had first relieved her necessities, and should continue to do so. It is instructive to follow the line of reasoning set forth by those who investigated the matter. They found: (1) she was "born and bred up in Chesham, came into the Profession of the Truth there, walked for divers years amongst Friends there & was then acknowledged by them for a member of that meeting"; (2) during that time she was relieved by them; (3) to support herself she then "went forth to service"; (4) she had difficulty in finding a position, and to make matters worse "could not bear living in Chesham, the air of that Place being disagreeable to her" — but still applied to that meeting for relief; and finally (5) Chalfont Meeting had relieved her as an object of charity, without acknowledging her right to their help. A foul climate did not discharge Chesham Meeting of its duties, and the meeting agreed to assume them. It had at one time acknowledged Mary Littlepage as a member, and therefore she was still their responsibility.

But even if there had not been such an acknowledgment, there were other things which constituted a tacit recognition of membership. When disputes over settlement arose, Friends sought to find out first where a person had lived at the time of his convincement; thus Somerset Quarterly Meeting on 7 April 1736 asked to get information from George Mall concerning his place of convincement and "severall places of his abode," since a dispute over his place of settlement had arisen with Dorset Quarterly Meeting. Other than place of convincement, the most important criteria of membership were having been allowed to sit in the monthly meeting for business and having made a contribution to the "stock" of a business meeting. In the "lower side" of Buckinghamshire some Northamptonshire Friends spoke with Stephen Webb, asking him "what meetinge he did belonge to or collect to." His answer was that he "collected" at Chackmore and thus belonged to the Biddlesden Monthly Meeting. That meeting, however, on 27 February 1699 declared that he did not belong to them, but rather to Perry Park Meeting, where he used to live — "for he hath not bin at our monthly meetinge since he went from thence and his giving of collection was only one day." So clearly was contribution a sign of membership that members under discipline were not allowed to give. Norwich Monthly Meeting, at considerable expense to itself since he was their richest member, returned the contribution of James Halls towards the building of the first meetinghouse, and when William Smith of Wells was married "by a priest" his collection to Wells Monthly Meeting on 4 April 1711 was taken "only in hopes of his return."

Inevitably there were disputes as to the precise meaning and applicability of these criteria. As early as 1693 the Yearly Meeting attempted to clarify them, especially in an effort to protect the Friends of London from the responsibility for the considerable numbers of poor Friends from the country who came there hoping to improve their fortunes and instead fell destitute. This early attempt was ineffectual; quarrels between meetings in London and in the provinces were particularly hard to compose. For example, Southwark Friends complained to Biddlesden Monthly Meeting that Henry Ward, who had moved there between 1699 and 1709, had now become a charge upon them, only to receive the unsympathetic reply that "the sence of this meeting is not to send any money to Hen: Ward and iff they be aweary of him they may send him down to the parish where his settlement is." This was to propose an unacceptable alternative if Henry Ward were fully accepted as a Friend, and on 26 February 1711 the Biddlesden Monthly Meeting was making preparations to take the case to the quarterly meeting.[34]

In 1710 the Upperside and Longford, Middlesex, Monthly Meetings were embroiled in a long controversy which contributed to the definition of new "rules of settlement" by the

34. The Norfolk Quarterly Meeting heard with apparent distress a complaint that a Quaker widow living in the Lynn Meeting House received some poor relief from the parish and wore the town's poor badge. Lynn Meeting was strictly charged on 30 December 1713 to maintain the widow for the future "according to our Christian principles and Antient practice ever since we were a people."

Yearly Meeting. The disagreement arose from the poverty of Daniel Tokefield, a farmer who had moved from Chesham to Colnbrook. The latter town, though also in Buckinghamshire, was in the area of the Longford Monthly Meeting, and four years after he had moved, Longford complained that he had been sent there without sufficient capital to make a success of farming. On 10 March 1710 Upperside Monthly Meeting answered that he had £100 and £20 or £30, if not £40, in "stock" when he left. This they considered ample, and they deemed him to be a member of Longford Monthly Meeting. The latter responded with the claim that the rules of settlement of 1693 prohibited the poor from settling there; Daniel Tokefield was now one of the poor, being worth no more than £50 and having a large family. To this Upperside countered that they took the rules of 1693 to apply only to London and the Friends of that city, not to embrace all of the London and Middlesex Quarterly Meeting. On 4 September 1710 they drafted another letter, since Longford Friends had now brought more serious charges — that Daniel Tokefield was a simpleton, too deficient in "natural capacity" to avoid striking bad bargains at fairs and markets. Friends of the Upperside Monthly Meeting, who presumably knew of this weakness, had helped him to settle within the compass of the Longford Monthly Meeting — with the intention, so the letter implied, of ridding themselves of someone who they knew might cease to be self-supporting. The Upperside Monthly Meeting disclaimed any responsibility for Tokefield's "want of capacity." As for the fact that members of their meeting had helped him to settle, they did so only as private persons, and not as agents of the meeting. "Since every faithful Friend is, or ought to be a Member of some Meeting" — a significant phrase — what they did as private persons could not be laid to the meetings they belonged to, without ungovernable disorder in the church.

This and other cases were referred to the Yearly Meeting,

which adopted new and more extensive rules of settlement
in 1710. Friends moving from the compass of one monthly
meeting to another were to get a certificate of removal, attest-
ing their good behavior and their freedom from engagements
of marriage. If the meeting into which they had moved accepted their collections for the "stock," or if it appointed them
to "the service of the church" — to attend a monthly or
quarterly meeting — they were to be considered as settled in
the new meeting. But some Friends were wanting in capacity
either to contribute or to sit in business meetings. If these
lived for three years "behaving him or themselves according
to Truth and not any ways chargeable" they were to be considered members of the meeting. Servants, including maid-
servants, were to gain a settlement after one year of good
service. These rules were to be good only for four years, unless
subsequently renewed.[35]

From time to time the London Yearly Meeting interpreted
these rules to various meetings, as it did on 3 July 1721 when
it wrote to the Wiltshire Quarterly Meeting that "All who
were not denied are to be esteemed members of the Several
Monthly Meetings in whose Compass they then resided."
Refinements were added to the rules in 1711, 1725, and
1729; and in 1737 an attempt was made, very much in the
spirit which led to the compilation of the Christian and
Brotherly Advices in the following year, to draft a statement
codifying and elaborating all of Friends' practice and advice
on the subject of the relief of the necessitous poor.

The 1737 rules were considered, paragraph by paragraph,
in the Meeting for Sufferings during March and April, 1737.[36]
The original draft had only five paragraphs, but four others
were subsequently added, making explicit the proper practice
in various cases. On 29 April 1737 clauses relating to the

35. London Yearly Meeting, minutes, IV, 142–144.
36. Meeting for Sufferings, minutes, VIII, 255, 259, 263, 271, 274,
279.

settlement of apprentices (to become clause six of the finished document) and of wives and children (subsequently clause eight) were read and adopted by the Meeting for Sufferings. The latter, for the first time, specifically mentioned that children of Friends shared in the settlement of their parents, and like them should be "deemed Members of the Quarterly, Monthly, or Two-Weeks Meeting within the Compass of which they Inhabited or dwelt the first Day of the fourth Month 1737." [37] The 1737 rules were much the longest, and were destined to be the last, of a series of enactments, as one might as well call them. As the latest rules, they found their way into the Quaker law book, the Christian and Brotherly Advices, and into the minds of all subsequent Quakers. But while the lawyer must consult the last enactment, the historian should give equal, if not greater, attention to the earlier ones in a series. It is hard to believe that anyone doing this could single out the rules of settlement of 1737 as "for the first time defining membership" or "instituting birth-right membership." The 1737 rules used language about members which did not differ from earlier ones; enough examples of the use of the word "member" have already been quoted from both seventeenth- and eighteenth-century documents to show that it was already a familiar concept in the minutes of monthly and quarterly meetings as well as of the London Yearly Meeting. What the 1737 rules attempted was merely to establish *where* membership existed. Rather than requiring Chesham Meeting to pay towards the relief of someone who lived in Chalfont St. Giles, it made membership (and the responsibility for relief) coincide with the place of residence at a given time.

It would in fact be truer to say that the 1737 rules of settlement *last* defined membership in the Society of Friends,

37. London Yearly Meeting, minutes, VIII, 314. An exception to the general rule that responsibility for relief coincided with residence on this date was made for "such who are Settled Pensioners to, or have within One Year last past, been Relieved by any other Such Meeting."

at least for the eighteenth century; and it was a conception of membership so bound up with responsibility and eligibility for relief that some references to it are incomprehensible in any other context. For example, Anna Brooker, an aged widow who had lived for many years in High Wycombe, became needy, and the Upperside Monthly Meeting claimed on 4 December 1732 that she belonged to the Horsleydown Monthly Meeting. That meeting disagreed, and the matter was referred to the London and Middlesex Quarterly Meeting, which decided on 2 April 1733 that she had no settlement at Wycombe. Horsleydown then appealed to the Yearly Meeting, which decided that the two monthly meetings should equally share the burden. The Upperside Monthly Meeting thereupon appointed someone to write to the Horsleydown Monthly Meeting about their joint responsibility. The anomaly occurred when Anna Brooker filed a bill in chancery against Alice Stevens, widow, who was her sister-in-law. Friends did not believe in settling disputes among themselves by bills in chancery. Someone, therefore, must visit Anna Brooker to let her know of Upperside Friends' displeasure; but she "belonging to Southwark Monthly Meeting equally with this," someone must also inform that meeting what was being done. Membership could thus be divided between two monthly meetings, almost as neatly as a stack of shillings.

If this seems strange to us, it is because we are accustomed to thinking of membership in terms of the warm personal relationships within the religious sects. Anna Brooker's "membership" is more nearly understandable if one thinks, let us say, of the nonresident burgesses of many an eighteenth-century town. Membership was a juridical right and relationship, not necessarily inhering in residence or common worship. This explains such an action as that of the Hogsty End Monthly Meeting on 8 May 1765 — an action similar to many taken in that decade, when Friends, under the influence of a new conception of discipline, purged themselves of many useless members. After dealing with some laggards in their midst, the meeting further declared that there were "several others both men and women who are likewise born of parents professing with us who are removed at such a distance that it may be difficult to find them (but yet according to the rule of our Society, they may lay claim to membership with us if they should stand in need of assistance)." However, the meeting had reason to believe that they had joined other "Societies" or had not walked "consistent to our Profession"; therefore in order to prevent having to support them at some future date, the meeting declared all such to be henceforth not members of the meeting.

It was not until a generation after 1737 that most monthly meetings acted on the Yearly Meeting suggestion that they draw up lists of their members. Only one did so at the time requested, and that was the Horsleydown (Southwark) Monthly Meeting, which had been pestered with so many indigent Friends from the country.[38] This makes it very unlikely that any formal procedure for the reception of members went into effect in the years immediately after 1737.

Disputes about the settlement of children had been very rare, which is another reason to think the reference to them in the rules of 1737 was of little importance. The evidence is that the membership of children was already accepted in regard to the responsibility for their relief. Thus when Thomas Davey removed from Docking, near Wells, to Lammas, the certificate sent by his meeting to the Lammas Monthly Meeting (dated 3 September 1729) says that there is no objection to him, his wife, or their three children as members. The only disagreement about the settlement of children which I found arose between Norwich and Wells Monthly

---

38. George W. Edwards "Some Early *Members* of the Society of Friends," is a valuable and entertaining account of how the Horsleydown Meeting went about compiling its list. It is possible that some other meetings did compile lists which have not survived, but it is not likely that this would not have been mentioned in the minute books.

Meetings over William Dowdy and his family. Dowdy requested a certificate from Wells on 2 January 1717, but Norwich Monthly Meeting objected against it that there "was no mention made of his Children, & of what Particular meeting they were Intire members of." On 6 November Wells Monthly Meeting answered this objection (which seems to have been only of a formal character) by specifying that "they had two Children, when they went away . . . and were members of Wells perticular meeting." This, too, would seem to indicate that the "membership" of children — in this sense — was taken for granted.

But, since membership was primarily a category in the administration of Friends' poor relief, it is not surprising that the tidying-up in 1737 did not really change, or even signal any change in, the status of children in the Society of Friends, or in the expectations entertained by their parents about their normal spiritual development. Speaking of the rules of settlement of 1737, John Stephenson Rowntree said that after them "the Society of Friends increasingly assumed the character of a corporation, existing for ends partly religious, partly social, and partly civil; and containing a number of persons unconverted to God." [39] In the next chapter we shall consider the adequacy of this description of eighteenth-century Quakerism: but whether it be considered as decadent or simply mature, it was far from being the simple product of the rules of settlement. These were a characteristic, but not especially important, production of the Quakerism of the Augustan Age. What they do show is that the development of the concept of membership, implicit as it was in a number of the earliest impulses within Quakerism, nevertheless prevented the universalism of the early Quaker hopes from rooting itself in their enduring common life. The memory of this universalism lingered — especially in the Quaker disownment

39. *Quakerism, Past and Present*, p. 112. Later, in an (unpublished) paper, "The Friends' Registers of Births, Deaths, and Marriages, 1650–1900," he revised his views of the 1737 rules.

procedures — but this memory did little to alter the logic of events, that accumulation of day-to-day decisions which Friends were learning to call "precedents." In this way — unwittingly, as most historical changes come about — Friends were making themselves into only the most picturesque of His Majesty's Protestant Dissenters.

V Traditional Quakerism

The early eighteenth century was scarcely a glorious period in English religious life. The established church was so wracked by political strife that convocation, its representative body, could no longer meet, and it seemed deep in the spiritual torpor from which it was to be aroused by the Wesleys. The older Dissenting churches were split by schisms and weakened by the growing inability of their members to take their doctrines seriously. But eighteenth-century Quakerism has been judged with especial severity. John Stephenson Rowntree, sighing over its "retrograde condition," speaks of the "degeneracy of the second generation of Quakers." "The first impressions made by the effusions of the Spirit," he quotes, "are generally the strongest . . . But human depravity, overborne for a time, arises afresh, particularly in the next generation." [1] Similarly, though without attributing its later history to the recrudescence of human depravity, Neave Brayshaw, Rufus Jones, Arnold Lloyd, and even William Charles Braithwaite have regretted that the number of Friends declined, that the society sank into quietism and self-contemplation, and that the growing wealth and respectability of Friends blunted the boldness of their testimonies.

1. John Stephenson Rowntree, *Quakerism, Past and Present* (1859), pp. 63, 104, 93–94. The quotation is from Joseph Milner, *History of the Church* (1794), I, 143.

Obviously eighteenth-century Quakerism — by which, exercising the usual license of not starting the eighteenth century exactly in 1700, I mean the Quakerism which followed the Toleration Act of 1689 — had a character quite different from that of the earliest days. In this chapter I shall attempt to give some account and explanation of its distinctive character, particularly insofar as it was the result of the institutional changes which are the theme of this book. It is a story, certainly, of developments quite different from those anticipated by the founders, but they are not necessarily perverse or contrary to the Holy Spirit. "Degeneration" of course suffers from all the notorious difficulties of "progress" as a category of historical explanation, and I doubt that it is a useful one. It seems preferable to start with some external measures of the vitality of eighteenth-century Quakerism, and then look further into the spirit of its operation.

The Concentration of Quakerism

One familiar symptom of the supposed decline of Quakerism was the decrease in its members. To support his complaint that the Society of Friends quickly passed the peak of its numerical strength and soon went into a precipitate decline, Rowntree estimated that in 1680 there were about sixty thousand persons "professing with Friends" in Great Britain, against only thirty-two thousand in 1800. He calculates that the proportion of Friends in the nation declined from one in 130 to one in 470.[2] Barbour places the numerical peak in the 1670's. Braithwaite estimates that there were about fifty thousand Friends by 1680, but does not think the number declined sharply thereafter; he feels that it remained stationary for a considerable time, with emigration draining away any natural increase.[3] The impression of at least one

2. Rowntree, *Quakerism, Past and Present*, pp. 68–73. This is the longest discussion of the question of Friends' numbers.

3. Hugh Barbour, *The Quakers in Puritan England* (New Haven: Yale University Press, 1964), pp. 231–232; William C. Braithwaite,

eighteenth-century Friend supports Braithwaite; John Richardson, asked in 1731 whether English Friends were more or less numerous, said he thought there had been no great alteration in his time; decreases in some areas had been balanced by increases in others.[4]

One man's guess is almost as good as another's here, for it is almost impossible to determine whether there were fewer Friends in the eighteenth century than there had been in the seventeenth. It is even harder to calculate their numbers in the eighteenth century, in part because of toleration itself. In attempting to suppress Friends, church and state did at least succeed in making rough censuses of them. Presentments for absence from church, in particular, provide a veritable roster of Dissenters. The fact that such sources of evidence cease in 1689 would by itself produce the impression that there were more Friends before that date. Even if one depends entirely on the registers of births, marriages, and burials, it is easy to be misled, since the registers were kept with increasing carelessness in the eighteenth century. There is much direct evidence of this, and enough indirect evidence even to allow an estimate of how serious under-registration was.

The direct evidence indicates that Friends were often concerned at the laxity of registration procedures. Buckinghamshire Quarterly Meeting on 28 December 1709 noted that for several years past three of the four constituent monthly meetings (Sherington, Biddlesden, and Hogsty End) had not brought in proper accounts of Friends' marriages, births, and burials. Similarly Wymondham Monthly Meeting on 7 August 1717 "found that friends have been very Remiss in Bringing in their Marrage Certificates to be incerted." In Cambridgeshire such minutes are a chronic lament, though here as

The Second Period of Quakerism (2nd ed.; Cambridge, Eng.: Cambridge University Press, 1961), p. 459.

4. *An Account of John Richardson* (Philadelphia, 1856), pp. 215–216.

elsewhere little improvement followed the detection of these shortcomings.

Where complete monthly meeting minutes survive, it is possible to make a statistical survey of the extent of under-registration of marriages. This is made possible by the fact that every marriage taking place among Friends had to have the prior approval of the monthly meeting, which was duly inserted in the minutes. Often there were marriages thus permitted which were not recorded in the marriage register, even though the recorded birth of children to the couple shows that it did take place. At some periods up to 20 per cent of marriages which took place were not recorded, and in some areas — as in Norfolk in the 1720's and 1730's — more than half of Friends' marriages were not entered in the registers. There is also one source which gives independent evidence of burials and thus shows the extent to which they also were omitted from the registers. This is the diary of Rebecca Butterfield, which takes keen and somewhat naive interest in the funerals of Friends buried at Jordans. Of the burials in the 1740's and 1750's which are reported in this diary, fewer than 10 per cent were registered by the Upperside Monthly Meeting.[5] Though the degree of under-registration of births is the most difficult to estimate, there were times in Buckinghamshire when more than 30 per cent of the marriages taking place appear to have been childless, which strongly suggests the failure to register births.[6]

As a consequence of such defective registration, there were many persons — 385 in Buckinghamshire alone — whose

5. The Diary of Rebecca Butterfield is a manuscript in Friends' House Library. Also there are in Friends' House marriage certificates in the hand of Thomas Ellwood which were not entered in Buckinghamshire Quarterly Meeting's register of marriages.

6. Nineteen per cent of the marriages of British ducal families made between 1730 and 1829 were childless; see T. H. Hollingsworth, "A Demographic Study of the British Ducal Families," in *Population in History*, ed. D. V. Glass and D. E. C. Eversley (London: Edward Arnold, 1965), p. 371.

births were registered among Friends, but about whom no further information is available. Such a large component of "lost" population, together with the other problems outlined above, clearly makes Table 11 a matter of guesswork; but based on the principles outlined in the Appendix, I have estimated the number of Friends between 1689 and 1740.

Table 11. Total of adult friends, 1689–1740.

County	Number at end of:				Percentage change		
	1689	1700	1720	1740	1689–1700	1700–1720	1720–1740
Buckinghamshire	525	486	428	327	−7.4	−11.9	−23.6
Norwich	253	333	412	428	+31.6	+23.7	+3.9
Norfolk	831	1,143	1,186	984	+37.5	+3.8	−17.0

In Buckinghamshire the peak in numbers seems to have been reached in the 1680's, whereas in Norfolk it was touched in the first decades of the eighteenth century. (Norfolk Friends in their reports to the London Yearly Meeting spoke of the period from 1698 to 1708 as one of "great openness" and eagerness to attend Friends' meetings; in the former year it was reported that Truth had prospered so much that the priests in Norfolk were "inraged at the increase of Truth in them parts, for when the People know that a Publick Friend is like to be at Friends' meetings, in many part of the Country, they can get hardly any of the People at their Church." [7] But the subsequent decline in the number of Friends in these two counties does not necessarily mean an over-all decrease. Even leaving aside the difficulties posed by the lacunae in the registers, we know that many country Friends went to live in London; eighty-six from Buckinghamshire alone removed to

7. Letter from John Tomkins to Sir John Rodes, 3 January 1698/9, printed in *A Quaker Post-Bag: Letters to Sir John Rodes and to John Gratton*, ed. Mrs. Godfrey Locker Lampson (London: Longmans, 1910), p. 149.

London, many of them to Southwark.[8] The undoubted increase of Friends in London, the size of which is impossible to measure, must be set against the evidence of decline in the country.

The great increase of Friends in Norwich during the period from 1689 to 1720 further suggests the importance of the tendency for Friends to be clustered in the towns. It is easy to observe the withdrawal of Friends from the countryside. In Buckinghamshire, there had been Friends in sixty parishes in 1700; by 1740 there were none in sixteen of these, and in another eighteen only one or two adults remained. Some of the particular meetings in the county were abandoned, and others were much reduced. In 1740 almost half the Quakers in Buckinghamshire lived in the five parishes of Sherington, Chesham, Amersham, Chalfont St. Giles, and High Wycombe. The number of Friends in High Wycombe had doubled since 1662, and there were twenty-two adults in Chesham and seventeen in Aylesbury, compared with one in each town in 1662. In Norfolk, Friends reported in 1763 that "the state of things in this county is low and by the removal of divers Members, meetings in some places are reduced to a very small number." [9] But at the same time, more and more Friends were found in such towns as East Dereham, Wells, and Wymondham, not to mention Norwich. In 1740 almost a quarter of the Friends in Norfolk lived in these three towns, about double the proportion in 1700, whereas only six Friends had lived in East Dereham and Wymondham and none at all in Wells at the end of 1662.

There was of course a general tendency for eighteenth-century Englishmen to move into the towns, but the urban

8. It appears that in Norfolk, on the contrary, more Friends moved into the county than moved out; in the period from 1700 to 1745, there were twenty-five certificates issued for Friends moving elsewhere and thirty-two received from newcomers to the county. See Muriel F. Lloyd Prichard, "Norfolk Friends' Care of their Poor, 1700–1850," *J.F.H.S.*, 40 (1948), 13.
9. Quoted in *ibid.*, 12.

concentration of Friends was much in excess of that in the general population. It is not too much to say that a tendency to residential segregation was at work, which by the end of the eighteenth century made such towns as Adderbury in Oxfordshire or Hitchin in Hertfordshire strongholds of Quakerism, while others of equal size might have no Quakers at all. It was difficult to live in accordance with a Quaker conscience without the support of some fairly sizeable community — especially when there were children of marriageable age who had to find Quaker spouses. Also, the painful Quaker testimony against tithes was a further deterrent to embracing Quakerism, or remaining faithful to it, for those who lived on the land.

As we have seen in Chapter II, Quakerism in the eighteenth century was becoming, in both senses of the word, a somewhat more bourgeois religion. Besides the growing concentration of Friends in the towns, an increasing number were drawn from the ranks of traders and artisans, while the old gentry and landed families and also the very poor had almost entirely ceased to be represented. What this seems to mean is not so much that the wealth of Friends increased or that their numbers declined — both of which would be very difficult to prove — but rather that there was an increased concentration within a smaller geographical and social range. Invariably this had the effect of isolating Friends to a greater extent from the full impact of English society as a whole, thus encouraging a greater corporate self-absorption.

More important than the absolute numbers of Friends or their distribution among towns and occupations was the changing composition of the society. In the early eighteenth century, for the first time, the majority of Friends were the children of Friends. Through the method of family reconstitution, and by noting the appearance of new surnames in the registers, it is possible to judge the extent of conversions. Many were certainly converted in the decade after the Act of

Toleration, but afterwards there were comparatively few converts. Perhaps noticing a decline in conversions, Friends added (in 1726) an explicit query about the numbers convinced during the course of the last year to the old question which had been addressed by Yearly Meeting to each constituent meeting as to "How the Truth has prospered amongst them since the last Yearly Meeting, and how friends are in Peace & Unity." The answers returned to this query during the first thirty years show that in only two of these thirty years did as many as half the meetings reporting say that there was some convincement during the past year; in several years three quarters or even four fifths of the meetings reported very little, if any, convincement.

New converts were particularly scarce in the cities. Norwich and Colchester reported some convincement in only one year out of the thirty; Bristol in only three years. The Midlands was another area where Truth made little progress; Bedfordshire, Derbyshire, Dorset, Gloucestershire, Lincolnshire, Nottinghamshire, Staffordshire, and Worcestershire all reported few conversions, and several counties remarked upon an actual decline in Truth's prosperity. The most remarkable example is Surrey. If one is to take literally their annual accounts, the conversion of one person in 1732 was their greatest success in the entire thirty years.

On the other hand, the original center of Quakerism seemed to retain its vitality in attracting converts. Yorkshire returned optimistic accounts year after year, and Lancashire, Westmorland, and Cumberland were not far behind. There were some conversions almost every year in London, and the counties of East Anglia and of the West Country were often able to give account that some had been converted and added to the church.

The impression given by this summary is that the number of conversions in most parts of England was sufficient to prevent the Society of Friends from entirely shrinking into a hereditary corporation — except in such places as Surrey and the Midlands counties. Friends were still far from the disastrous decline in numbers of the first half of the nineteenth century, when almost half again as many persons resigned or were disowned as were converted.[10] By 1750 in some places as many as one quarter of Friends might have been converts, but in most from 80 to 90 per cent of the members were children of Friends.

It is important to note that, if one can judge by the amount of energy expended, Friends were still making a considerable effort to preach their message to "the world." The appearance of a traveling minister would be widely advertised, and on these "publick occasions" Friends often saw a great concourse of their neighbors, who would probably not have attended the ordinary meetings for worship. As Kent reported in 1735, their regular meetings were somewhat decayed, "as our meetings are mostly attended with Silence, a Manner of Worship comprehended but by few." Even where it was reported that first day meetings were well attended by "sober people of the World," Friends usually added, as Derbyshire did in 1733, that "Our Neighbours seem affected . . . to hear the truth declared, yet there seems little Convincement, or at least Conversion . . . amongst them." Time after time similar accounts appear; it is hoped that there is some convincement, or there are some who appear to be inclined towards Friends; yet for the many who might be "convinced of the truth of our Principles," as Buckinghamshire said in 1738, "few appear in open Profession."

This left the direction of the affairs of Friends to an increasing extent in the hands of those who had never known any other religion and who had never known the struggle of associating themselves with a despised religious minority. But

10. Rowntree, *Quakerism, Past and Present*, p. 75. The demographic consequences of Friends' discipline in this period were particularly severe, since many disownments were for "marrying out" and thus deprived Friends of their progenitive members.

insofar as the community of faith and the community of blood came to coincide, Quakerism was to become not so much a sect as a great clan — or, as the eighteenth century would have put it, a "connection." And as their own children succeeded them as Friends, it became necessary for Quakers to reconsider their teachings on the family — a social institution which had been neglected or even condemned in early Quaker thought. By the end of the first century of Quakerism, when as many as 90 per cent of Quakers were children of Quakers, the family clearly stood at the heart of the Quaker way of life, animating all of the institutions which Friends had developed for their common concerns. The story of its rise to this position thus appropriately completes the history of the social development of English Quakerism.

The Reconstruction of the Family

Friends were generally so quick to take up the pen, and so adept at mutual exhortation, that one can reasonably judge the direction and intensity of their corporate attention to any subject by the volume and character of their literary productions. It is singular, therefore, that scarcely anything was written about the proper kind of domestic life or the upbringing of children during the first two decades of Quakerism. The first mention of the care of children in Yearly Meeting epistles does not come until 1688, and, as far as I can discover, there were only two small books addressed specifically to the duties of parents and children before the 1680's.[11] But by the turn of the century, advice, which Friends were liberal with on almost every other subject, was flowing copiously on this one; and by the middle of the eighteenth century concern for the nurture and education of children was expressed so frequently as to seem a corporate preoccupation.

11. Humphry Smith, *To all Parents of Children upon the Face of the Whole Earth* (1660); William Salt, *The Light, the Way, that Children ought to be Trained up in, wherein the Holy Men of God Walked* (1660).

This lack of emphasis on nurture in the family in the earliest Quaker writing is probably, in part, an index of the vitality of eschatological belief; the curve of titles borrowing apocalyptic imagery falls as steeply as that of wholesome advice to parents and children rises. The sense of an ending which was so strong in the Interregnum militated against that sense of the continuity of the family which governs most men's conception of the future. In addition, the era of mass conversions, most of them involving a breach in the family, was hardly propitious for expounding the advantages of religious nurture.

The tension between nurture and conversion exists in all religions. It was held to a minimum within Roman Catholicism, where the sacraments — especially baptism, confirmation, and ordination, which could only be administered once — served to solemnize the stages of development of a steadily deepening spiritual life. Any overpowering religious experience within Roman Catholicism was almost always interpreted as a call to a clerical or monastic vocation. Under the conditions of clerical celibacy no one who had passed through such an experience could expect to have children; there was no possibility of expecting such an experience to be repeated in the next generation. But the tension between nurture and conversion was bound to be heightened within Protestantism. Having abandoned the separate vocation of "the religious" and clerical celibacy, Protestants who themselves had passed through a conversion experience and believed that such experiences were essential were committed to the attempt to secure, over a series of generations, similar conversion experiences both from their children and from persons who had not grown up within the group.

The Friends' conceptions of conversion, as we have seen in Chapter I, were informed by a powerful sense of unexpected encounter with God, preceded by such intense feelings of sin and deliverance as would hardly allow religion to be seen as a gradual process of development within a matrix of parental love and discipline. But Friends as they became parents could hardly deny the family some role in the economy of salvation; and so they emphasized both the necessity of nurture and its futility. At first, as one might expect, Friends were concerned to emphasize the folly of depending on tradition or upbringing for faith. They did this in a series of theological arguments which demand close attention, because at first glance it appears that they were upholding beliefs in the innocence or positive virtue of infants and in the possibility of universal salvation which would seem to lead straight to the position that all that was necessary was tender cultivation of these good instincts within the infant.

Friends certainly rejected the doctrine of original sin and with it the beliefs in predestination which they found in the Calvinist sects — "Conceited Personal Election," as George Whitehead termed it, "Unchangeably Design'd from Eternity; in which they (viz. *Baptists*, and their Followers) must only be the Sharers . . . [and] but very Few (if any) besides." [12] Robert Barclay the Apologist thought that the doctrine of predestination was absurd in itself and contrary to nature and justice, not to say mercy. Since there was also no biblical warrant for believing it, "it is manifest, that Man hath invented this opinion out of self-love, and from that bitter Root from which all error springs; for the most part of Protestants that hold this, having as they fancy, *the absolute decree of Elections* to secure them and their Children, so as they cannot miss of Salvation, they make no great difficulty to send all others, both Old and Young, to hell." He goes on to argue that there is no law to infants, as they are "utterly incapable of it, the Law cannot reach but such as having in some measure, less or more, the exercise of their understand-

12. George Whitehead, *The Dipper Plung'd or Thomas Hicks his Feigned Dialogue between a Christian and a Quaker Proved, an Unchristian Forgery* (n.p., 1672), p. 4.

ing, which infants have not." It is therefore possible to settle the matter syllogistically: "Sin is imputed to none, where there is no Law. But to infants there is no Law: Therefore sin is not imputed to them." [13]

Friends did not consider infants to be merely sinless moral ciphers, awaiting knowledge of the law in order to infringe it. Humphry Smith stated that *"In many tender Babes and young children,* there is a meek, innocent, harmless principle from God, who willeth not the death of any; and they have a light from Christ, that lighteth every man that cometh into the world." "Look upon young Children," he exclaimed, "and see how innocent and lamb-like they look; and consider if every thing were not good as God made it." [14]

Seen in their proper context, these arguments, paradoxically, make for the necessity of conversion. The error of the Baptists and other Protestants who believed in predestination and original sin was the assumption that they and their children were assured of salvation in any event. Thus, although the belief that children were born in a state of perfect innocency often leads to the belief that if they survive to be brought up in a Christian home they will gradually acquire the saving graces of Christian life, Friends would not have accepted this consequence. We must therefore reject the claims made by some writers that Friends espoused what William James called the "once-born" conception of religious life.

Rowntree in 1859 attacked them for taking this position. "It might have been early discovered," he wrote, "that to make membership in a Christian Church dependent on the accident of birth, was very much to abandon the New Testament idea of a Church." [15] In 1872 he found this notion of "birthright membership" more attractive: "the practice of the

13. *Apology for the True Christian Divinity* (1678), proposition 4, section 4.
14. *To all Parents,* pp. 3–4.
15. *Quakerism, Past and Present,* p. 112.

Roman Catholic and Anglican Churches and of the Society
of Friends, in admitting children into their communions in
infancy, is amply supported by scriptural authority, and
commends itself to the instinct and judgment of those who
have had practical occasion to consider the position of children in the fold of Christ." [16] Walter Joseph Homan, writing
from the perspective of Deweyan liberalism, contended that
the early Friends "believed religion was a gradual growth";
that children "belonged to the Society as fully as did their
parents. They were limited only by their physical, mental,
social, and religious immaturity. As they developed these four
characteristics they shared more fully in the theory and practice of the Society of Friends." [17]

Much of the basis for such statements derives from confusion about the significance of the 1737 Rules of Settlement,
which I attempted to clarify in the last chapter. In addition,
it may not have been realized that belief in the innocency of
infants was compatible with a belief in the necessity of
radical and profound conversion; yet, even if we leave Friends
out of account, the General Baptists believed in both.[18] Notwithstanding Rowntree's admiration for it, the first Quakers
attacked the Anglican practice of infant baptism, and they
were equally opposed to the Federal Theology — a variant of
Calvinism emphasizing that children might stand in a covenant to God originally entered into with their parents —
which they encountered in New England.

"God casts the line of election in the loins of godly parents"

16. "Membership in the Society of Friends," *Friends' Quarterly
Examiner*, 6, no. 22 (April 1872), 257.

17. *Children and Quakerism* (Berkeley: University of California
Press, 1939), pp. 78, 23.

18. Among the articles of faith of one of the English congregations
in Amsterdam in the early part of the seventeenth century was the
proposition "That infants are conceived and born in innocency without
sin, and that so dying are undoubtedly saved, and that this is to be
understood of all infants, under heaven." Quoted in Robert Barclay of
Reigate, *The Inner Life of the Religious Societies of the Commonwealth*
(1876), appendix to Chapter VI, viii.

was a comfortable maxim in seventeenth-century Massachusetts, a state that has known election through inheritance even in more recent times. "If you be not in the Covenant, but your whole desire is, that you may, you must labour to bring yourselves into a good family," advised John Cotton. William Stoughton rose to a rhetorical pitch in contemplating genetic salvation: "Consider and remember alwayes, that the Books that shall be opened at the last day will contain *Genealogies* in them. There shall then be brought forth a *Register of the Genealogies of New-Englands* sons and daughters." [19] To George Keith (while still in his Quaker phase) the doctrine that God had entered into a covenant guaranteeing salvation to the children of the faithful was quite incomprehensible: "What that Holiness or Cleanness is, that the Children of one, or both the believing Parents have, is a great Mystery, I am sure to many who have that Scripture place oft in their Mouthes, and greatly glory in it, that they are in Church-Covenant, and therefore they are holy, and their Children, also some call it federal or Covenant-Holiness, but what it is they know not . . . for many, yea, very many, Children of professed Christians of all sorts, when they grow up to Youth, are as unholy, and sometimes worse, as the Children of Unbelievers." [20] Similarly Edward Burrough controverted the doctrine of Samuel Eaton, an Independent minister of Cheshire, that "the Profession of the Faith entitles both such as make it, and their Infants" to the covenant. The covenant, said Burrough, "is not outward, but Spiritual." [21]

Just as they attacked the various theological devices by

19. John Cotton, *The Covenant of God's Free Grace* (1645), p. 20, and William Stoughton, *New Englands True Interest, Not to Lie* (Cambridge, Mass., 1670), p. 33, both quoted in Edmund S. Morgan, *The Puritan Family: Essays on Religion and Domestic Relations in Seventeenth-Century New England* (Boston: Boston Public Library, 1944), pp. 99–102.

20. George Keith, *The Presbyterian and Independent Visible Churches in New-England and else-where, Brought to the Test, and examined according to the Doctrin of the holy Scriptures* (1689), pp. 84–86.

21. Edward Burrough, *The Memorable Works of a Son of Thunder and Consolation* (1672), p. 489.

which children were attached to the church without conversion, so Friends warned against depending on a merely inherited faith. John Crook exhorted all children of believing parents, and servants of believing masters, "to Examine your selves, how you came by your Profession? Whether you, that are Children and Servants, received it by Tradition, only because of your outward Relations, &c. or from the inward Work of God upon your own Spirits, as those did that received the Truth (*in the Love of God*) at the beginning." [22] Stephen Crisp recommended the same examination. More was required "than that you were educated therein, and brought up to it by your Parents, Guardians, or Masters." " 'Except ye be born again, ye cannot see the Kingdom of God,' " he reminded them; their testimony for Truth would be worthless until "rooted and grounded in it, through an experimental Warfare in their own particulars." [23]

The same note was sounded in the eighteenth century, though with a recognition that it was increasingly unheeded. "I can say by living Experience," wrote Deborah Bell, "that to be the Child of faithful Parents (although it is an unexpressible Privilege to all those that rightly prize it) will not save you, *for the Soul that sins must die*, unless they repent." All confidence to the contrary came from Satan: "the Enemy was seeking to perswade me, (as I am afraid he is seeking to perswade too many in this Day) that the Faithfulness and Integrity of my Parents, would stand me in great stead when I came to dye . . . but I saw clearly, in that Day, by that Eye the Almighty had opened, that unless I came to be acquainted with the same Power that had wrought a Change and Alteration upon my dear Parents . . . I should be miserable and undone for ever." [24]

22. "An Epistle to all that Profess The Light of Jesus Christ (within) to be their Guide," (1678) in *The Design of Christianity, Testified, in the Books of John Crook* (1701), p. 320.
23. Stephen Crisp, *An Epistle of Tender Counsel and Advice* (1680), pp. 15, 17.
24. Deborah Bell, "Testimony concerning her Dear Father John

The conversion experiences of the first generation of Friends had usually taken place not in emulation but in defiance of parents. The impact of Quakerism, and of the religious ferment of the Interregnum generally, was to shatter families and ruin the effective exercise of paternal power. Thus Sir Isaac Penington threatened to disinherit Isaac the Younger, but the old man could not prevent his family from pursuing the most divergent paths. While one of the daughters also became a Friend, another of his sons took Holy Orders in the Roman Catholic Church.[25] Walter Ellwood had locked up and assaulted young Tom; he seems also to have disinherited him.[26] A good many of the early Quaker ministers suffered the disapproval of their fathers "in the outward." Nicholas Gates "became as an Alien to my Father's House . . . and was Rejected by my Father, and many times threatened with being Cast off; but the Lord was exceeding good to me in all my Trials . . . though I can say I loved my Father tenderly . . . the Lord was more to me than my earthly Father." [27] Edward Burrough had the same scale of priorities, as can be seen from this letter to Francis Howgill, reporting the death of both his parents: "The old man and old woman, my father and mother according to the flesh, is both departed this world, ten days one after the other, and I am sent for down, but truly I cannot go; it is only pertaining to outwards, and I feel no freedom to it at present." [28]

Wynn," in *The Memory of the Just Reviv'd: in divers Testimonies Concerning John Wynn* (1715), pp. 23–24.

25. The pained letters of Isaac Penington the Elder to Isaac Penington the Younger, on the occasion of the latter's conversion to Quakerism, are preserved in Friends' House Library.

26. In the course of controversy with John Raunce and Leonard Key, Ellwood discusses his financial relations with his father, saying that he received no inheritance at all, though his father had offered him £500 if he would be married by a priest. See *A Fair Examination of a Foul Paper* (1693), pp. 20–21.

27. Nicholas Gates, *A Tender Invitation to all, to embrace the Secret Visitation of the Lord to their Souls* (1708), pp. 26–27, 23.

28. Quoted in Elisabeth Brockbank, *Edward Burrough, A Wrestler for Truth 1634–1662* (London: Bannisdale Press, 1949), p. 132.

The tension between Quaker children and their parents was often brought into the open by adherence to the plain testimonies. John Crook recalled that the first converts suffered from outward as well as inner turmoils, "in Gestures, and Postures, and Language, and Behaviour, divers from all People; which made them become a Gazing-stock to Men and Angels, and to be hated of their own Mothers Son, and near Relation." [29] Certainly Friends like John Love knew of what they spoke when they addressed *An Epistle to all Young Convinced Friends, whom the Lord hath reached by His mighty Power, and separated from the World, and turned their Hearts, so as to forsake Father, and Mother, Wife, and Children, for his Name sake* (1696).

We need not depend on literary evidence to establish the extent of family fragmentation brought about by early Quakerism. By checking Friends' records against those of the parishes and, more simply, by noting how many Friends in a place shared a common surname, I have established that the great majority of early converts in Norfolk and Buckinghamshire were the only ones of their families to join Friends. Only once did I discover three brothers who all became Quakers.[30] Sometimes a father and some of the adult children became Friends, but just as often fathers failed to convert even their wives, much less their children. More often a wife, but not her husband, joined Friends; and in landed families, as we have seen, it was almost always the younger sons and not the heir who became converts.

29. "Truth's Progress" (n.d.), in *Design*, p. 264.
30. Thomas, William, and Henry Glidwell, sons of Robert Glidwell and Elizabeth Sexton of North Crawley, Buckinghamshire. Some other families contributed two and possibly more early converts. The sister and uncle of Daniel Wharley, Isaac Penington's son-in-law, also became Friends, but not his brother, and his uncle must have returned to the established church, since his three children, born in 1646, 1648, and 1654, were all baptized on 19 January 1668. The Hawes family of Snareshill and the King family of North Walsham, Norfolk, must have had several members among early Friends, but it is impossible to disentangle their exact relationships.

Many times the breach in the family was not irreparable, for non-Quaker relatives are piously and sometimes affectionately mentioned in many wills. Family ties which remained unruptured despite religious differences no doubt account for many of the incidents in the records of sufferings in which friendly neighbors refused to buy goods which had been distrained, or defended persecuted Quakers in other ways. But there is ample evidence of the painful family scenes produced by the hostility which the older churches felt for Quakerism, particularly in the beginning, and the consciousness of the breach they had made in their own families helped to muffle any emphasis on the family's role in religious life in the writings of the early Friends. Holding to the absolute principle that everyone must follow the inward light, the most that they could expect of the family was that it allow this following and thus tolerate diversity of religion within the household.

However, the principle that diversity of religion within the household be tolerated was purely ancillary to the one that everyone must follow the inward light. Consequently, when rebellious Quaker sons in their turn became fathers, they forgot their pleas that wives, children, and servants should have freedom of conscience — when conscience had inclined them to Quakerism — and upheld a rigorous standard of filial obedience.[31] The claim to obedience was the reciprocal of the obligation which parents had to give their children a godly upbringing. Thus, at the same time that they attempted to induce the same sort of religious experience in their children that they themselves had undergone, Friends were also introducing and defending a new doctrine of Christian nurture.

This can easily be illustrated from their devotional literature. John Banks was particularly concerned that parents

---

31. This point is made in Keith Thomas, "Women and the Civil War Sects," *Past and Present*, 13 (1958), 55–57.

should restrain their children from all evil impulses: "Sometimes I have heard, to the grief of my Soul, *Parents* say to their *Children*, Do such a thing; they have replied (*I will not*:) And whether ought the *Child*, that doth not yet understand what's good either for its *Soul* or *Body*, to have its *Will*? Or ought not the *Parents* rather to Constrain them to do what they know is good for them, tho' they be stiff and stubborn?" [32] The lenient parent was more culpable than the disobedient child: "the Rod of God is for their Backs, who (through a foolish Pity) are ready to say, *I cannot find in my heart to whip my Child*. What! Hast thou not a Heart and Mind to do thy Child good?" [33] Ambrose Rigge, in an Epistle written in 1692, reminded parents of their responsibilities for keeping to plain and sound language, dress, and behavior: "this is your Duty, the Lord requires it of you, even to watch over your Children, as those that must give an Account to God, while they are under your Wings: *Elie's* not Restraining his Sons became his Sin." [34] It is not surprising that one of the things Friends found admirable about the redoubtable William Edmondson was that "the Lord raised him up and made him as a BATTLE-AX in his Hand, and a ROD to correct stubborn Children." [35]

The Quaker opinion about the locus of authority in the family was shared by all religious men. Richard Baxter spoke for all divines in defining the authority of parents as "most unquestionable." "They will dispute the authority of minis-

32. John Banks, *An Epistle to Friends Shewing the Great Difference between a Convinced and Converted Estate* (1692), p. 13.
33. *A Rebuke to Unfaithful Parents and a Rod for Stubborn Children* (1710), p. 2. Banks would clearly have had a rebuke, if not a rod, for Walter Joseph Homan, whose *Children and Quakerism* endows early Friends with a conception of childhood which is quite admirable and totally unhistorical.
34. *Constancy in the Truth Commended: Being a True Account of the Life, Sufferings, and Collected Testimonies of Ambrose Rigge* (1710), p. 309.
35. *A Journal of the Life of William Edmondson* (Dublin, 1715), p. liv.

ters, yea, and of magistrates," he wrote, "But the parents' authority is beyond all dispute . . . Therefore father and mother as the first natural power are mentioned rather than kings or queens in the fifth commandment." [36] A manual of family duties much in favor among Puritans warned: "If maisters then or parents doe not governe, but let servants and children doe as they list, they doe not onely disobey God, and disadvantage themselves, but also hurt those whom they should rule: for when any have such libertie to do as they list, it maketh them grow out of order, to the provokeing of God's displeasure, and curse against themselves, wheras if they had beene held in by the bridle of Government, they might be brought to walke, so as the blessing of God should follow them in their courses." [37]

The Puritans, in fact, had turned to domestic religion and the establishment of family worship in part because their program of ecclesiastical and political reform had been blocked. As one of their ministers put it, "such Householders, as pretend to be great Protestants, and sound professors of the Gospell, may long enough talke of discipline, and still complaine of the want of Church-government; but all in vaine, and to no purpose, unlesse they will begin this most necessarie discipline in reforming their owne houses." [38] Not only the Puritan tradition, but the same sense that any change

36. Richard Baxter, *Christian Directory* (1673), II, 517, quoted in Richard B. Schlatter, *The Social Ideas of Religious Leaders, 1660–1688* (London: Oxford University Press, 1940), p. 5. Schlatter's discussion of the religious justification of paternal authority (pp. 1–30) is admirable; see also G. C. Cragg, *From Puritanism to the Age of Reason* (Cambridge, Eng.: Cambridge University Press, 1950), pp. 170–172.

37. *A Godlie Forme of Householde Government for the Ordering of Private Families according to the Direction of God's Word. First gathered by R.C. And now newly perused, amended, and augmented by John Dod and Robert Clever* (1612), p. 16. The work seems to be entirely by Clever, and the alleged augmentations and corrections in fact amount to very little; nevertheless the prestigious name of Dod served as a further recommendation to Puritan purchasers.

38. *Godlie Forme of Householde Government,* "Epistle Dedicatorie," Sig A. 3.

in the established church and state was beyond their powers led Friends to look to the family, the inescapable social unit, as the paramount religious one.[39]

Schooling and Apprenticeship

This is evident in all Quaker institutions, from provisions for schooling and apprenticeship to the establishment of procedures for marriage. In fact, Quaker schools had only a feeble development during the first century of Quakerism, and the first thought of meetings who had the care of orphan children was not to educate them but to apprentice them, thus introducing them into a substitute family. A minute from the Norfolk Quarterly Meeting, agreeing to terms for apprenticing an orphan child, with provision for a year of instruction so that the child could learn to read and write, fairly represents the early Quaker emphasis on education. Friends fully shared the conventional expectation of their times that poor children should learn elementary subjects only, whereas richer ones should have a more polite (and capital-intensive) education.[40] John Bellers felt that Friends could well do without the accomplishments typical of a gentleman's education, and in the same spirit the Clerkenwell workhouse (which was more or less the embodiment of Bellers' ideas for a "college of industry") preferred for its sewing mistress a less skillful (and less expensive) teacher, since all they wanted to teach was "sewing work as far as is necessary for good servant maids . . . as that is what we chiefly aim at for them." In their view "education of them in seamstry of a nicer sort tends rather to destroy the end

39. So deeply rooted was the idea that the family was the first political unit that male servants coming into the Massachusetts Bay colony were arbitrarily assigned to artificial "families" (Morgan, *Puritan Family*, p. 85).

40. L. John Stroud, "The History of Quaker Education in England (1647–1903)," unpub. diss., University of Leeds, 1944, p. 78.

proposed, by begetting apprehensions in them (& probably in their parents, &c.) that they are qualified for seamstresses, governesses, mantua-makers, quilters, &c. or some business by which they may live at their own hands (as they call it) and from whence we apprehend very ill consequences to arise." [41]

It was not upward social mobility per se, but rather the independence of "living at their own hands" outside the discipline of a family, which seemed to threaten such ill consequences. Friends, as we have seen, put the duty of masters in the religious instruction and correction of their servants and apprentices only slightly below the responsibility of fathers; indeed a proper apprenticeship was necessary to confirm the effects of a sound education. William Dover, writing in the middle of the eighteenth century, proposed a great increase in schools, especially Protestant schools for Catholic children; but he warned, "if those Children after Instruction in Learning and Industry, either in *Ireland* or the Highlands of Scotland, are not placed as Apprentices, or Servants, with Protestant Masters or Mistresses, but are permitted to return to their Popish, Bigotted, Rude and Rebellious Parents, the Benefits which might issue from their Education, may be expunged and annulled." [42]

It will be obvious from these examples that "education" did not generally mean intellectual stimulation or training; and consequently it did not have to be conducted in schools. Though Yearly Meeting in 1695 urged all quarterly meetings to establish schools for their children, the response was mixed. In Lancashire in 1703 it was reported that "Not one friends child but what goes to friends schools," but this was the only county and only year where such a claim could

---

41. T. Frederick Ball and William Beck, *The London Friends' Meetings* (1869), p. 370, quoted in Stroud, p. 88.

42. William Dover, *Reasons for Erecting an Additional Number of Schools, for the Better Education of Youth in Learning and Virtue* (1752), pp. 9–10.

be made. In Norfolk and Buckinghamshire there were no Friends' boarding schools, and only the intermittent presence of a schoolmaster testifies to any effort to provide instruction. Today, when university graduates are several times more numerous among English Friends than in the general population, it is hard to believe that in the early eighteenth century there was such widespread indifference to intellectual cultivation on the part of Friends; yet, except for a few well-established schools in or near the largest cities, it is hard to find anything which approaches systematic schooling for Quaker children, let alone any attempts at higher education.[43] In England, as in New England, Friends made only a tardy and small contribution to education, in comparison to the educational impulses so strongly marked in the Presbyterians and Congregationalists; there is little to match the early Dissenting academies, not to mention Harvard or Yale.

The Quaker Doctrine of Marriage

If the family were to serve as the chief agent of religious instruction, it was necessary that both parents speak with a single voice. Despite their own deviations from religious uniformity within the family, the early Friends were determined that none of their numbers be "unequally yoked" — that is, married to someone who was not a Quaker. It was the common doctrine of all Christians that no Christian should marry an infidel, heretic, or schismatic — classes much multiplied by the progress of the Reformation. For Protestants, marriage was charged with a particular intensity, since Protestant thought, rejecting the medieval glorification of celi-

43. Dorothy G. B. Hubbard, "Early Quaker Education (*c*. 1650–1780)," unpub. Master's thesis, University of London, 1940, considers the first half of the eighteenth century a particularly slack period in the Quaker educational effort; see especially pp. 151–155, 262–265. Much of the material in this paragraph comes from Miss Hubbard's work, though she puts a somewhat different emphasis on it.

bacy as a higher state than marriage, had tended steadily to the reverse conclusion. The marriage of priests was not a legalization of old license, but an act of positive holiness; and of course the moral duties of the priest differed not a whit from those of the godly layman. Milton had produced a justification of divorce which was in fact an exaltation of marriage, conceived as the highest union between free spirits.[44]

It was fully in this Miltonic spirit that George Fox projected his marriage to Margaret Fell in 1669. As Braithwaite writes, "In his mind the union seems to have had a mystical fitness at a time when the Church, through the Quaker movement, was come up out of the wilderness, and the gospel order had been again set up." [45] His marriage, he thought, was commanded of God, and was meant for a sign to all the faithful. To one who objected that marriage was only for the procreation of children (Margaret Fell was 55 at the time) Fox answered that it was "a testimony that all might come uppe Into the mariage as was in the beginninge . . . out of the wildernesse to the mariage of the lamb." [46] In a substantial and, it must be admitted, obscure tract *Concerning Marriage* (1663), Fox grounded his answers to queries about marriage on the state of matrimony as it exists in paradise. Fox claimed, on the usual arguments for perfection, that God's will was capable of being infallibly known with regard to marriage as to all other things; and he held that Friends married to those not (or not yet) converted need not despair about the spiritual health of their children: "there is a state where the believing wife sanctifies the unbelieving husband, and the believing husband sanctifies the unbelieving wife." However he warned

44. William Haller, *Liberty and Reformation in the Puritan Revolution* (New York: Columbia University Press, 1955), pp. 78–85, gives a characteristically complete and sensitive discussion of this.

45. *Second Period*, 2nd ed., p. 262.

46. George Fox, *Journal*, ed. Norman Penney (Cambridge, Eng.: Cambridge University Press, 1911), II, 154.

Friends against contracting marriages with unbelievers, and notwithstanding the assertion that God's will about marriage can be manifestly known, the pamphlet concluded with a marriage order approved by Fox.

Since this order developed into the normative Quaker procedure for marriages, it is worth detailed examination. "First, after the thing is known between the parties themselves, before any thing is concluded, let it be declared unto friends, who are able in the wisdom and power of God to see and feel into it, if they see the thing in the light and power of God, to stand." Next the couple were to declare it to the meetings to which they "belonged." If there were any objections, these were to be laid before the "next general meeting." The marriage itself could take place in a meeting of twelve or more Friends, where the couple would "declare their testimony how the Lord hath joyned them." They were not to be "married in a corner by one called a Minister, for mony." After the marriage, there was a certificate to be made out; if they were moved to do so, Friends might declare it to the magistrate or in the market-place.[47]

This marriage order predates the establishment of monthly and quarterly meetings, but it provided most of the elements of the eventual marriage discipline. There are nevertheless instructive changes made in the course of the first generation of Quakerism, particularly in reinforcing the parental power at one of its most sensitive points: the right to regulate the marriages of the children.

Most writers on domestic relations in the seventeenth century — though not all — took the position that parental consent was always essential for marriage.[48] Although there

47. Thomas Lawrence and George Fox, *Concerning Marriage* (n.p., 1663), pp. 2–3, 6, 14.
48. C. L. Powell, *English Domestic Relations 1487–1653* (New York: Columbia University Press, 1917), pp. 131–135. Manuals by clergymen on domestic duties reach a compromise: children should certainly not be married without their parents' consent, but neither should the parent arrange a marriage without the child's consent. I am quite

is abundant literary evidence of the concern of parents that their children should contract suitable marriages, nothing dramatizes it like the arrangements made by some fathers. The will of Edward Cook is unusually explicit, but it does not strike one as eccentric. Cook, a Quaker who left an estate of over £1,000, nominated executors to oversee the administration of his considerable landed property. His three daughters were all left annuities of £5 (£5 10s. to the youngest) until the dates of their marriages. When these occurred the annuities were to cease. If the executors, after a careful investigation, were satisfied with the marriages that the daughters had made, they were to have a portion of £140 or £120. But if they failed to make an acceptable marriage (the canons for which were emphatically set forth) the daughters were to be deprived of any share in the estate.[49]

Such executors were to do after death what a living father could do for himself. The proper ordering of marriages among Friends required that they frame a procedure which added the sanctions of the church to the exhortations of the father. And this mechanism was not used only against marriage to outsiders. Even though they were both Friends, the bride and the bridegroom had to produce evidence that both sets of parents were in full agreement with the marriage before it was allowed. In fact, Friends required the approval of the parents before the proposal of marriage was made. The Yearly Meeting Epistle of 1690 directed that children and young persons make no "motion or procedure . . . upon the account of Marriage, without first acquainting their Parents or Guardians therewith, and duly waiting upon them for their Consent and agreement therein." It was prudent also to ask for Friends' approval before suggesting marriage. The Somerset Quarterly Meeting, in the course of denouncing

unable to make out from the Delphic text of Fox's *Concerning Marriage* what his sentiments were on this question.

49. Will of Edward Cook, Archdeaconry Court of Buckinghamshire, 1703.

"Such as walke disorderly" decried persons' "letting their affections one to another so inordinately before a proposall be made to friends, according to the good order of truth." Such couples gave the impression that the matter was already concluded before Friends had had a chance to give their helpful advice; the Meeting was merely asked to "consent to answer their inordinate affections . . . & they haveing so joyned themselves in their affecons that its hard to receive a denyall." If Friends do not "bow to their corrupt wills, they then farther run into the enemys snare, & goe to the priest" to be married. It was therefore in accordance with good order that a Bristol Friend asked the consent of Men's Meeting before he asked it of the girl.[50]

The various delays to get monthly meeting approval and parental consent might be expected to put a considerable chill on marital ardor. This is one of the themes of a satirical poem about Quaker marriage procedure called *Aminadab's Courtship*. The hero had to go through considerable vexation, even though the poet says:

> But Reader, by the Way, I'd have thee know,
> Here were no Parents to refer unto;
> No Guardians, or Trustees, or such as those,
> Both *'Dab* and *Phebe* were at their own dispose;
> For otherwise, Friends are so nicely bent,
> They could not finish without their consent;
> Nay, if their Parents ne'er so distant live,
> They unto them a full Account must give
> Of their Intentions, and with Patience wait
> Till from them they receive Certificate.[51]

50. Russell Mortimer, "Quakerism in Seventeenth Century Bristol," unpub. Master's thesis, Bristol University, 1946, p. 191.

51. [Elias Bockett], *Aminadab's Courtship: or, The Quaker's Wedding. A Poem being an Impartial Account of their Way of Courtship, Method of Marrying, etc.* (1717), pp. 31–32. We may well doubt this work's impartiality, since we leave the happy couple at the wedding feast, where "some incline to be exceeding Merry And drown the inward Light in outward Sherry" (p. 45).

Obedience to parents' wills was enjoined even if they were not Friends. Elias Osborn wished to marry a Quaker girl whose mother was a Friend, but not her father. The father at first refused his consent, though later he finally agreed. This gave Osborn the opportunity to recommend "that young People take Care to be subject to Parents as much as in them lyes, tho' they are not of our Way; Truth will lead to it if truly minded." [52]

And if not truly minded, of course, Friends punished breaches of procedure. Isaac Bond found himself under the displeasure of the Scotby, Cumberland, Preparative Meeting on 15 November 1721 because he, after getting his own parent's consent to marry Jane Bowman, "did aquaint the young woman's parents time after time & waited severall months for their consent yet could not have it, which became a great exercise to me." Finding "the concerne continuing" he was "willing to Impart my minde to the young woman not in contempt to the order in the least yet in so doeing friends is so uneasye with me that I canot have their unitye in my marrying untill I acknowledge my miss: for which mis I am sory." [53]

52. *A Brief Narrative of the Life, Labours, and Sufferings of Elias Osborn* (1723), p. 21.

53. It must be said that Friends were not always insistent on paternal consent, so long as there had been consultation and a reasonable period of waiting. The Upperside Monthly Meeting allowed one marriage without the permission of one parent — who was not a Friend. Those who visited him "could receive no reasonable answer from him, nor discover any real ground he had to refuse his consent, but rather a stiff & resolute wil, which appeard more plain by the old man's words . . . that he had sworn he would never give his consent, & he would not be forsworn; which the meeting not judging a reasonable or righteous impediment, exprest their consent that John and Sarah might take each other in marriage" (minute of 7 October 1674). The Norwich Monthly Meeting in October 1696 heard the reason of John Wells, Sr., against the marriage of John Wells, Jr., which was "that he did believe it will be his Absolute ruin if he hath her, and likewise if he had her not." The meeting "upon a mature consideration, are of a contrary perswasion in that respect," and the marriage was allowed. In 1779 the Horsham Monthly Meeting allowed a Friend to marry "though not so successful as to obtain her

Not every Friend was willing to humble himself thus. This explains why the offense of "marrying by a priest" — that is, marrying another Quaker, though with a clergyman officiating — was more common than the one of marrying "one of the world." In Norwich the monthly meeting disowned two members who married outside the society, but had to visit and reprove fourteen who were "married by a priest." In almost every other meeting whose records I have examined the latter was the more common offense; and when we note that most of the offenders were in late adolescence or in their early twenties, it seems likely that in most of these dramas the offending "priests" had in fact played the role of Friar Lawrence, parental objection having made the regular Quaker procedure impossible.

The effects of the testimony against mixed marriages in diminishing the numbers of Quakers — at least during later Quaker history — are well known. Given the suspiciousness which Friends showed towards attenders who seemed drawn to a Quaker girl rather than the inward light, it is clear that this testimony helped to isolate Friends. Less rigorous judges might have taken such potential bridegrooms as a useful source of converts. When we consider that "marriage by a priest" was a distinct offense from marrying outside the society — and by and large a more common one — we can see the full resources which Quakerism put into the hands of parents. When it came to insubordinate and irregular marriages of one Friend to another, the censures of the elder merely amplified the complaints of the father. Often, indeed, these would be the same man. In not having any clergy themselves and forbidding marriage before a clergyman, Friends eliminated the possibility of any appeal to religious authority against the paternal.

In making available the maximum power to parents,

---

father's consent" (T. W. Marsh, *Early Friends in Surrey and Sussex* [1886], p. 103).

Friends were entrusting to them the vital task of forming character. It was, increasingly, reliable behavior according to their distinctive norms which distinguished the Quaker from the children of the world. The way in which the family operated in the formation of character, and the peculiar development which it gave the Quaker ideas of conversion, can be seen in the history of the "public testimonies."

The Public Testimonies

As we have seen, the early Friends distinguished between convincement, which might be mere intellectual assent, and full-fledged conversion. The latter, which normally took several months to complete, involved a complete reconstruction of conduct, and this could be discerned by Friends. Quakers often — especially in the eighteenth century — spoke of those who seemed to be convinced, yet did not "take up a public testimony."

To Friends, "public testimonies" of course meant not relations of conversion experiences, as with the Baptists or Independents, but conformity to righteous deeds — especially those judged peculiar, rude, or subversive by their fellow Englishmen. As has been well said by Theodor Sippell, "Quakerism is above all a testimony; it is a permanently-declared appeal to the consciences of all men. In word, deed, and outward sign it proclaims without any compromise what the spirit of God says." [54] In the course of the eighteenth century Friends began to put an enormous emphasis on these testimonies, especially the ones which manifested the importance of plainness. But in the course of the century which had elapsed since the beginning of the movement the significance of these testimonies had subtly changed, so that the

54. "Denn das Quäkertum ist in erster Linie Zeugnis; es ist der in Permanenz erklärte Gewissensappell an alle Menschen. In Worten, Taten und äusseren Zeichen soll das, was der Geist Gottes sagt, ganz kompromisslos verkündet werden" (*Werdendes Quäkertum* [Stuttgart: W. Kohlhammer, 1937], p. 109).

insistence upon them by ministers and meetings for discipline in fact amounted to a preference for the cultural habits which Friends' children automatically acquired in the family. As the cultural divergence of Friends from "the world" became much more pronounced, this expressed itself as a tension between "plain Friends," who adhered to the last rigors of dress and speech, and laxer ones — "wet Quakers," as they were disparagingly called.[55]

The aims of the Quaker testimonies were peace, honesty, and humility. The testimony against "carnal strivings and fightings," which had assumed a definitive form by the year of the Restoration, was originally important for its declaration that Friends had no intention of resorting to "apostolic blows and knocks" and would not participate in any further civil wars. Since there was no military conscription, most Friends had no other occasion to make a personal testimony. Merchants could not arm their ships, and ironmasters were obliged to decline contracts for cannon; but aside from this, the most that Friends could do was to avoid enlisting in the army and to keep their windows dark when other Englishmen were celebrating feats of arms.

A great many of Friends' customs were justified on the single grounds of honesty. If one always told the truth, there was no reason to be put on oath. If goods were offered for sale, the only honest course was to announce the price at which a fair profit would be gained; setting a higher price in the anticipation of bargaining was merely to multiply deceit. These testimonies touched upon the most important ventures of life, and that against oaths perhaps cost more Friends their

55. Writes T. Edmund Harvey in *Quaker Language* (*J.F.H.S.*, Supplement 15, 1928), 6: "In the eighteenth and earlier nineteenth centuries the plain language, along with the traditional Quaker dress of later origin, which by that time accompanied it, were the invariable mark of the consistent Friend and were adopted, often after great inward struggles, by the converts to Quakerism as well as by a number of birthright members, who after a deep spiritual crisis had resolved to take up the cross, as they felt it, of this testimony."

lives than any other. But the concern for honesty was pushed into the most commonplace aspects of life. The Quakers made an attempt to purify the English language of the taint of popery and paganism. Place-names, redolent of a millenium of Catholicism, were denuded; Chalfont St. Peter became "Peter's Chalfont." Just as such names imputed existence to the saints, so did the names of the days of the week and of the first eight months refer to nonexistent pagan gods. The Quaker terminology of "first day," "second day," and so on had last been heard in Christendom in the days of the early Church Fathers; Tertullian and others had sought to substitute it for the naming of the days after the planets, which in turn were named for the Roman gods. Indeed, astrology owed no little of its historical impact to this linking of days, planets, and gods.[56] But no matter how soundly based was Friends' testimony against heathenish survivals in the calendar, it was shared by few contemporary Englishmen; and even clerks of meetings sometimes forgot.[57]

Honesty also compelled Friends to avoid saying "you" to a single person; but to take up the use of "thou" involved, at least in southern England, a breach with customary usage which had the further disadvantage of exposing one to resentment or ridicule.[58] James Parnel explained Friends' principles

56. The French calendar still preserves almost all the Roman deities in the names of the days of the week; the English mingles them with the Norse gods. See Jean Seznec, *The Survival of the Pagan Gods,* trans. Barbara Sessions (New York: Harper & Bros., 1961), p. 43.

57. From 1732 to 1757 the Lynn Monthly Meeting continuously used the heathen names in its accounts, as did the Biddlesden Women's Monthly Meeting in "June" and "July," 1684. Sarah Fell, daughter of Margaret and stepdaughter of George Fox, did not use the "plain" names of the months in her household account book and also used such titles as Duke, Sir, and Esquire. See *The Household Account Book of Sarah Fell of Swarthmoor Hall,* ed. Norman Penney (Cambridge, Eng.: Cambridge University Press, 1920), pp. 59, 132, 375, 413. George Fox enunciated the accepted doctrine with regard to titles: "You do not read of Mr. Paul, and Mr. Peter, &c." ("Great Mistery" in *Works* [1831 ed.], III, 73).

58. Hugh Barbour, *Quakers in Puritan England,* pp. 164–165 makes the attractive suggestion that the North Country background of so many

by claiming that the use of "you" to a single person was "an Invention of Proud *Lucifer* in man to exalt himself, as it will plainly appear; for amongst the Great and Rich Ones of the Earth, they will either *Thou* or *You* one another, if they be equal in Degree, as they call it; but if a man of low Degree in the Earth come to speak to any of them, then he must *You* the Rich Man, but the Rich Man will *Thou* him." [59]

Humility, therefore, as well as honesty, dictated the use of "thou." Further to abase themselves, Friends issued advice which had the effect of a series of thoroughgoing sumptuary laws, prohibiting everything from lace to tombstones. In their effort to protect themselves from the novel seductions of more comfortable times, Irish Friends furnish us with the most picturesque examples. In November 1713 the Dublin Half-Yearly Meeting cautioned against putting glasses and china cups on shelves "as seems to be more for mode & shew than Use or Service" and against "that undecent & immodest fashion of going with bare necks and breasts." Two years later snuff was anathematized, along with "the accustomary & fashionable using of tea"; apparently it was all right to use tea, so long as it was done unfashionably, since "real occasion" — presumably medicinal — might be a justification. In May 1723 the meeting noted with sorrow that "several friends Children and some young People are unnecessarily Enclined to, and in the practice of learning French, the method of Teaching whereof as also the learning the same as now taught

---

early ministers helped to establish the testimony against "you." "Thees" and "thous" are still in common use in the northern counties, as shown by the story of the London teacher, in her first day of teaching in a Derbyshire school, who was looking for a place to dispose of the wrappings of her luncheon sandwiches. "Where's the bin?" she asked a small boy, only to receive the reply: "Ah've bin 'om, of course. Weer does tha think ah've bin?" (*The Listener,* 9 April 1959, p. 1567.) The most complete study of the plain speech is Thomas Finkenstädt, *You und Thou: Studien zur Anrede im Englishchen* (Berlin: de Gruyter, 1963), pp. 120–213.

59. "A Shield of the Truth," in *A Collection of the Writings of James Parnel* (n.p., 1675), p. 94.

having a Tendency to corrupt our youth." In November 1714 even wigs were brought under the care of the Meeting: "if any Friend wants hair, they should acquaint the mens meeting they belong to, and have their approbation and consent, before they get any."

Since clothing was a principal vehicle of pride, Friends lavished much care on a due simplicity of costume. In its origins, the plain dress of Friends was the "simple, unadorned costume of the men of [Fox's] generation . . . The dress of the Quaker, when he first arose, was in custom and fashion simply the dress of everybody, with all extravagance left off." The frontispiece, a seventeenth-century youth "in his converted state," would serve just as well for a Quaker. In fact, the only difference between the ordinary dress of George Fox and of Charles II (a youth in his natural state) was in ornament; Fox's trousers had no "points" or jewelled ribbons at the knees; there were no ribbons on the instep of his shoes, which were heavy and square of toe; and his stockings were of homespun, not silk.[60] The simplicity of the costume was not only to mortify the flesh and its pride. The money saved could be given to the poor; as William Penn finely said, "The trimming from the vain world would clothe the naked one."

But the distinctive Quaker clothing is a particularly good example of the way that, for all their admirable features, the Quaker testimonies did come in the course of a century to contribute powerfully to setting Friends off as a separated people. We have already noted the importance laid on the plain testimonies by eighteenth-century Friends, and I have argued that adherence to them was often the chief sign by which the sincerity of converts was tested by Friends. It is very clear that by the eighteenth century, deviation from plain speech and dress was generally attributed to association with "people of the world." John Kelsall laments that he was

60. Amelia Mott Gummere, *The Quaker: A Study in Costume* (Philadelphia: Ferris and Leach, 1901), pp. 15, 17.

allowed, through the negligence of his relatives in allowing him "the society and fellowship of the World's children both at School and elsewhere," to become "addicted to" the evil customs of "saying Good Morrow, Good Evening, putting off the Hat." So much was this to be avoided, he thought, that parents and overseers of children ought not to permit them to associate at all with the children of the world.[61]

It is not hard to see why the plain testimonies should have come to be peculiar to Friends. The use of "first day," for example, is quite often found among Independents and Baptists in the Commonwealth period, but it quickly died out, not being supported by the weight of argument and administrative sanction which Friends brought to it. Changes in general English usage of "thou" and "you" were irreversible, and in fact have totally obscured the meaning of the testimony, since some Friends today use "thou" in their families and to close friends, reserving "you" for outsiders. This is the only form of *tutoiement* that can exist in English, and is entirely untrue to the egalitarian meaning of the testimony in the seventeenth century. We do not know at exactly what rate the use of "thou" to social inferiors was dying out, but by the middle of the eighteenth century, at least in southern England, "thou" was probably reserved for Friends and God.

The fate of the plain dress is an even more striking example. Since the first Friends found constant temptations to vanity in wigs, cuffs, points, and other accoutrements of men's fashions, one can imagine the ceaseless vigilance required against the snares which the devil spun out in women's dress. George Fox found it necessary to caution against "skimingdish hatts and your unessessery buttens on the topps of your sleeves shoulders backs." In the next century there were new and numerous abominations. David Hall ex-

61. John Kelsall, "A Journal or Historical Account of the Chief Passages, Concerns, and Exercises of My Life since my Childhood" (1731), p. 17. This journal is a manuscript in Friends' House Library.

claimed: "of all the giddy Modes, antick and fantastick Inventions, that ever old Satan or his Agents, with respect to external Dress, have hitherto vampt up, since the Fall of *Adam*; was there ever any Thing contriv'd so much for the Ruin of Female Modesty, and the Incitement to Sensuality and Corruption, as these immodest, indecent, odious, extravagant Hoops." [62]

The conception of simplicity in dress which the first Friends adhered to was the simple, unadorned costume of the men of George Fox's generation, and it was exactly the same standard which Friends a century later were still prescribing. But in a century even the costume of male Englishmen changes somewhat. Even the dowdiest or most old-fashioned of the world did not quite duplicate the fossilized mid-seventeenth-century dress of Friends. That dress thus became, for all intents and purposes, a uniform. John Wesley, with characteristic acuteness, regarded this as a virtue of Friends, and wanted to make the early Methodists dress uniformly ("like the people called Quakers or the Moravians") but did not succeed.[63]

Conversion to Quakerism, at least insofar as it had to be judged by "taking up a public testimony," thus entailed the necessity of buying a new set of clothes; the pathway to heaven commenced in a tailor's shop. It is true that the earliest converts felt that the whole of their being had been transformed by their encounter with Truth. As Luke Howard put it: "And then as to my whole Life and Course thereof, I had all to learn again the beginning of, both Eating and Drinking, and wearing Apparel, and Talking, and Buying and Selling; yea all to be made New." [64] But it is hard to deny the

62. *Brief Memoirs of the Life of David Hall* (1758), pp. 87–88. The quotation from Fox is in Mortimer, "Quakerism in Bristol," pp. 224–225.
63. Quoted in Gummere, *Quaker Costume*, p. 14.
64. Quoted in L. V. Hodgkin, *The Shoemaker of Dover* (London: Friends' Book Centre, 1943), p. 30.
65. *A Brief Collection of Remarkable Passages Relating to Margaret Fox* (1710), pp. 534–535.

cogency of Margaret Fox's last "Epistle to Friends," which warns, "let us all take heed of touching any thing like the Ceremonies of the Jews . . . Let us beware of being guilty, or having a hand in ordering or contriving that which is contrary to Gospel-Freedom . . . It's a dangerous thing to lead young Friends much into the observation of outward things, which may be easily done; for they can soon get into an outward Garb, to be all alike outwardly; but this will not make them true Christians." [65]

Margaret Fox's own household retained its Gospel-Freedom; she and her daughters had ribbons, colored stockings, looking-glasses, and even vizard-masks, all of which would have struck a plain eighteenth-century Friends as intolerable frippery.[66] No doubt Friends of an aristocratic or gentry background were more inclined to personal adornment, and the increasing emphasis on plainness is probably in part a reflection of the virtual extinction of this group among Quakers. But the transformation of the testimony of plainness into "an outward Garb, to be all alike outwardly" had clearly altered its original meaning. The plain dress was no longer simple; the precise construction of a Quaker costume became an increasingly exacting art, and no doubt proportionately expensive. Bonnet-making for Quaker women had become, by the middle of the nineteenth century, such a specialized trade that sometimes women had to get bonnets from extremely remote towns.[67]

In short, the plain dress had become a uniform and the plain speech a set of passwords. The same fate had even overtaken the testimony against oaths — recall how Somerset Friends were indignant when someone who was not a Friend testified without swearing, on the grounds that this amounted to falsely pretending to be a Quaker. These testimonies both

66. *Household Account Book of Sarah Fell*, ed. Penney, pp. xix-xx, 145, 367.
67. Samuel Fothergill of Scarborough, *An Essay on the Society of Friends* (1859), p. 156.

symbolized and helped to create the clannishness of Friends. They help us to understand why there was a rift between "plain Friends" and the others, and why there were so many meetings in the early eighteenth century that reported that there was a body of attenders besides the recognized members, receiving spiritual nourishment from Quaker ministry and doubtless admiring Friends' style of life without feeling fully able to join in it. It was obviously much more difficult for an outsider to adjust himself to the sort of learned behavior that the plain testimonies represented. The easiest place for their inculcation was the family; and so long as outward conduct and adherence to the public testimonies were the criteria by which the reality of conversion was judged, it is clear that the bias of Quaker institutions was against the conversion of the world and in favor of the organization of family life for the conversion of Quaker children.

VI   From Movement to Sect

With its peculiarities of dress and of speech, its clannish marriage customs, and the internal discipline which held it as a pure example to the world, the Quakerism of 1755 would have seemed in some ways strange to men who had lived through the heroic days of the Interregnum. But we can only speculate what the first Friends would have felt; and even more important, there is no reason to assume that the perspective of the early Quakers is in any sense a privileged or correct one. If we aim at understanding rather than lamentation we should exploit all the advantages of our own point of view — especially since, unfortunately, we shall not be able to escape its unconscious limitations.

If we should try to understand the transition from seventeenth-century Quakerism to its eighteenth-century forms by employing the categories of sociology, we would have to begin with the two ideal types of church and sect.[1] The main characteristic of the church as an ideal type is that it embraces, or aspires to embrace, the whole of a culture. It has members of all ages, drawn from every occupational group and social

1. See Ernst Troeltsch, *The Social Teaching of the Christian Churches,* trans. Olive Wyon (2 vols; New York: Macmillan Company, 1931), I, 331–349; *From Max Weber: Essays in Sociology,* ed. and trans. H. H. Gerth and C. Wright Mills (New York: Oxford University Press, 1946), pp. 59–60, 323–326; Reinhard Bendix, *Max Weber: An Intellectual Portrait* (New York: Doubleday, 1960), pp. 280–286.

class. Children are consequently brought into membership immediately — in Christianity, through infant baptism. One could no more enter the church by willful choice than one could will to be born, or choose to grow up entirely un-affected by the cultural values of one's parents.

The religious sect is distinguished by sociologists exactly by the element of voluntary association of all its members. This makes it necessary for everyone — even the children of members — to enter the sect by an authentic act of their own (typically, by the experience of conversion). The sect, as an ideal union of hearts and wills, expels any of its members who diverge in any important respect from its theological or moral consensus; its doctrines tend to elaborate upon the differences between its own members, conceived as a pure seed, a saving remnant, or the elect, and the "mixed multi-tude" or external "world." It is most unlikely that the mem-bers of a sect will come from the entire range of social back-grounds; instead the sects are likely to be, as Ernst Troeltsch says, "connected with the lower classes, or at least with those elements in Society which are opposed to the State and to Society." [2]

Ideal types are useful as analytical models, not as descrip-tions of any actually existing religious organization, since there are none which have all the characteristics either of a pure "church" or a pure "sect." Troeltsch believed that the medieval Roman Catholic Church was the closest approach to an historical embodiment of the church type, and that as a consequence, one should also look to the Middle Ages for the purest sects.[3] As analytical tools, ideal types are also static, being more suitable for classification at a given moment of time than for describing the historical evolution of a religious group.

Some scholars have argued that the sect can exist in ap-

2. Troeltsch, *Social Teaching*, I, 331.
3. *Ibid.*, I, 333.

proximately pure form only for a generation; after that, as H. Richard Niebuhr writes, the pure "sectarian" religious body must inevitably adopt some of the institutions of the "church." [4] In fact, as soon as one attempts to use these ideal types to understand the historical development of Quaker institutions, it becomes apparent that neither is altogether appropriate and that subtle manipulation of them is essential. I have used the word "movement" to describe the first few years of Quakerism because it, rather than either "church" or "sect," seems to catch the essentials of the situation: fluidity and mobility. Mobility, in the basic sense of moving about the country, was a necessity for the origins of Quakerism. Since there was virtually no local organization during the first ten or fifteen years, the locus of power lay with the traveling ministers. The most mobile elements in the population, wholesale traders and former army officers, were the principal carriers of the new religion. It also seems that Quakerism made its greatest appeal to men who had changed their place of residence at least once, and perhaps several times, since their births. Even the gentry converts were not, for the most part, from "established" families, which may be another way of saying that they were at least relative newcomers.

As we have seen from the spiritual autobiographies of the early Friends, they were inclined to the images of wandering and pilgrimage, visualizing the temporal flow of their lives, particularly the historical sequence of religious changes, in these spatial terms. Along with this sense of mobility went a fluidity of doctrine and practice. Since there were no precedents to appeal to, and indeed no relevant history at all, the "experimental" knowledge in which Friends trusted had full play. Spontaneity and even extravagance of behavior were at their height, only infrequently restrained by the occasional admonition of some traveling minister.

4. H. Richard Niebuhr, *The Social Sources of Denominationalism* (New York: H. Holt, 1929), p. 10.

The first phase of other religious groups — Methodism, or early Christianity itself, for example — might be better understood by emphasizing the degree to which they shared these characteristics of a "movement." It is certainly not easy to elucidate their character by employing the terms "church" and "sect." If one defines the sect by the wholly free adherence of its members, the first years of Quakerism were in one sense the most sectarian, since it was then composed entirely of converts. But in other ways it was more like a church. It had a greater social range, though, as we have seen, it had few if any representatives from the old ruling class, and most of its gentry leaders could perhaps be described as "opposed to the State and to Society." It avoided the self-definition entailed in taking a name, and its discipline of offenders operated as if there were no clear and visible lines of membership. Most important, from the very completeness of its desire to separate from the established church, it had perforce to provide for itself institutions analogous to those of that church. The registration of the births of Friends' children and the provision of comprehensive poor relief, both begun almost immediately and destined to develop eventually into "birthright membership," were institutions of this sort. By choosing a territorial principle for the organization of their business meetings, rather than the congregational principle favored by the Baptists and Independents, and by arranging them in a hierarchy (no matter how loose) Friends were in a way imitating the centralized institutions of church and state. It is a fine example of Hegel's historical insight that the struggle against the church and the effort to achieve complete separation from it led Friends in this fashion to "mirror" the structure of the church.

Quakerism as a "movement" had drawn to a close as early as 1670. This was largely the consequence of persecution, which disrupted the network of traveling ministers and required Friends, in self-defense, to establish local and national business meetings. Since persecution put an exorbitant premium on Friends' innocence, they had to discipline everyone who compromised the purity of their testimonies. Besides this winnowing of the society, which helped to eliminate any antinomian tendencies remaining from the enthusiasm of the first meetings, the establishment of business meetings drove from the ranks of Friends a considerable number of the early leaders who objected to George Fox's notions of organization. The secession of these leaders, and the death in prison of many others, meant that for the most part a new generation of local leaders came to operate the new administrative machinery. Though there was still some chance for ordinary Friends to travel in the ministry and take a prominent place in the meetings for church business, the public status of recognized ministers or "Public Friends" and the evidence that comparatively few members formed the core of the business meetings represented some constraint of earlier freedoms.

Quakerism after 1670, and especially after 1689, was more nearly sectarian, if one thinks not of the element of voluntary association of the members but of the completeness of their separation from their culture and particularly from other religious organizations and of the relative standardization of their behavior. The impulse towards uniformity of behavior again was largely owing to persecution. Besides the role it played in making necessary the organization of business meetings, with all that they did to maintain the reputation of Quakerism, persecution focused Friends' attention on the public testimonies. We must remember that persecution was not only martyrdom in prison or ruinous distraint for matters of high consequence. Many of the sufferings of the Quakers were of a more everyday kind — for their manners, not their beliefs or morals. These persecutions were not so amenable to political pressure and tended to survive the legislative relief of Friends' disabilities achieved during the reign of

William III. The persistence of this petty persecution tended to have the effect of making manners, as defined by the testimonies of plain speech and dress, seem as important as their morals. Indeed, the plain Friends of the eighteenth century spoke of adopting the plain testimonies as "taking up the cross."

In their conception of membership, Friends after 1670 came much closer to the sectarian norm. The theory of "invisible membership" faded away as disownments came more and more to be spoken of as directed against the person, rather than the action, and as meetings freely referred to converts as "joining" and "coming into membership." Conversion itself was still insisted upon; there could be no genuine inward relationship with God by mere tradition and education. But Friends felt the same difficulty that all Puritan sects encountered in bringing their children to an authentic conversion, or to a reasonable substitute. The only sect to have devised an entirely satisfactory mechanism assuring that none of its new members were making a merely traditional or inertial assent to its faith was the Shakers, who were entirely celibate. Unwilling to take such heroic measures, the Puritan sects sooner or later had to make some provision for children who were neither vicious enough to excommunicate nor zealous enough to welcome, but who merely, as Cotton Mather said of the second generation of New England Puritans, "could not come up to that experimental account of their own regeneration, which would sufficiently embolden their access to the other sacrament." [5]

In New England, political power rested in the hands of members of the church; consequently the inability of many to give an "experimental account of their own regeneration" led to a political crisis, which was resolved in 1662 when the so-called Half-Way Covenant was devised, giving some political rights to the children of believers who themselves could

5. Quoted in Perry Miller, *Orthodoxy in Massachusetts* (2nd. ed.; Boston: Beacon Press, 1959), p. 202.

not qualify for full church membership. This is the most dramatic example of an accommodation with the problem, because the concerns of state made such a solution urgent. Elsewhere the inadequate regeneration of the second and subsequent generations was perceived as a general "declension" in the spiritual vitality of the group. John T. McNeill thus speaks of eighteenth-century Presbyterianism as "decayed," afflicted by "dull and ineffective ministers" and suffering from a "decline in numbers and significance." [6] William Haller sees "populist Puritanism" as "destined to run out upon the flats of sectarianism sunned by commercial prosperity . . . [its] early enthusiasm congealed into the fundamentalism and asceticism of indurated dissent." [7] If it did not "congeal into fundamentalism" the Puritan sect ran the opposite risk of declining into Unitarianism, as the English General Baptists and Presbyterians did. Both fates have been attributed to the "crisis of conversions" arising in the second generation of believers.

I began my researches for this book in the belief that there was an establishment of a new category of membership among Quakers, birthright membership, which was formally recognized in 1737; and that this category, whose name has been incorporated into the vocabulary of the sociology of religion, was the analogous stage in Quaker development to the Half-Way Covenant in the life of the New England Puritans. It now seems clear that the 1737 rules of settlement are, in themselves, irrelevant to the Half-Way Covenant. They are not concerned with whether a person was a member, but where he was a member; their reference to children, added in the latter stages of discussion as part of a general effort to close all loopholes, was not predicated in any way on spiritual experiences, or the lack of them.

6. John T. McNeill, *The History and Character of Calvinism* (New York: Oxford University Press, 1954), p. 370.
7. William Haller, *The Rise of Puritanism* (New York: Columbia University Press, 1938), p. 272.

Although the traditional interpretation of these rules is a misunderstanding of their historical importance, it is nevertheless a misunderstanding which is itself important historical evidence. What nineteenth-century Quakers thought of eighteenth-century ones testifies to the differences between early Quakerism and that of the eighteenth century. Nineteenth-century Friends thought that Quakerism had chosen, by these rules of settlement, the pattern of a church in which children were never to know any kind of alienation from their families, their society, or from God. They considered that Quakers had come to share the attitude of the Anglican and Roman Catholic churches towards Christian nurture, rather than that demand for conversion typical of the Nonconformist sects. Though they may have been wrong about what the early eighteenth-century Friends thought they were doing in the rules of settlement, their error indicates that nineteenth-century Friends, at least, were settling questions of the spiritual state of children by reference to the notion of "birthright" membership; and though this may have been a mistake in historical thinking, it was the natural result of all the changes which had made this idea of "birthright membership" consonant with other Quaker institutions.

I think it is fairly easy to see how this came about. As we have seen, the reality of conversion was judged by adherence to Friends' public testimonies, as manifested during a "novitiate" of at least several months' duration — even though these testimonies or customs were to some extent losing their original meaning, and perhaps were suitable indicators precisely because of their being cherished only by Friends. The necessity of judging the external fruits of conversion tended to endow these with more importance, and at the same time facilitated the acceptance of the habits inculcated in the family as signs of conversion.

This meant, as we have seen, the displacement of Friends' energies into the creation of character through the agency of the family. By the end of the first century of Quakerism the family was regarded as the key to any future progress. The first really systematic membership lists which Friends compiled were family lists, which were used for the regular family visitations which began in the 1760's. These visitations began because the reformers who felt that the Society of Friends was in a low state regarded them as one of the chief remedies for this decay — a decay particularly visible in disregard for the public testimonies. Even those meetings which had reported little or no convincement for thirty-five years seem to have regarded this internal discipline as more important than any enhanced effort at evangelism.

In their doctrines and practice of family religion the Quakers worked out the fullest implications of an idea common to all Protestants, the priesthood of all believers. Seeing marriage as a higher state than celibacy, Protestants even in the seventeenth century were moving towards the virtually obligatory matrimony which is imposed on American Protestant ministers today. A married priesthood might be expected to refrain from exercising its clerical authority in ways which impaired the integrity of the family; but as long as the clerical office remained, it represented at least a potential countervailing power to that of the father. This power was actually brought into play when clergymen married children without their parents' consent, or taught them in schools things of which their parents did not completely approve. But the Quakers, consistently hostile to any institutional distinction between clergy and laity, reduced the tension between the religious organization and the family to a minimum. Church discipline was paternal (as can be seen most clearly in the regulations governing marriage); and since most Quaker children did not go away to school — the foundation of the great Quaker schools was in the last half of the eighteenth century — and were not yet exposed in any numbers to that other, grimmer, educational institution, the factory, the only escape from the nexus of the family was to spend in adolescence some time as "servants" in another Quaker family.

Though Friends expected their children not to acquire a merely hereditary or traditional faith, they gave them few institutional helps. The absence of a required public profession of faith seems to suggest no institutionalized expectation of conversion experiences, and the low number of converts from the outside shows that the "twice-born" must have been a small minority of eighteenth-century Quakers. Nevertheless this need not be taken as a sign of decadence. In part we have been victimized by an enormous emphasis on the entrance into the Christian life, from which historians have been no more exempt than revival preachers. The vast and adulatory literature on the beginnings of Quakerism, as contrasted to the much smaller amount devoted to the development of Quaker institutions, naturally imbues conversion with glamour. Nonetheless, in historiography as in pastoral care it is well to avoid a fixation on conversion (or the "fallacy of origins"). The convert wants some further ideas as to how the Christian life is to be lived, and it was to this question that the eighteenth-century Friends addressed themselves; it is a question to which the historian also owes some sympathy.

In their attempt to provide guidance for the Christian life, eighteenth-century Friends began to speak of "pertinent precedents," "the rules of our society," and "our constant practice ever since we were a people." Thus after about half a century, or two generations of Friends, it had no longer become absurd to speak of "traditional Quakerism," and we need no longer be surprised at the interest and skill which Quakers manifested in writing history. But if the inner form of Quakerism had hardened into a mold, it was because of the concern for a distinctive character structure. Homogeneity was the sign that the process was working. In trusting in the family as the supreme earthly institution for the creation of character, and in going so far as to merge the authority of the family with that of the church, the Quakers of the eighteenth century were doubtless departing from the spirit of Burrough, Nayler, and Hubberthorne. But if anything is eccentric in the history of a social group, it is the undisciplined, vital extravagance of its formation; this can hardly be used as the standard from which degeneration is dolefully measured.

For all their sectarian connotations, the Quaker public testimonies did in the main point the way to a more humane and civilized culture. As G. M. Trevelyan says, in a fine and deserved tribute to the Quakers:

> They settled down in the Eighteenth Century as a highly respectable and rather exclusive 'connection' . . . possessing their own souls and guiding their own lives by a light that was indeed partly the 'inner light' in each man, but was also a tradition and a set of spiritual rules of extraordinary potency, handed on from father to son and mother to daughter in the families of the Friends.
>
> The finer essence of George Fox's queer teaching . . . was surely this — that Christian qualities matter much more than Christian dogmas. No Church had made that its living rule before. To maintain the Christian quality in the world of business and of domestic life, and to maintain it without pretension or hypocrisy, was the great achievement of these extraordinary people . . . The Puritan pot had boiled over, with much heat and fury; when it had cooled and been poured away, this precious sediment was left at the bottom.[8]

In all of this, Quaker tradition played a great part. Furthermore, although it has not been my purpose to describe it, one

8. G. M. Trevelyan, *English Social History* (London: Longmans, Green, 1942), p. 267.

also senses in eighteenth-century Quakerism more than can be precisely analyzed. That part of Quaker inspiration from the inward light does not always generate the kind of evidence which the historian can handle. Meetings for worship kept no minutes; but they were nevertheless of transcendent importance for Friends themselves.

I hope that my comparative and statistical study of Quakerism has shed new light, but all new light creates new shadows. We should not leave in utter obscurity a criterion which is of utmost importance in the evaluation of any tradition: a capacity for renaissance. It has been observed that one of the remarkable things about Quakerism is that none of the "testimonies" with which it has come to be publicly identified — penal reform, abolition of slavery, and pacificism itself — were typical concerns of the earliest Friends.[9] Penal reform and the abolition of slavery were the particularly distinctive concerns of late eighteenth-century and early nineteenth-century Quakerism. Despite the way that Quaker history threw power to the prudent, there was still room for the saintly eccentricities of John Woolman; and no student of mid-eighteenth-century Norwich Quakerism should be altogether startled by the thought that a generation later, a Gurney girl would grow up there who was to be known to all the world by her married name, Elizabeth Fry. These two should be enough to remind us that in their zeal for order Friends had not altogether abandoned a creative tenderness to the spirit, and that it was a spirit which could lead them beyond the vision of their ancestors.

9. Hugh Barbour, *The Quakers in Puritan England* (New Haven: Yale University Press, 1964), p. 242.

Appendix, Bibliography, Index

Appendix

A Note on Methodology

Most of the evidence for this book was obtained by reordering several series of Quaker and other records. The basic series was the Quaker registers of births, marriages, and deaths for the relevant areas, which were analyzed by the method of "family reconstitution." [1] A 3″ x 5″ card was made out for each person listed in the register, with a note of each demographic event pertinent to him. The cards were subsequently sorted and arranged by families. In addition to all those mentioned in the Quaker registers, I prepared separate cards for each person mentioned in minutes of business meetings (as a Friend); in the Quaker records of sufferings; and in the presentments before the Norwich and Norfolk Quarter Sessions for those attending more than one Friends' meeting. (A large number of persons were presented for attending only once; but I suspect that these attenders were merely curious.)

1. The process and rationale of "family reconstitution" is described in detail in *An Introduction to English Historical Demography,* ed. D. E. C. Eversley, Peter Laslett, and E. A. Wrigley (New York: Basic Books, 1966), pp. 96–159. Since I worked from digests of the registers which had already been arranged alphabetically, the procedure was less laborious than that which Wrigley carried out on parish registers.

The 3″ x 5″ cards were then copied on McBee punchcards, which have a series of holes and numbers printed around the perimeter, so that information which is expressed in numbers can be stored by punching out the appropriate holes. The information can be recovered and correlations made by running a knitting needle through the mass of cards, so that those which have been punched at that particular hole fall out. On every card the following information (where known) was recorded: (1) date of birth; (2) parish and county of principal residence (assigned a number from a coded list); (3) occupation and occupation of father (from a coded list); (4) age when converted or (for children of Friends) age when first appearing in business meetings; (5) year when first identifiable as a Friend; (6) age when first married; (7) number of children and number of these surviving to the age of fifteen — recorded for women only; (8) year of death — or of leaving Friends in some other way, as by moving away or disownment; and (9) age at death. In addition, by punching or not punching one hole for each category, I encoded the sex; number of marriages; religious affiliation of the father; whether the person was a Public Friend; whether a member of business meetings; whether literate; if ever on relief; whether the person left an extant will; and whether he was ever disowned or adhered to the schismatics. Once the cards were all punched, it became relatively easy to tell who the adult Quakers were in any given year and to establish the correlations which are herein reported, as well as others which produced nothing of interest.

Lest this account be taken as prescriptive rather than descriptive I should point out that the use of manually sorted punchcards, though well adapted to the study I had in mind, prevented me from doing justice to the possibilities of purely demographic analysis which the data might support. Punched cards, whether they are to be manually or electronically sorted, suffer from two difficulties: there simply is not enough room on them for all the information available, and the number of runs required for a really complicated calculation such as age-specific mortality ("life expectancy") is so great that the cards sometimes fall apart before the computation is finished. I have therefore transferred the data from the registers to tape for computer analysis.[2]

There were two problems of judgment rather than of technique. The first was deciding whom to count as Quakers, discussed above. Since there is reliable evidence that some persons were entered in the registers or records of sufferings who were not regarded as Friends, my figures undoubtedly overstate the number of Friends by including a number of "attenders." I doubt, however, that I have overstated by more than 10 per cent.

The second and more troublesome problem was posed by the large number of Friends whose deaths were not registered. In order to assign the most nearly appropriate date of death, I made a crude actuarial table, giving the numbers of Friends who died at various ages. I could then assign a date of death by calculating a retrospective "life expectancy," as follows: if a man was last mentioned in 1713, at which time he was 75, I averaged the ages at death of all men in the county who lived to the age of 75. If the average turned out to be 81, I presumed that the man would live six more years and die in 1719. In a few even more speculative cases, where neither the date of birth nor death were known, I assigned a birth date from the median age at first marriage and then assigned a death date as above.

Though this is demography of an exceedingly rough-and-ready sort, I think that its crudities do not matter too much. In the first place, I had to resort to it for a comparatively small number of my subjects. In the second place, because

2. A purely demographic analysis which will cover a wider geographical area for the period from 1655 to 1840 is being carried out in collaboration with D. E. C. Eversley and the Cambridge Group for the History of Population and Social Structure.

of the multiplicity of sources consulted, the subjects remained in observation much longer than just the entries in the registers would have allowed. Finally, since it is based throughout on medians and averages, I hope that individual deviations will have canceled one another out.

The Editing and Censorship of Friends' Journals

The literary activity of the early Quakers was nothing if not copious, as any glance at their bibliographies will show. Francis Bugg speaks of administering "the Goods of a Poor Widow a Quaker, whose Substance was not 10£, yet she had more than 200 Quaker Books and Pamphlets." [1] Clearly family reading was expected, and it is also clear that the journals and spiritual autobiographies of Friends were a staple of devotional literature. Many of them have didactic forewords which make clear the intent of the publishers, if not altogether of the writers.

After the first few years of the Quaker movement, when new converts often published an account of their experiences, it became usual for journals to be published only after the authors' deaths. Louella Wright has shown that the earliest Quaker journals were in print on the average only three years after their author had died, while those in the late seventeenth and early eighteenth centuries were printed an average of five years after the authors' deaths. [2]

Such spiritual autobiographies, written up at the end of life largely for didactic purposes, have a tendency to resemble one another, and can properly be spoken of as a genre.

1. Francis Bugg, "An Address to Private Gentlemen and Tradesmen" prefixed to *The Pilgrim's Progress, from Quakerism to Christianity* (1698).
2. Louella M. Wright, *The Literary Life of the Early Friends* (New York: Columbia University Press, 1932), pp. 160–164.

In addition, Friends' journals were under another and less subtle compulsion, the censorship exercised by the Morning Meeting of ministers in London. This censorship was sufficiently notorious to attract the attention of the adversaries of Truth. Francis Bugg pictured the Morning Meeting exercising "the fiery Tryal of their Infallible Examination" on such works as *THIS IS THE WORD OF THE LORD, TO THEE, O BRISTOL!* "where they . . . will Alter . . . Words and Sentences; put in, and leave out, what they conceive suit best with the Times; and yet, let it go as *THE WORD OF THE LORD*." ³ Similarly, Charles Leslie, speaking of "their Laudable Custom . . . to chop and change the Writings of their Dead Prophets, to answer the Exigency of the Times" warned Friends not to do this "in the new-design'd Edition of their great Apostle G. Fox's worthy Remains." ⁴

As we now know, this mock-pious wish was not honored; Thomas Ellwood, the first editor of Fox's *Journal*, made wholesale omissions of many cures which Fox claimed to have performed.⁵ Charles Leslie's charge that the editors of collected works omitted passages of pamphlets written under the Protectorate which expressed loyalty to Cromwell is also correct.⁶ These alterations were discovered because the manuscript "Book of Miracles" and the first editions of the pamphlets have survived; unfortunately there are few other surviving manuscripts of seventeenth-century journals, and thus little evidence to judge the extent of changes made by the Morning Meeting. Besides their sensitivity to changes in the

3. Bugg, *Pilgrim's Progress*, pp. 73–74.
4. Charles Leslie, *The Snake in the Grass* (1696), pp. cclxx-cclxxi.
5. These omissions are the subject of Henry Cadbury's edition of *George Fox's Book of Miracles* (Cambridge, Eng.: Cambridge University Press, 1948). The best discussion of the censorship is in Wright, *Literary Life*, pp. 97–109. One can see it in action in the minutes of the Second Day Morning Meeting: e.g., 24 November 1673; 24 January 1676, when omissions are directed in *The Life and Death of Jane Whitehead*; 23 July 1677; 25 April 1681; and 23 July 1694.
6. Alan Cole, "The Quakers and the English Revolution," *Past and Present*, 10 (1956), 39–54.

political climate, it seems that they were most concerned to avoid flights of mystical language which suggested excessive "enthusiasm." On 23 July 1694 the Morning Meeting found Stephen Crisp's *Short History of a Long Travel from Babylon to Bethel* full of "many Misterious Expressions." It judged that it should not be printed as part of Crisp's collected works, which appeared in that year; if Colchester Friends wished to publish it separately, they should write an explanatory preface. It eventually saw the light in 1711.

It is thus true that to some extent the similarities between the various journals owe more to their editors than to their writers; especially if one wishes to recapture the political milieu of the earliest years of Quakerism and the apocalyptic imagination which was appropriate to it one should search for manuscripts and read separate first editions rather than collected works.

Bibliography

PRIMARY SOURCES

I. *Manuscripts*

A. Friends' House Library, London

DIGESTED COPIES OF REGISTERS OF BIRTHS, MARRIAGES, AND BURIALS

Bedfordshire and Hertfordshire Quarterly Meeting: births, 1643–1838; marriages, 1658–1836; burials, 1655–1837; supplemental registers of births, marriages, and burials, 1656–1796.

Berkshire and Oxfordshire Quarterly Meeting: births, 1612–1837; marriages, 1648–1837; burials, 1655–1837.

Buckinghamshire Quarterly Meeting: births, 1645–1837; marriages, 1658–1835; burials, 1656–1837.

Cambridgeshire and Huntingdonshire Quarterly Meeting: births, 1631–1837; marriages, 1658–1836; burials, 1657–1837; supplemental registers of births, marriages, and burials, 1645–1837.

Cheshire and Staffordshire Quarterly Meeting: burials, 1655–1837.

Cumberland and Northumberland Quarterly Meeting: births, 1648–1837.

Derbyshire and Nottinghamshire Quarterly Meeting: births, 1632–1837.

Devonshire Quarterly Meeting: births, 1627–1837.

Dorset and Hampshire Quarterly Meeting: births, 1638–1837.

Gloucestershire and Wiltshire Quarterly Meeting: births, 1642–

1837; marriages, 1656–1836; supplemental registers of births, marriages, and burials, 1647–1776.

Herefordshire, Worcestershire and Wales General Meeting: births, 1635–1837; marriages, 1657–1836; burials, 1650–1838; supplemental registers of births, marriages, and burials, 1657–1776 and 1680–1804.

Lincolnshire Quarterly Meeting Registers, 1618–1837, transcribed and indexed by Harold Brace. Typescript.

London and Middlesex Quarterly Meeting: births, 1644–1720 and 1720–1837; marriages, 1657–1720 and 1720–1837; burials, 1661–1700, 1700–1751, and 1751–1837.

Norfolk and Norwich Quarterly Meeting: births, 1613–1837; marriages, 1658–1836; burials, 1657–1837; supplemental registers of births, marriages, and burials, 1688–1806.

Northamptonshire Quarterly Meeting: births, 1647–1836; marriages, 1659–1837; burials, 1657–1837; supplemental registers of births, marriages, and burials, 1658–1824. The first entries in the latter actually date from 1655.

Suffolk Quarterly Meeting: births, 1653–1837; marriages, 1662–1836; burials, 1655–1837; supplemental registers of births, marriages, and burials, 1641–1757.

Sussex and Surrey Quarterly Meeting: births, 1640–1837.

Warwickshire, Leicestershire and Rutland Quarterly Meeting: births, 1623–1837; supplemental registers of births, marriages, and burials, 1636–1836.

Yorkshire Quarterly Meeting: births, 1587–1776.

MINUTE BOOKS

Alban's Men's Monthly Meeting Minutes, 1703–1724; 1724–1768.

Biddlesden [Buckinghamshire] Monthly Meeting Minutes. The volumes are entitled as follows:

Hogshaw House and Biddlesden, Vale of Aylesbury, Men's Monthly Meeting Minute Book. The minutes begin 29 April 1678 and end 26 February 1735. Book for the Sarvise of Friends belonging to the Monthly Meeting called

Biddlesden. Contains minutes from 25 March 1735 to 15 December 1779. Book of the Women's Meeting at Hogshaw House. Contains collections and disbursements, ca. 1678 to 1700 and from 1700 to 1733, and minutes of meetings from 29 July 1700 to 27 September 1762 (dealing entirely with proposed marriages) and from 1761 to 1793.

Buckinghamshire Men's Quarterly Meeting Minutes, 1669–1761.

Buckinghamshire Quarterly Meeting Collection, 1650–1759.

Hogsty End [Buckinghamshire] Monthly Meeting Book, 1742–1794.

London Yearly Meeting Minutes, 1668–1693; 1694–1701; 1702–1708; 1709–1713; 1714–1720; 1721–1728; 1729–1733; 1734–1740; 1741–1747; 1748–1754. There are no minutes for the years 1669–1671.

Markyate [Bedfordshire] Men's Monthly Meeting minutes, 1699–1778.

Meeting for Sufferings Minutes. Volumes I–VIII.

Morning Meeting Book of Records, 1673–1692; 1692–1701.

North Somerset Men's Monthly Meeting Minutes, 1667–1688; 1688–1712; 1713–1740.

Pulloxhill [later Ampthill, Bedfordshire] Men's Monthly Meeting Minutes, 1734–1756.

Sherington [Buckinghamshire] Monthly Meeting Accounts, 1750–1822. From 10 June 1761, minutes of the Monthly Meeting are interspersed with the accounts.

Somersetshire Men's Quarterly Meeting Minutes, 1668–1684; 1684–1716; 1716–1756.

Stotfold and Clifton [Bedfordshire] Men's Monthly Meeting Minutes, 1718–1746. On the spine this volume is described as "Pulloxhill Monthly Meeting Collections."

Upperside [Buckinghamshire] Men's Monthly Meeting Minutes, 1669–1690; 1690–1713; 1713–1762; 1762–1785. From references to meetings in March 1669 and December 1668, minutes of which are not included, it appears that the first eight pages have been torn from the first book. The first minute book has been published: Beatrice Saxon

Snell, ed., *Publications of the Records Branch, Buckinghamshire Archaeological Society*, vol. I (High Wycombe, Eng., 1937).

Upperside Women's Monthly Meeting Minutes, 1678–1737; 1737–1795.

Hunger-Hill [Upperside] Monthly Meeting Account Book, 1689–1751.

Upperside Monthly Meeting Account Book, 1750–1813.

Westminster Men's Monthly Meeting Minutes, 1674–1690; 1690–1701; 1701–1712; 1712–1721; 1721–1739.

Wiltshire Quarterly Meeting Minutes, 1678–1708; 1708–1734; 1734–1785. Bound with the first volume are rough minutes for 1678–1683, partially duplicating the fair-copy minutes, and accounts for 1683–1708. The duplication of minutes was the result of the Separatists' carrying off the original minute book.

ACCOUNTS OF SUFFERINGS

A Memorial of the Sufferings of the people of God called Quakers, in the County of Bucks, and parts adjacent, for their Testimony of Truth. This is the Quarterly Meeting book of sufferings, covering the period from 1655 to 1792.

Original Records of Sufferings, 8 vols.

The Record of Friends' Sufferings, 6 vols. These large folios, covering the years from 1654 to 1690 for the entire nation, were compiled by Ellis Hookes, though some entries are in the hand of Richard Richardson.

JOURNALS OF EARLY FRIENDS

Butterfield, Rebecca. Diary. Kept from 1744 until 1797, although the entries after 1770 are in a different hand.

Kelsall, John. A Journal or Historical Account of the Chief Passages, Concerns and Exercises of my Life since my Childhood.

MISCELLANEOUS

Parliament (Petitions, 1659): "These Several Papers were sent to the Parliament the 20th day of the 5th month 1659." A Petition of 7,000 women Friends against tithes.

B. Norfolk and Norwich County Record Office, Norwich

MINUTE BOOKS

Lynn Monthly Meeting Minutes, 1677–1733; 1734–1775.
Lynn Monthly Meeting Accounts, 1698–1719; 1704–1772. The 1698–1719 volume is concerned almost entirely with the building and upkeep of Upwell Meeting House.
Norfolk Quarterly Meeting Minutes, 1709–1739; 1739–1784. Undoubtedly there was an earlier volume, but it is now lost.
Norwich Monthly Meeting Minutes, 1670–1690; 1690–1745.
Norwich Yearly Meeting Minutes, 1694–1794. This was a meeting for worship and evangelism, not for business.
Tivetshall Monthly Meeting Minutes, 1667–1690; 1711–1767.
Wells Monthly Meetings Journall, 1712–1738; Wells, Holt, and Fakenham Monthly Meeting Minutes, 1738–1759.
Wymondham Monthly Meeting Minutes, 1701–1726.
Wymondham Monthly Meeting Accounts, 1693–1749; 1747–1784; 1767–1797.

ACCOUNTS OF SUFFERINGS

Lynn Monthly Meeting Sufferings, 1699–1761. No entries between 1717 and 1758. In the back are accounts of disbursements for the poor, 1709–1725 and 1747–1753.
Norfolk Quarterly Meeting Accounts of Sufferings, 1654–1733. By far the most complete record for all parts of the county.
A Booke of ye Sufferings of the People of God cald Quakers in the Citty of Norwich. The first entry is for 1654, although there are no consecutive entries until 1666. There are no entries for 1683–1699 or 1732–1746.

A Record of Ye Sufferings of Friends in Ye Citty of Norwich. Devoted entirely to the "Norwich case." The first entry is for March 30, 1682 and the last for August 4, 1685.

A Record of Friends' Suferings for ye Division of Tivitshall Monthly Meeting. The beginning date is stated to be 1740, but as the first few pages are torn out, the first entry which remains is for 1744.

PARISH REGISTERS (Microfilms)

St. Stephen's, Norwich
Great Yarmouth
Wymondham

QUARTER SESSIONS RECORDS

Norfolk Quarter Sessions Indictments, 1654–1670. Loose papers arranged by year in boxes. No papers for 1656.

Norfolk Quarter Sessions Indictments for Religious Offences, calendared by D. E. H. James. Loose papers, covering dates 1665–1685.

Norfolk Quarter Sessions Book, 1661–1666/7; 1667–1676.

Norfolk Quarter Sessions Order Book, 14 July 1657 — 12 January 1668/9.

Great Yarmouth Quarter Sessions Roll.

Norwich Mayor's Court Book, 1654–1666.

Norwich Quarter Sessions Indictment Files, vols. LXIII–LXXXIX (August 1653 through July 1690). The volumes are roughly chronological in arrangement, though with a good many anomalies. Binding follows the Old Style calendar: thus January 1666/7 is bound before April 1666.

Norwich Quarter Sessions Minute Books: Vols. 9–12, 1639–1654; 1637–1664; 1654–1670; 1665–1687.

WILLS

Archdeanery Court of Norwich.

Consistory Court of Norwich.
Archdeaconry Court of Norfolk.

OTHER ECCLESIASTICAL RECORDS

Archdeaconry Court of Norwich Act Book, 1663–1684. Covers
only Breccles Deanery.
Archdeaconry of Norwich Inquisition Books, 1664; 1666;
1670–1673.
Archdeaconry of Norwich Visitation Book, 1668–1681.
Churchwardens' Presentments: Lynn Deanery, 1679; Holt and
Walsingham Deaneries, 1680–1682, 1684; Ingworth and
Sparham Deaneries, 1681; Breccles Deanery, 1683; Brisley
Deanery, 1684; Blofield Deanery, 1684.

C. Other Collections

MINUTE BOOKS

Cambridgeshire Quarterly Meeting Minutes, 1673–1756. Cam-
bridgeshire County Record Office, Cambridge.
Cork Six Weeks Meeting Minutes, 1675–1694. Friends' Meeting House, Dublin.
Cumberland County Meeting Minutes, 1672–1723; Cumberland Quarterly Meeting Minutes, 1731–1785. Friends'
School, Brookfield, nr. Wigton, Cumberland. There are no
minutes surviving for 1673–1684.
Dublin Half-Year Men's Meeting Minutes, 1671–1688; 1689–
1707; 1708–1757. Friends' Meeting House, Dublin.
Huntingdon Men's Monthly Meeting Minutes, 1672–1723.
Huntingdonshire Quarterly Meeting Minutes, 1673–1699;
1700–1754. The latter volume also contains some minutes
of Huntingdon Men's Monthly Meeting. This and the last
entry are in the Cambridgeshire County Record Office,
Cambridge.
Lammas Monthly Meeting Minutes, 1678–1728, Arthur J.
Eddington, compiler. A typed transcript of minutes now

lost. Library of Mrs. Doris Eddington, 2 Christ Church Road, Norwich.

Leinster Province Meeting Minutes, 1670–1706. A contemporary transcript. Friends' Meeting House, Dublin.

Middlewich Preparative Meeting Minutes, 1694–1727; 1727–1764. Friends' Meeting House, Morley, nr. Wilmslow, Cheshire.

Moorehouse Preparative Meeting Minutes, 1701–1776. Friends' Meeting House, Carlisle.

Newgarden Monthly Meeting Minutes, 1678–1704. Friends' Meeting House, Dublin.

Summary of Disciplinary Actions by Norwich Monthly Meeting, 1670–1868, Arthur J. Eddington, compiler. 2 Christ Church Road, Norwich.

Pardshaw Preparative Meeting Minutes, 1707–1725; Accounts and Minutes, 1711–1756. Friends' Meeting House, Cockermouth, Cumberland.

Stockport Preparative Meeting Minutes, 1694–1731; 1731–1780. Friends' Meeting House, Morley, Cheshire.

Wells, Holt, and Fakenham Monthly Meeting, Selected Minutes, 1697–1723, Arthur J. Eddington, compiler. Typed transcript; the minute book for 1687–1712 cannot now be found. 2 Christ Church Road, Norwich.

ACCOUNTS OF SUFFERINGS

Frandley Preparative Meeting Sufferings, 1680–1714.

Newton Meeting of Sufferings Minutes, 1684–1725. This and the preceding book are in Friends' Meeting House, Morley, Cheshire.

North Walsham Sufferings, Arthur J. Eddington, compiler. A collation of the Norfolk Quarterly Meeting Book of Sufferings and the Lammas Monthly Meeting Book of Sufferings, 1672–1785 (since lost). 2 Christ Church Road, Norwich.

CHURCH BOOKS

Church Book belonging to a Society of Christians who assemble for divine Worship at the Old Meeting Norwich. Consecutive entries begin in 1642 and go to 1681; then there are two pages torn out, and consecutive entries resume from 1767 to 1839. Consulted by permission of the pastor and trustees of the Old Meeting, Norwich.

The Entire Records of the Congregational Church at Great Yarmouth, 1642–1813, copied from the Church Book by Joseph Davey, 1846. Dr. Williams' Library, London.

PARISH REGISTERS

Amersham
Chesham
Farnham Royal
St. Andrew's, Norwich
St. Augustine's, Norwich
St. Clement with St. Edmund, Norwich
St. George Colegate, Norwich
St. Gregory's, Norwich
St. Mary de Coslany, Norwich
St. Michael de Coslany, Norwich
St. Michael's at Plea, Norwich
St. Peters Hungate, Norwich
St. Peter Mancroft, Norwich
Sherington. The surviving original books for this parish begin in 1698.

PARISH REGISTERS (Bishop's Transcripts), all in the Bodleian Library, Oxford

Farnham Royal
North Crawley
Padbury
Penn
Sherington

PARISH REGISTERS (Modern Transcripts)

Bedfordshire Parish Registers: Dunstable, Eaton Bray, Luton, Studham, Totternhoe, F. G. Emmison, transcriber.

Buckinghamshire Parish Registers: Vol. IV, Iver, Lillingstone Dayrell, Lillingstone Lovell. The Iver register was copied by K. S. Block and indexed by Esme Pole-Stuart; the other two were copied by W. E. C. Cotton and indexed by C. Vivian Appleton.

Chalfont St. Giles, Mrs. G. D. Law, transcriber.

St. Benedict's, Norwich.

St. Giles, Norwich. Transcribed by the Rev. J. P. Hill and indexed by Vera London.

St. James with Pockthorpe, Norwich, Rev. J. P. Hill, transcriber.

St. Martin at Oak, Norwich.

St. Saviour's, Norwich.

SS. Simon and Jude, Norwich, Rev. J. P. Hill, transcriber. Indexed by Vera London.

Ware, Herts., Parish Register, P. S. Moody and P. Boyd, transcribers. All these are in the library of the Society of Genealogists, 37 Harrington Gardens, London, S.W. 7.

WILLS

Archdeaconry Court of Buckinghamshire. Somerset House, London.

Prerogative Court of Canterbury. Somerset House.

II.   *Published Material*

A.   Documents

CHURCH BOOKS

The Church Book of Bunyan Meeting, 1650–1821. G. B. Harrison, ed. London: J. M. Dent and Sons, 1928.

Records of a Church of Christ Meeting in Broadmead, Bristol, 1640–1687. Edward Bean Underhill, ed. London: Hanserd Knollys Society, 1847.

Records of the Churches of Christ, gathered at Fenstanton, Warboys, and Hexham. Edward Bean Underhill, ed. London: Hanserd Knollys Society, 1854.

PARISH REGISTERS

Bedfordshire Parish Registers, vol. XVII: Ampthill, 1602–1812; Tingrith, 1572–1812. F. G. Emmison, ed. Bedford, Eng.: Bedford County Record Office, 1938.

Bradbrook, William. "Wavendon Parish Register," *Records of Buckinghamshire,* vol. IX, 31–53. Aylesbury, Eng., 1909.

Buckinghamshire Baptisms, Marriages, and Burials, vol. I (new series): Aston Abbots, 1559–1837; Edgcott, 1538–1837. William Bradbrook, ed. London: Bucks Parish Register Society, 1912.

Buckinghamshire Parish Registers: Marriages, vol. VIII: Chesham and Iver. W. P. W. Phillimore and Thomas Gurney, eds. London: Phillimore and Co., 1912.

Downs, R. S. "The Parish Church of High Wycombe IV: The Parish Register," *Records of Buckinghamshire,* vol. VIII, 249–275. Aylesbury, Eng., 1903.

Leckhampstead Parish Register, 1558–1754. Aylesbury, Eng., 1912. Reprinted from the "Bucks Advertiser," Aylesbury.

Long Crendon Parish Registers, 1559–1684. Aylesbury, Eng., n.d. Clippings from the "Bucks Advertiser" preserved in the library of the Society of Genealogists, 37 Harrington Gardens, London, S.W. 7.

The Parish Registers of Hunsdon, County Hertford, 1546–1837. Herbert Cokayne Gibbs, ed. Rev. ed. London: St. Catherine Press, 1918.

A Transcript of the First Volume, 1538–1636, of the Parish Register of Chesham in the County of Buckingham. J. W. Garrett-Pegge, ed. London, 1904.

MISCELLANEOUS

Calendar to the Bucks. Sessions Records: vol. I, 1678–1694, ed. William Le Hardy; vol. II, 1694–1705, ed. William Le Hardy and Geoffrey Ll. Reckitt; vol. III, 1705–1712, and Appendix, 1647, ed. William Le Hardy and Geoffrey Ll. Reckitt. Aylesbury, Eng.: Standing Joint Committee of the Buckinghamshire Quarter Sessions and County Council, 1933, 1936, 1939.

Early Quaker Letters from the Swarthmore MSS. to 1660. Calendared, indexed, and annotated by Geoffrey Nuttall. London, 1952. Should be used in preference to *Letters, &c. of Early Friends Illustrative of the History of the Society*, A. R. Barclay, ed. (1841), which, as Nuttall notes, seldom quotes even a single sentence verbatim.

Episcopal Visitation Book for the Archdeaconry of Buckingham, 1662. E. R. C. Brinkworth, ed. Buckinghamshire Record Society, vol. VII, 1943.

Extracts from State Papers Relating to Friends, 1654 to 1672. Norman Penney, ed. London: Headley Brothers, 1913. Almost all from the Calendar of State Papers, Domestic.

The First Ledger Book of High Wycombe. R. W. Greaves, ed. Buckinghamshire Record Society, vol. XI, 1956.

The First Minute Book of the Gainsborough Monthly Meeting of the Society of Friends. Harold W. Brace, ed. Lincoln Record Society Publications, vols. XXXVIII and XL, 1948 and 1949.

"The First Publishers of Truth" Being Early Records (Now First Printed) of the Introduction of Quakerism into the Counties of England and Wales. Norman Penney, ed. London: Headley Brothers, 1907.

The Freemen of Norwich, 1714–1752, A Transcript of the Third Register. Percy Millican, transcriber. Norwich, Eng.: Norfolk Record Society, vol. XXIII, 1952.

"Friends in Buckinghamshire, 1668," *Journal of the Friends' Historical Society*, 16 (1919), 70.

The Household Account Book of Sarah Fell of Swarthmoor Hall.

Norman Penney, ed. Cambridge, Eng.: Cambridge University Press, 1920.

Keith, George. "Gospel Order and Discipline," *Journal of the Friends' Historical Society*, 10 (1913), 70–75.

King, Gregory. "Natural and Political Observations and Conclusions upon the State and Condition of England," in *Two Tracts of Gregory King*, edited with an introduction by George E. Barnett. Baltimore: Johns Hopkins University Press, 1936. Written in 1696.

Letters to William Dewsbury and Others. Henry J. Cadbury, transcriber and ed., in *Journal of the Friends' Historical Society*, Supplement 22, 1948.

Norfolk Quarter Sessions Order Book. Calendared by D. E. Howell James. Norwich, Eng.: Norfolk Record Society, vol. XXVI, 1955.

A Quaker Post-Bag: Letters to Sir John Rodes of Barlborough Hall, in the County of Derby, Baronet, and to John Gratton of Monyash 1693–1742. Mrs. Godfrey Locker Lampson, ed. London: Longmans, 1910. The first letters date from 1690.

The Register of the Freemen of Norwich, 1548–1713. Percy Millican, transcriber. Norwich, Eng., 1934.

Some Westmorland Wills, 1686–1738. John Somervell, ed. Kendal, Eng.: T. Wilson and Son, 1938.

Steven Crisp and his Correspondents, 1657–1692. Charlotte Fell Smith, ed. London, 1892.

Sudbury Quakers 1655–1953: Extracts from Various Sources Collated by Stanley H. G. Fitch. n.p., n.d. Useful material from minute books.

Tawney, A. J., and R. H. Tawney. "An Occupational Census of the Seventeenth Century," *Economic History Review*, 5 (1934), 25–64.

Transcript of Three Registers of Passengers from Great Yarmouth to Holland and New England. Charles Boardman Jewson, ed. Norwich, Eng.: Norfolk Record Society, vol. XXV, 1954.

Turner, G. Lyon. *Original Records of Early Nonconformity under Persecution and Indulgence.* 3 vols., London: T. F.

Unwin, 1911. The first two volumes consist of excerpts from Archbishop Sheldon's censuses of 1665, 1669, and 1676; vol. III is "historical and expository."

The Visitation of Norfolk Anno Domini 1664 Made by Sir Edward Bysshe, Knt., Clarenceux King of Arms, vol. I, A–L, vol. II, M–Z. A. W. Hughes Clarke and Arthur Campling, eds. Norwich, Eng.: Norfolk Record Society, vols. IV and V, 1934.

Wigfield, W. M. "Recusancy and Non-Conformity in Bedfordshire, illustrated by Select Documents, 1622–1842," *Publications of the Bedfordshire Historical Record Society,* vol. XX (1938), 145–229.

B. Books

An Account of the Life and Death of our Faithful Friend and Fellow-Labourer in the Gospel, Thomas Markham; with Several Testimonies concerning him. 1695.

Aldam, Thomas, Jr. *A Short Testimony Concerning that Faithful Servant of the Lord Thomas Aldam of Warnsworth in the County of York.* 1690.

Ashby, Richard. *An Epistle to the Called of God, Every-where.* 1715.

[Ashby, Richard et al.] *The Defence of the People Called Quakers: Being a Reply, to a Book lately Published by certain Priests of the County of Norfolk.* 1699.

Ashby, Richard. *Work While it is call'd to Day, Recommended in a Brief Relation of the Exercise and Preparation for Death, of William Roe.* 1715.

Bache, Humphrey. *A few words in true love written to the old long sitting Parliament.* 1659. Reprinted, Eastgate, Gloucestershire, 1910.

Baily, Charles. *A True and Faithful Warning unto the People and Inhabitants of Bristol . . . also some Queries which deeply concern all who are in Authority in the Nation, to consider of, With a brief Account of some Tryals and sufferings, which the author hereof hath suffered.* 1663.

Baker, Richard. *A Testimony to the Power of God Being Greater than the Power of Satan: Contrary to all those, who hold No Perfection here.* 1699.

Banks, John. *An Epistle to Friends Shewing the great Difference Between a Convinced Estate and a Converted Estate.* 1692.

―――― *A Journal of the Life of John Banks.* 2nd ed., 1798.

―――― *A Rebuke to Unfaithful Parents and a Rod for Stubborn children.* 1710.

[Barclay, David.] *Advice to Servants.* N.d. Broadside.

Barclay, Robert. *The Anarchy of the Ranters and other Libertines, the Hierarchy of the Romanists, and other Pretended Churches, equally Refused and Refuted.* 1676.

―――― *An Apology for the True Christian Divinity.* 1678.

Bathurst, Elizabeth. *Truth Vindicated by the Faithful Testimony and Writings of the Innocent Servant and Hand-maid of the Lord, Elizabeth Bathurst, Deceased.* 1691.

Baxter, Richard. *One Sheet against the Quakers.* 1657.

―――― *The Quakers Catechism, Or, the Quakers Questioned, their Questions Answered, and Both Published.* 1655.

Beck, Sarah. *A Certain and True Relation of the Heavenly Enjoyments and Living Testimonies of God's Love unto her Soul, Declared upon the Dying-Bed of Sarah the Wife of John Beck of Dockra in the County of Westmoreland.* 1680.

Beckwith, Sarah. *A True Relation of the Life and Death of Sarah Beckwith.* 1692. A journal prefaced by an account of the author's death.

Beevan, I[ohn?]. *A Loving Salutation to all People Who have any desires after the Living God, but especially to the people called Free-Will Anabaptists.* 1660.

Bennitt, William. *The Work and Mercy of God Conduceth to his Praise, or a Demonstration of the Visitation of Gods Love to my Soul in the dayes of my Youth.* 1669.

[Besse, Joseph.] *A Brief Account of Many of the Prosecutions of the People Call'd Quakers in the Exchequer, Ecclesiastical, and Other Courts, for Demands Recoverable by the Acts made in the 7th and 8th Years of the Reign of King William the Third, for the more Easie Recovery of Tithes, Church-Rates, etc.* 1736.

Besse, Joseph. *A Collection of the Sufferings of the People Called*

Quakers for the Testimony of a Good Conscience . . . from the Time of their first being distinguished by that Name in the Year 1650, to the time of . . . the Act of Toleration . . . Taken from Original Records and other Authentick Accounts. 2 vols. 1753.

Bettris, Jeane. *A Lamentation for the Deceived People of the World, But in Particular to them of Alesbury, and those small Villages round about her; who are carried away Captive by her Priests and Teachers.* 1657.

Bishop, George, Thomas Goldney, Henry Roe, Edward Pyott, and Dennis Hollister. *The Cry of Blood and Herod, Pontius Pilate, and the Jewes, reconciled, and in conspiracy with the Dragon, to devour the Manchild, Being a Declaration of the Lord arising in those people, of the City of Bristol, who are scornfully called Quakers and of the Manifold Sufferings . . . sustained by them.* 1656.

Blaugdone, Barbara. *An Account of the Travels, Sufferings and Persecutions of Barbara Blaugdone.* 1695.

[Bockett, Elias.] *Aminadab's Courtship: or, the Quaker's Wedding. A Poem being an Impartial Account of their Way of Courtship, Method of Marrying, etc.* 1717.

Bockett, Richard. *Fruits of Early Piety, Consisting of Several Christian Experiences, Meditations, and Admonitions.* 1722.

Bolton, John. *A Justification of the Righteous Judgement of God on Nathaniel Smith.* 1669.

Boweter, John. *Christian Epistles, Travels and Sufferings of That Antient Servant of Christ John Boweter.* 1705.

Bowles, George. *A Tender Exhortation in the Love of Christ, to the Youth Amongst the People called Quakers.* 1720.

Bownas, Samuel. *A Description of the Qualifications Necessary to a Gospel Minister.* 1767.

A Brief Account of the Life and Death and Some of the Gospel Labours, of that Faithful Servant and Minister of Jesus Christ, William Ellis. 1710.

A Brief Narration of the Life, Service, and Sufferings, of that Faithful Servant of Jesus Christ John Peters. 1709.

A Brief Relation of the Life & Death of Elizabeth Braytwhaite.
N.p. [1684?]

Briggs, Thomas. *An Account of Some of the Travels and Sufferings of that Faithful Servant of the Lord, Thomas Briggs.*
1685.

Browne, Samuel. *An Account and Testimony of Samuel Browne Concerning his dear Mother Sarah Browne, Widow.*
[1694?]

Browne, Sarah, and Thomas Browne. *Living Testimonies Concerning the Death of the Righteous, or the blessed End of Joseph Featherstone and Sarah his Daughter: Written by Sarah his Wife, and Thomas Brown, her second Husband . . . Also something concerning Charles Wray, Grace Browne, and Katherine Browne her Daughter, Writ by Thomas Browne the Elder, in Partney in the county of Lincoln.* 1689.

Brush, Edward. *The Invisible Power of God Known in Weakness, with a Christian Testimony of the Experience and Sufferings of Edward Brush, Aged Ninety-One Years.* 1695.

Bugg, Francis. *The Pilgrim's Progress, from Quakerism, to Christianity.* 1698.

―――― *Quakerism Withering, and Christianity Reviving.* 1694.

―――― *The Quakers Detected, Their Errours Confuted, and their Hypocrisie Discovered.* 1686.

Bunyan, John. *Grace Abounding to the Chief of Sinners.* 1666.

Burnet, William. *The Capital Principles of the People Called Quakers Discovered and Stated out of their Own Writings.* 1668.

Burnyeat, John. *The Truth Exalted in the Writings of that Eminent and Faithful Servant of Christ John Burnyeat.* 1691.

Burrough, Edward. *The Memorable Works of a Son of Thunder and Consolation.* 1672.

Camm, Thomas. *The Line of Truth and True Judgement Stretched over the Heads of Falsehood and Deceit, in a Short, yet Serious Examination, of a Printed Book, Entituled (The Memory of that Servant of God John Story Revived).* 1684.

Carleton, Thomas. *The Memory of that Faithful Servant of the*

Lord Thomas Carleton, Revived, Being a Collection of Several of his writings . . . Also some Testimonies. 1694.

Caton, William. *A Journal of the Life of that Faithful Servant and Minister of the Gospel of Jesus Christ Will.ᵐ Caton.* 1689.

Chandler, John. *A True Relation of the Unjust Proceedings, Verdict (so called) & Sentence of the Court of Sessions at Margaret's Hill in Southwark, against divers of the Lord's People called Quakers.* 1662.

Chester, Elizabeth. *A Narrative of the Life and Death of Edward Chester.* 1709.

Chevers, Sarah. *A Short Relation of Some of the Cruel Sufferings (for the Truths Sake) of Katharine Evans and Sarah Chevers, in the Inquisition in the Isle of Malta.* 1662.

Claridge, Richard. *The Life and Posthumous Works of Richard Claridge.* Joseph Besse, ed. 1726.

C[lever?], R[obert?] *A Godlie Forme of Householde Government for the Ordering of Private Families according to the Direction of God's Word.* 1612. First edition, 1598, perhaps written by Roger Carr.

[Coale, Benjamin]. *Miscellanies, or Sundry Discourses concerning Trade, Conversation, and Religion: Being the Advice of a Father, to his Children, on those Subjects.* 1712.

Coale, Joseph. *Some Account of the Life, Service, and Suffering, of an Early Servant and Minister of Christ, Joseph Coale, Collected out of his own Writings.* 1706.

Coale, Josiah. *The Last Testimony of . . . Richard Farnworth.* 1667.

——— *A Song of the Judgments and Mercies of the Lord.* 1662.

The Continued Cry of the Oppressed for Justice, Being a farther Account of the late Unjust and Cruel Proceedings of Unreasonable Men against the Persons and Estates of many of the People CALL'd Quakers, only for their peaceable meetings to worship God. 1675.

The Copie of a Paper Presented to the Parliament: and read the 27th of the fourth Moneth, 1659 Subscribed by more than fifteen thousand hands. 1659. A petition against tithes, forced maintenance, and other burdens of conscience.

Crisp, Stephen. *An Epistle of Tender Counsel and Advice.* 1680.

────── *A Memorable Account of the Christian Experiences, Gospel Labours, Travels and Sufferings of that Ancient Servant of Christ, Stephen Crisp.* 1694.

C[risp], S[tephen]. *A Short History of a Long Travel from Babylon to Bethel.* 1711. Written in 1691.

Croker, John. *A Brief Memoir of the Life of John Croker.* 1839.

Crook, John. *The Design of Christianity, Testified, in the Books, Epistles and Manuscripts, of that Ancient Faithful Servant of Christ Jesus, John Crook.* 1701.

────── *A Short History of the Life of John Crook.* 1706.

────── *A True and Faithful Testimony Concerning John Samm.* 1664.

Crouch, William. *Posthuma Christiana, or a Collection of Some Papers of William Crouch.* 1712.

A Cry out of the Forrest: Or a short Relation of the Barbarous and Cruel Actings of Jeremeel Tarrent, Minister of Winkfield Parish, in Berk-shire: against John Cotterell, an Honest Harmless Man of the same Parish. N.p., 1676. Broadside.

Curwen, Alice. *A Relation of the Labour, Travail and Suffering of that faithful Servant of the Lord Alice Curwen.* N.p., 1680.

Curwen, Thomas, Margaret Fell, William Houlden, Henry Wood, William Wilson, and others. *This is an Answer to John Wiggan's Book Spread up and down in Lancashire, Cheshire and Wales, who is a Baptist & a Monarchy-man.* 1665.

Danks, John. *The Captives Return or the Testimonys of John Danks of Colchester, and Elizabeth Danks, his wife, to the mercy and goodness of God, in calling them back to his Everlasting truth, after their out-runnings and seperation from the same.* N.p., 1680.

Davies, Richard. *An Account of the Convincement, Exercises, Services, and Travels, of that Ancient Servant of the Lord, Richard Davies,* 3rd ed. 1771.

Deacon, John. *An exact History of the Life of James Naylor with his Parents, Birth, Education, Profession, Actions, & Blaspheemies.* 1657.

Dewsbury, William. *The Faithful Testimony of that Antient Servant of the Lord, and Minister of the everlasting Gospel, William Dewsbery.* 1689.

D[imsdale], W[illiam]. *The Quaker Converted, or the Experimental Knowledge of Jesus Christ Crucified, in Opposition to the Principles of the Quakers, declared; In a Narrative of the Conversion of one in Hartfordshire, who was for some Years of their Faith and Principle, and inclined unto them . . . Likewise an Epistle Dedicatory by W. Haworth, Minister of the Gospel at Hartford.* 1690.

Dole, Dorcas. *A Salutation and Seasonable Exhortation to Children.* 1700. Written in 1683.

Dover, William. *Reasons for Erecting an Additional Number of Schools, for the Better Education of Youth in Learning and Virtue.* 1752.

Edmondson, William. *A Journal of the Life, Travels, Sufferings, and Labour of Love in the Work of the Ministry of that Worthy Elder, and Faithful Servant of Jesus Christ, William Edmondson.* Dublin, 1715.

Ellwood, Thomas. *The Account from Wickham (Lately published by John Raunce and Charles Harris) Examin'd, and found False.* N.p., 1689.

—— *An Answer to George Keith's Narrative of His Proceedings at Turners-Hall, on the 11th of the Month called June, 1696.* 1696.

—— *A Fair Examination of a Foul Paper, called Observations and Reflections, etc. Lately Published by John Raunce and Leonard Key.* 1693.

—— *History of the Life of Thos. Ellwood.* 1714.

Estaugh, John. *A Call to the Unfaithful Professors of Truth.* Philadelphia, 1744.

Farnworth, Richard. *The Heart Opened by Christ.* N.p., 1654.

—— *The Ranters Principles & Deceits Discovered and Declared Against, Denied and Disowned by Us whom the World cals Quakers.* 1655.

F[ield], J[ohn], and Richard Scoryer. *Friendly Advice in the Spirit of Love unto Believing Parents and their Tender Offspring in relation to their Christian Education.* 1688.

Fisher, Samuel. *The Testimony of Truth Exalted by the Collected Labours of . . . Samuel Fisher.* 1679. The bulk of this enormous folio of almost 1,000 pages is *Rusticus ad Academicos or The Rustick's Alarm to the Rabbies; Or, the Country Correcting the University and Clergy.* 1660.

Forster, Thomas. *A Guide to the Blind Pointed to, Or a True Testimony to the Light Within.* 1659.

Foster, Mary. *A Declaration of the Bountifull Loving-Kindness of the Lord, Manifested to His Hand-maid Marry Harris, who stood idle in the Market-Place, till the Eleventh hour, yet then received her Penny . . . that none might Dispair. Also, a Discovery of her Sufferings thorow her Disobedience and Rebellion against God's precious Truth, that none might presume, or harden their hearts in the day of God's visitation.* N.p., 1669.

Fox, George. *Gospel Truth Demonstrated in a Collection of Doctrinal Books.* 3 vols. Philadelphia, 1831. Originally published in 1706, and commonly referred to as the *Doctrinals.*

———— *The Great Mystery of the Great Whore Unfolded: and Antichrist's Kingdom Revealed unto Destruction.* 1831. First printed in 1659.

———— *Journal.* Thomas Ellwood, ed. 1694. On Ellwood as editor, see *George Fox's Book of Miracles*, Henry J. Cadbury, ed. Cambridge, Eng., 1948.

———— *The Journal of George Fox.* Norman Penney, ed. 2 vols. Cambridge, Eng., 1911. A verbatim reprint of the extant manuscript, which does not have the beginning account of Fox's own spiritual pilgrimage.

———— *The Short Journal and the Itinerary Journals of George Fox.* Norman Penney, ed. Cambridge, Eng., 1925.

———— *The State of the Birth Temporal & Spiritual and the Duty and State of a Child, Youth, Young-Men, Aged-Men and Fathers in the Truth.* 1683.

———— *A Testimony concerning Our dear Friend and Brother George Watt.* 1689.

Fox, George, the Younger. *A Collection of the Several Books and Writings Given Forth by that Faithful Servant of God and His People, George Fox, the Younger.* 1662.

Fox, Margaret. *A Brief Collection of Remarkable Passages and Occurrences Relating to the Birth, Education, Life, Conversion, Travels, Services, and Deep Sufferings of that Ancient, Eminent, and Faithful Servant of the Lord, Margaret Fell; but by her Second Marriage Margaret Fox.* 1710.

Freame, John. *Scripture Instruction Digested into Several Sections.* 1713.

Fuller, Samuel. *A Serious Reply to Twelve Sections of Abusive Queries.* Dublin, 1728.

Furly, John. *A Testimony to the True Light . . . Also, a True Relation how the Lord made manifest strength in weakness, and raised up a living Testimony to his Eternal Truth, in a child of his.* 2nd ed., n.p., 1670.

Gates, Nicholas. *A Tender Invitation to all, to embrace the Secret Visitation of the Lord to their Souls.* 1708.

Goymer, Abraham, and Edward Harvy. *The Words of a Dying Man, which may be a Warning to Old and Young, to prize the Day of their Visitation, before it be too late.* 1700.

Gratton, John. *A Journal of the Life of That Ancient Servant of Christ, John Gratton . . . with a Collection of his Books and Manuscripts.* 1720.

Green, Theophilus. *A Narrative of some Passages of the Life of Theophilus Green.* 1702.

Green, Thomas. *A Declaration to the World of my Travel and Journey out of AEgypt into Canaan.* 1659.

Halhead, Myles. *A Book of some of the Sufferings and Passages of Myles Halhead.* 1690.

Hall, David. *Some Brief Memoirs of the Life of David Hall.* 1758.

Hawkins, Richard. *A Brief Narrative of the Life and Death of . . . Gilbert Latye.* 1707.

Hayes, Alice. *A Legacy; or, Widow's Mite: Left by Alice Hayes to her Children and Others.* New York, 1807. Original edition, 1723.

Hebden, Roger. *A Plain Account of Certain Christian Experiences, Labours, Services and Sufferings, of That Ancient*

Servant and Minister of Christ, Roger Hebden, Deceased. 1700.

Hobbs, Richard. *The Quakers Looking-Glass Look'd upon: and turned towards Himself.* 1673.

Hobbs, Richard, and others. *A True and Impartial Relation of some Remarkable Passages of Charles Bailey, a Quaker.* 1667.

Hobson, Joseph. *Memoirs of the Life and Convincement of that Worthy Friend Benjamin Bangs . . . mostly taken from his own mouth.* 2nd ed., 1798.

Holme, Benjamin. *An Epistle of Tender Counsel to Parents, School-Masters, and School-Mistresses; and likewise to the Youth.* 1749.

Hooker, Richard. *Of the Laws of Ecclesiastical Polity,* books I–IV. 1907. First published in 1593.

Howard, Luke. *A Warning from the Lord unto the Rulers of Dover.* 1661.

Howgill, Francis. *The Dawnings of the Gospel-Day.* 1676. A collection of his works.

Hubberthorn, Richard. *A Collection of the Several Books and Writings of that Faithful Servant of God, Richard Hubberthorn.* 1663.

Hubberthorn, Richard, and James Nayler. *A Short Answer to a Book called the Fanatick History.* 1660.

Keith, George, and Thomas Budd. *An Account of the Great Divisions, Amongst the Quakers in Pensilvania, &c.* 1692. This book was published in Philadelphia in 1692 under the title *The Plea of the Innocent against the False Judgment of the Guilty.*

Keith, George. *An Exact Narrative of the Proceedings at Turners-Hall, the 11th of the Month called June, 1696 Together with the Disputes and Speeches There between G. Keith and other Quakers, Differing from Him in Some Religious Principles.* 1696.

——— *George Keith's Explications of Divers Passages Contained in His Former Books.* 1697.

——— *George Keith's Fourth Narrative, of his Proceedings at Turners-Hall.* 1700.

———— *The Magick of Quakerism.* 1707.

———— *A Plain Short Catechism for Children & Youth.* Philadelphia, 1690.

———— *The Presbyterian and Independent Visible Churches in New-England and else-where, Brought to the Test, and examined according to the Doctrin of the holy Scriptures.* 1689.

———— *The Standard of the Quakers Examined or An Answer to the Apology of Robert Barclay.* 1702.

———— *A Third Narrative of the Proceedings at Turners-Hall, The Twenty First Day of April 1698.* 1698.

———— *Truth and Innocency Defended against Calumny and Defamation, in a late Report spread abroad concerning the Revolution of Humane Souls.* N.p. [1692?].

Kiffin, Benjamin. *War with ye Devill.* 1676.

Lake, Clement. *Something by Way of Testimony Concerning Clement Lake of Crediton in Devonshire, with Something he wrote in his Life time, by way of Answer, unto John Flavell, Independent Preacher of Dartmouth.* 1692.

The Last Words and Testimonies of and for William Allen, late of Earles Cowln in Essex. 1680.

Lawrence, Thomas, and George Fox. *Concerning Marriage.* N.p., 1663.

Lawson, Thomas. *A Serious Remembrancer to Live Well, Written Primarily to Children, and Young People. Secondarily, to Parents. Useful (I hope) for All. Lastly, Compendious Remarks on the Death of Jonah Lawson.* 1684.

Laythes, Thomas. *Something Concerning my Convincement of God's Truth, the Way, Work, and Manner Thereof.* N.p. [1686?].

Leslie, Charles. *The Present State of Quakerism in England, Wherein Is Shew'd, That the Greatest Part of the Quakers in England are so far Converted, as to be Convinced.* 1701.

[Leslie, Charles.] *The Snake in the Grass: or, SATAN Transform'd into An Angel of Light.* 1696.

Lilburne, John. *The Resurrection of John Lilburne, Now a Prisoner in Dover-Castle, Declared.* 1656.

A *Lively Testimony to the Living Truth, Given forth by Robert Jeckell upon his Death-bed.* 1676.

The Living Words of a Dying Child, Being a True Relation of some part of the Words that came forth, and were spoken by Joseph Briggins on his Death-Bed. N.p., 1677.

Livingstone, Patrick. *Selections from the Writings of Patrick Livingstone.* 1847.

L[oddington], W[illiam]. *The Twelve Pagan Principles, or Opinions for which Thomas Hicks Hath Published the Quaker to be no Christian Seriously Considered.* 1674.

Lodge, Robert. *Several Living Testimonies Given forth by divers Friends to the Faithful Labours and Travels of . . . Robert Lodge . . . also Two General Epistles, written by Himself long since, to the Believers in Christ; and are now printed for their Edification and Refreshment.* 1691.

Love, John, the Younger. *An Epistle to all Young Convinced Friends, whom the Lord hath reached by His mighty Power, and Separated from the World, and turned their Hearts, so as to forsake Father, and Mother, Wife, and Children, for his Name sake.* 1696.

Lucas, Margaret. *An Account of the Convincement and Call to the Ministry of Margaret Lucas.* Philadelphia, n.d. First published in 1797.

Lurting, Thomas. *The Fighting Sailor Turn'd Peaceable Christian: Manifested in the convincement and conversion of Thomas Lurting.* 1710

Mason, Martin. *The Boasting Baptist Dismounted, and the Beast Disarmed and Sorely Wounded without any Carnal Weapon. In a Reply to Some Papers, Written by Jonathan Johnson, of Lincolne.* 1656.

[Matern, John.] "A Testimony to the Lord's Power and Blessed Appearance in and Among the Children at Waltham Abbey School" (1679), reprinted in *An Account of a Divine Visitation and Blessing.* Philadelphia, 1797.

Mather, William. *A Novelty: Or, a Government of Women, Distinct from Men, Erected amongst some of the People call'd Quakers, Detected.* N.d.

Mellidge, Anthony. *A True Relation of the former Faithful and long service, with the present most unjust Imprisonment of Anthony Mellidge, Sometime called a Captain; now in scorn called a Quaker.* N.p., [1657?].

The Memory of that Faithful Man of God, Thomas Stordy, Late of Cumberland, Deceased, Revived by the Testimonies of several Faithful Friends given concerning him, his Sincere Life and Blessed End. 1692.

The Memory of that Faithful Servant of Christ William Carter Late of Cumberland (Deceased) Revived. 1690.

Moore, William. *Newes out of the East . . . Or a True Account of the Tryals and Sufferings, Jeopardies, and Tortourings, which John Philly and William Moore passed through of late.* N.p., 1664.

Myers, George. *The Spiritual Worship and Service of God Exalted: and Capably performed only in the Spirit of Our Lord Jesus Christ.* 2nd ed., 1721.

A Narrative and Testimony Concerning Grace Watson. 1690.

News from the Country. 1705. A satirical dialogue against the collusion of priests and lawyers in actions for tithe recovery.

One Wonder More, Added to the Seven Wonders of the World, Verified in the Person of Mr. George Keith, once a Presbyterian, afterwards about Thirty Years a Quaker, then a Noun Substantive at Turners-Hall, and now an Itinerant Preacher (upon his Good Behaviour) in the Church of England: And all without Variation (as himself says) in Fundamentals. N.p., n.d. Written by "a Protestant Dissenter." The most likely date is 1701.

Osborn, Elias. *A Brief Narrative of the Life, Labours, and Sufferings of Elias Osborn.* 1723.

Padley, Benjamin. *Some Fruits of a Tender Branch, Sprung from the Living Vine: Being a Collection of Several Sound and Godly Letters, written by that Faithful Servant of God Benjamin Padley, with Diverse Living Testimonies to that Innocent Life.* 1691.

Pagitt, Ephraim. *Heresiography.* 5th ed., 1654.

Parnel, James. *A Collection of the Several Writings Given forth from the Spirit of the Lord, through that Meek, Patient and Suffering Servant of God, James Parnel.* N.p., 1675.

Patchet, Francis. *Living Words Through a Dying Man.* N.p., 1678.

Paye, Edward. *Antichrist in Spirit unmasked, or Quakerism a great Delusion.* 1692.

Pearson, Isaac. *The Implacable Cruelty of the People Call'd Quakers in the County of Cumberland, against Isaac Pearson, One of that Persuasion.* 1713.

Penington, Isaac. *Works.* 4th ed., 4 vols. Sherwoods, N.Y., 1861.

Penington, John. *The People Called Quakers Cleared by Geo. Keith, from the False Doctrines Charged upon them by G. Keith.* 1696.

Penington, Mary. *A Brief Account of My Exercises from Childhood.* Philadelphia, 1848. Written in 1680.

Penn, William. *An Account of the Blessed End of Gulielma Maria Penn and of Springett Penn, the Beloved Wife and Eldest Son of William Penn.* N.p., n.d.

—— *Christian Discipline: Or Certain Good and Wholsome Orders for the Well-Governing of My Family.* J. Forster, ed. 1751. Broadside.

—— *Fruits of a Father's Love: Being the Advice of William Penn to his Children.* 11th ed., 1841.

Pennyman, John. *A Short Account of the Life of Mr. John Pennyman . . . with Some of His Writings (Relating to Religious and Divine Matters).* 1696.

Pepys, Samuel. *Memoirs of Samuel Pepys.* 2 vols., 1825.

Piety Promoted by Faithfulness, Manifested by several Testimonies concerning that true Servant of God, Ann Whitehead. N.p., 1686.

Rack, Edmund, and others. *The Norffs President of Persecution (unto Banishment) against some of the Innocent People call'd Quakers.* 1666.

Raunce, John, and C[harles] H[arris]. *A Memorial for the present Generation, and also for that which is to come; Being an Account from Wickham, concerning the Difference amongst the People called Quakers, in those Parts.* N.p., [1690].

Richardson, John. *An Account of that Ancient Servant of Jesus Christ, John Richardson.* Philadelphia, 1856.

Rigge, Ambrose. *Constancy in the Truth Commended: Being a True Account of the Life, Sufferings, and Collected Testimonies, of . . . Ambrose Rigge.* 1710.

Roberts, Daniel. *Some Memoirs of the Life of John Roberts.* 3rd ed., Dublin, 1754.

Rofe, George. *The Righteousness of God to Man, Wherein he was created: . . . With a True Declaration how I lived before I knew the truth, and How I came to know the truth, and overcame deceit.* 1656.

Rogers, Richard, and Samuel Ward. *Two Elizabethan Puritan Diaries.* M. M. Knappen, ed. Chicago: University of Chicago Press, 1933.

Rogers, William. *A Brief Account of the Blessed Ends of the Two Sons of William Rogers . . . Recommended to the Serious Perusal of our Youth.* 1709.

Salt, William. *The Light, the Way, that Children ought to be Trained up in, wherein the Holy Men of God Walked.* 1660.

Sam, Mary. *An Exhortation to all People to prize their Time, in making their Calling and Election sure, before they go hence and be no more.* 1680.

Samble, Richard. *A Handful after the Harvest-Man: or a Loving Salutation to Sions Mourners, being a Collection of Several Epistles and Testimonies of that Faithful Labourer in the Lord's Vineyard, Richard Samble.* 1684.

Sansom, Oliver. *An Account of Many Remarkable PASSAGES of the LIFE of Oliver Sansom.* 1710.

Saul's Errand to Damascus, or the Quakers Turn'd Persecutors. 1728.

Scaife, William, and Issable Scaife. *A Short Relation of some words and expressions that were spoken by Barbara Scaife in time of her Sickness, a little before she departed this life.* N.p., [1686?].

Scoryer, Richard, and J[ohn] F[ield]. *Friendly Advice in the Spirit of Love unto Believing Parents, and their Tender off-spring in Relation to their Christian Education.* 1688.

A Seasonable Account of the Christian Testimony and Heavenly Expressions of Tudor Brain upon his Deathbed. 1698.

[Senhouse, John]. *Outragious Apostates Exposed*. N.p., 1718.

Sewel, William. *The History of the Rise, Increase, and Progress of the Christian People Called Quakers*. 1722.

A Short Relation Concerning the Life and Death of that Man of God, and faithful Minister of Jesus Christ, William Simpson. N.p., 1671.

A Short Relation of Some Part of the Sad Sufferings and Cruel Havock and Spoil, inflicted on the Persons and Estates of the People of God in Scorn called Quakers, For meeting together to Worship God in Spirit and Truth, Since the late Act against Conventicles. N.p., 1670.

A Short Testimony Concerning the Death and Finishing of Judieth Fell. 1682.

Sixmith, William. *Some Fruits Brought Through a Tender Branch in the Heavenly Vine Christ Jesus named William Sixmith*. 1679.

Sleigh, Joseph. *Good Advice and Counsel Given Forth by Joseph Sleigh of the City of Dublin in the Time of his Sickness to his Children*. 1696.

Smith, Humphry. *A Collection of the Several Writings and Faithful Testimonies of that Suffering Servant of God, and Patient Follower of the Lamb, Humphry Smith*. 1683.

—— *To All Parents of Children upon the Face of the Whole Earth*. 1660.

Smith, Nathaniel. *The Quakers Spiritual Court Proclaimed, Being an Exact Narrative of two several Tryals had before that New-High-Court of Justice, at the Peele in St. John's Street*. 1669.

Smith, Patrick. *A Preservative Against Quakerism*. 1732.

Smith, William. *Balm from Gilead: A Collection of the Living Divine Testimonies written by . . . William Smith*. 1675. This is probably the nearest Quaker equivalent to Richard Baxter's *Christian Directory*.

Some Testimonies Concerning the Life and Death of Hugh Tickell, as also His Convincement, Travels, Sufferings, and Service for the Lord, and his Eternal Truth. 1690.

Some Testimonies of the Life, Death and Sufferings of Amariah Drewet of Cirencester in Gloucestershire. 1687.

Stirredge, Elizabeth. *Strength in Weakness Manifest: in the Life, Various Trials, and Christian Testimony of that Faithful Servant and Handmaid of the Lord, Elizabeth Stirredge.* 1711.

Story, Christopher. *A Brief Account of the Life, Convincement, Sufferings, Labours and Travels of . . . Christopher Story.* 1726.

Story, John. *The Memory of that Servant of God, John Story, Revived.* 1683.

Story, Thomas. *A Journal of the Life of Thomas Story.* Newcastle-upon-Tyne, 1747.

Symonds, Thomas, *The Voyce of the Just Uttered: His Passing out of AEgypt through the Red Sea, through the Wildernesse to the Promised Land, where rest and peace is enjoyed.* 1656.

A Testimony concerning Our dear & well-beloved Friend and Brother in the Truth, William Coale. 1682.

This to Thee O King and Thy Council. N.p., n.d. Select Tracts, vol. 57, no. 2 in Friends' House Library. It deals with sufferings.

Thompson, Thomas. *The Quakers Quibbles, Set forth in an Expostulatory Epistle to William Penn: also the Pretended Prophet and last Witness Lodowick Muggleton and the Quakers Compared and Considered, by an Indifferent Penn.* 1674.

———— *The Second Part of the Quakers Quibbles Set Forth.* 1675.

Thompson, William. *The Care of Parents, is a Happiness to Children: Or, the Duty of Parents to their Children, and of Children to their Parents.* 1710.

Toldervy, John. *The Foot out of the Snare . . . Being a Brief Declaration of his Entrance into that Sect Called (by the Name of) Quakers.* 1656.

Tompkins, Anthony. *A Few Words of Counsel and Advice to all the Sons and Daughters of Men: More Especially to the Children of Believers.* 1687. Printed with this is a short exhortation by Richard Needham.

Townsend, Theophila. *A Testimony Concerning the Life and Death of Jane Whitehead.* 1676.

Trapnel, Anna. *A Legacy for Saints; being Several Experiences of the dealings of God with Anna Trapnel, In, and after her Conversion,* (*written some years since with her own hand*) *and now coming to the sight of some friends.* 1654.

A True Copy of Some Original Letters Which Pass'd between John Hall of Monk-Hesleden in the County of Durham, an Eminent Quaker Teacher, and William Walker of East-Thickley in the same county, Farmer, whose Wife had the misfortune to be seduced to Quakerism. Newcastle-upon-Tyne, 1725.

Tyso, John. *Something written to the Magistrates of London and Middlesex.* 1663.

Vickris, Richard. *A Few Things of Great Weight.* 1697. An exhortation to Friends to have family meetings and otherwise instruct young people.

Voltaire. *Letters Concerning the English Nation.* 1733.

Ward, Samuel, and Richard Rogers. *Two Elizabethan Puritan Diaries,* M. M. Knappen, ed. Chicago, 1933.

Watson, Samuel. *A Short Account of the Convincement, Gospel Labours, Sufferings and Service of that Ancient and Faithful Servant and Minister of the Lord Jesus Christ, Samuel Watson: Being a Collection of his Works.* 1712.

West, Moses. *A Treatise Concerning Marriage.* Leeds, 1736.

Whitehead, George. *Antichrist in Flesh Unmask'd and the Quakers Christianity Vindicated from the Malicious and Injurious Attempts of Edward Paye, William Alcott & Henry Loader, in their late Defaming Confused Book Falsly Styled, Antichrist in Spirit Unmask'd.* 1692.

—— *The Christian Progress of that Ancient Servant and Minister of Jesus Christ, George Whitehead.* 1725.

W[hitehead], G[eorge]. *The Dipper Plung'd or Thomas Hicks his Feigned Dialogue between a Christian and a Quaker Proved, an Unchristian Forgery.* N.p., 1672.

Whitehead, George. *The Quakers Plainness Detecting Fallacy.* 1674.

Whiting, John. *Early Piety Exemplified in the Life and Death*

of Mary Whiting . . . with Two of her Epistles to Friends.
N.p., [1681?].

——— *Judas and the Chief Priests Conspiring to Betray Christ and his Followers; or An Apostate Convicted, and Truth Defended. In answer to George Keith's Fourth (False, Partial) Narrative, of his Proceedings at Turners-Hall.* 1699.

——— *A Memorial concerning Sarah Scott, and the Great Mercy & Goodness of God, expressed by her in the time of her Sickness.* 1703.

——— *Persecution Expos'd in Some Memoirs Relating to the Sufferings of John Whiting.* 1715.

Whitrow, Joan. *The Work of God in a Dying Maid, Being a Short Account of the Dealings of the Lord with one Susannah Whitrow, About the Age of Fifteen.* N.p., 1677.

Widders, Robert. *The Life and Death, Travels and Sufferings of Robert Widders.* 1688.

Willett, Joseph. *Some Observations on a Pretended Dialogue Between a Baptist and a Quaker.* 1720.

Wilson, Thomas. "A Brief Account of the Life, Travels, and Christian Experiences of Thomas Wilson," in *Friends' Library* (Lindfield, 1836), XIV, 289–350.

Wilson, William. *The Memorial of the Just Shall Not Rot. Or a short Collection of some of the Letters of that faithful Servant of the Lord William Wilson . . . together with Several Testimonys Concerning his faithfulness in his day.* 1685.

Wolrich, Humphrey. *A Declaration of the Tender Mercies of the Living Lord . . . With a few Words, from my own Experience, of what I have found and tasted of the Goodness of God in that Way the Professors of the World esteem Dangerous and Erroneous.* N.d.

Wynn, John. *The Memory of the Just Reviv'd; in divers Testimonies Concerning . . . John Wynn.* 1715.

Young, Arthur. *The Farmer's Tour through the East of England.* 4 vols., 1771.

Zachary, Thomas. *A Word to all Those who have bin convinced of the Truth and yet through the Strength of Fleshly Wis-*

dom, will not subject to the Requirings of that Spirit of Truth. N.p., n.d.

SECONDARY SOURCES

I. Manuscripts

A. Friends' House Library, London, N.W.1

Arnold, H. G. "Early Meeting Houses," typescript.
Cole, W. A. "The Quakers and Politics, 1652–1660," unpub. diss., Cambridge University, 1955.
"Guide to Quarterly and Monthly Meetings," 2 vols., typescript. Gives the composition of quarterly meetings by constituent monthly meetings, and the composition of monthly meetings, so far as is known, by constituent particular meetings, throughout the history of the Society of Friends.
Hubbard, Dorothy G. B. "Early Quaker Education (c. 1650–1780)," unpub. Master's thesis, University of London, 1940.
"Meeting Records Catalogue," 4 vols., typescript. Should be consulted for the latest whereabouts of local meetings records.
Mortimer, Russell S. "Quakerism in Seventeenth Century Bristol," unpub. Master's thesis, Bristol University, 1946.
Stroud, L. John. "The History of Quaker Education in England (1647–1903)," unpub. diss., University of Leeds, 1944.

B. Bodleian Library, Oxford University

Diocesan, Archdeaconry and Probate Records (Shelfmark R. 13. 12). A mimeographed index of MSS. in the Bodleian from the three archdeaconries now constituting the diocese of Oxford (Buckinghamshire, Berkshire, and Oxfordshire).

MS. Archd. Papers Bucks, W. J. Oldfield, ed. (Shelfmark c.248 = R. 13. 112a). A more detailed calendar of archdiaconal records of Buckinghamshire.

C. Others

Edwards, George W. "Some Early *Members* of the Society of Friends." In the possession of the author, 15 Westland Drive, Hayes, Bromley, Kent.

Watkins, Owen. "Spiritual Autobiography from 1649 to 1660," unpub. diss., University of London, 1952. In the University of London library.

II. *Published Material*

A bibliography of articles and books used as secondary sources in the preparation of this book has been deposited at the Friends' House Library, London; another copy has been placed in the Widener Library, Harvard University.

Index